UNDERSTANDING
ISLAM IN INDONESIA
—— POLITICS AND DIVERSITY ——

For our most recent grandchild
Alexander Clarence Pringle

First published in Singapore by
EDITIONS DIDIER MILLET PTE LTD
121 Telok Ayer Street, #03-01
Singapore 068590

www.edmbooks.com

Published in North America by
UNIVERSITY OF HAWAI'I PRESS
2840 Kolowalu Street
Honolulu, HI 96822 USA

www.uhpress.hawaii.edu

Library of Congress Cataloging-in-Publication Data

Pringle, Robert, 1936–
    Understanding Islam in Indonesia : politics and diversity / Robert Pringle.
      p. cm.
    Includes bibliographical references and index.
    ISBN 978-0-8248-3415-9 (pbk. : alk. paper)
    1. Islam—Indonesia—History. I. Title.
BP63.I5P746 2010
297.09598—dc22

2010002947

Printed in Singapore

COVER PHOTO: *A supplicating man in a mosque in*
Palembang, Sumatra. | *Abbas/Magnum Photos*

UNDERSTANDING
ISLAM IN INDONESIA
——— POLITICS AND DIVERSITY ———

ROBERT PRINGLE

University of Hawai'i Press
Honolulu

Contents

List of Maps

Introduction

This book is intended as a primer on Islam in Indonesia, which is home to more Muslims than any other country on earth. Indonesia is also the world's fourth most populous country and its third largest genuine democracy. Interest in Indonesian Islam has increased since the events of September 11, 2001, but most people know little about the country and much less about Indonesian Islam. Even those who know something about Indonesia tend to be in the grip of contending stereotypes. The first is that Indonesian Islam is "moderate," quite different from the frightening Middle Eastern variety. The second is that, notwithstanding the moderation of its Islam, Indonesia is a soft state, at risk of succumbing to a theocratic, extremist, sometimes violent Islamic minority.

To go beyond the stereotypes and make sense of what is happening today, it is necessary to know something about Indonesian society and especially about certain historical events which have great explanatory force. To draw a parallel: suppose you were an Indonesian trying to understand the social fabric of modern Europe, as it pertains to the health and stability of the continent. You would need, as a starter, to comprehend the significance of the term "Protestant Reformation," to know something about the Enlightenment and why it still influences perceptions today, and to understand the trauma of World War I and its stepchildren, the Great Depression and World War II. It would help to understand the great explorations, colonization, the wars of decolonization, and the migration of formerly colonized people to Europe in recent years. Without such understanding, however minimal, you would be lost.

Most readers will be interested primarily in the politics of Islam, and its ability to co-exist with, or even help nurture, a modern democratic state. With that in mind, the book is not about the theology of Islam, except insofar as doctrine relates to political culture, which of course it quite often does.

The first four chapters aim to provide base-level understanding of the history which has conditioned the development of Islam in Indonesia. The fifth chapter explores aspects of Islamic institutions in Indonesia which are of particular interest to foreigners, including Islamic law, Islamic education, and two mass organizations unique to the country, Nahdlatul Ulama and Muhammadiyah. The final three chapters examine two current topics of paramount importance: first, the sectarian and regional violence that followed the fall of President Suharto in 1998 and seemed to presage the disintegration of Indonesia, and second, the question of whether or not Indonesia's new democracy is at risk of being subverted or co-opted by an Islamic extremist minority. While I have tried to make the historical chapters as impartial as possible, my discussion of current and near-current events in the final three chapters reflects my personal opinions as to what can be concluded from the historical record, and – equally important – from the nature of Indonesia's diversity.

It is a fundamental premise of this book that Indonesian Islam cannot be understood apart from the complexities of Indonesian history and culture. I have therefore concentrated on national factors which in my view will continue to be important and in many cases determining. This does not mean that global factors are not also important, but it is the Indonesian element that is least understood outside the country and it is that deficit which this book is designed to address.

I have occasionally used parallels from American history, partly because I know something about it, but more because Indonesia and the United States are comparable in many respects. Both are large, multicultural democracies, often disorderly, hardly immune from violence or the inefficiencies that come with large size and complexity, but also endowed with considerable underlying cohesion. It is not an accident that the national mottos of Indonesia and the United States mean the same thing, in Old Javanese and Latin respectively. Equally fruitful comparisons could probably be made with other multicultural states with large Muslim populations – Pakistan, Nigeria and Iran all come to mind – but such comparisons would be far more difficult to present to a generalist audience.

I have necessarily compressed much material into little space. Some readers, including students, will want to know more, and there are several features of this book intended to make it easier for them. Instead of a full bibliography, there is a guide to further reading: a limited list of books and on-line sources annotated to explain why each is helpful or simply interesting. In order to make the book more useful as a desk-top reference, there is a glossary with a sentence or two about major institutions and foreign-language terms. In addition to the glossary, there is a list of major Indonesian political parties. Following this Introduction there is a note on the vexing issue of terminology, which almost no one seems to use the same way. Footnotes have been kept short and used sparingly. Finally I have taken special, personal care to make sure that the index is comprehensive.

This book is based on a combination of training in Southeast Asian history, service as a US diplomat in Jakarta from 1970 to 1974, and research (mainly interviews) in Indonesia and Australia in 2001 and 2007–2008. While it is not designed for scholars or other experts on Indonesia, it could not have been written without their writings and generous help. My exceptional debt to certain individuals requires special mention. In the case of Chapter 4, on the Suharto era, I have drawn particularly on Robert W. Hefner's *Civil Islam: Muslims and Democratization in Indonesia* and R.E. Elson's *Suharto: a Political Biography*. Chapter 6, an outline of post-Suharto sectarian violence and terrorism, leans heavily on the work of both the International Crisis Group and the UNDP's Crisis Prevention and Recovery Unit in Jakarta. Martin van Bruinessen and Julia Day Howell were instrumental in helping me to understand the renaissance of Traditionalist Islam and Sufism, a phenomenon of far-reaching significance only now being fully appreciated. The ongoing research of Saiful Mujani of the Lembaga Survei Indonesia in collaboration with Bill Liddle has been equally important in helping me to understand current trends in political Islam. Jamie Mackie, who encouraged me from the start, also arranged contacts in Australia, where there is now a critical mass of scholarship on Indonesia. Ambassador Chan Heng Chee did the same for me in Singapore, another hot spot for Southeast Asian studies generally. Jim Fox of the Australian National University introduced me to his talented cohort of Indonesian graduate students and offered much helpful advice himself. Julia Day Howell was similarly helpful and generous at Griffith University in Brisbane. My work also benefited greatly from the friendship and help of Merle Ricklefs, not to mention my reliance on his two remarkable volumes on Islamization in Java, and his indispensable *History of Modern Indonesia*. Some of those mentioned above read and offered advice on various chapters, as did Dick Baker, Judy Bird, Mary and Filino Harahap, Barbara Harvey, Al La Porta, and Margaret Sullivan.

Among the many others who were generous in sharing their knowledge and/or hospitality were Amin Abdullah, Taufik Abdullah, Rukmini Abidin and her family, Heddy Shri Ahimsa, Dewi Fortuna Anwar, Bahrissalim, Ramang Basuki, Anes Baswedan, T. Bramyanto, R. Philip Buckley, Robin Bush, Harold Crouch, Adjie Damais, Darni Daud, Nia Dinata, Hermawan Kresno Dipojono, Don Emmerson, Gregg Fealy, Michael Feener, Abdullah Gymnastiar, Sandra Hamid, Hal Hill, Virginia and M.B. Hooker, Harris Iskandar, Fuad Jabali, Dorodjatun and Emy Kuntjoro Jakti, Sydney Jones, Yudi Latif, Tim Lindsey, Burhan Magenda, Nono Anwar Makarim, Syafi'i Ma'arif, John MacDougall, Goenawan Mohamad, Ahmed Muttaqin, Melinda Nathan, A.D. Pirous, Douglas Ramage, Zainul Abidin Rasheed, H. Jusny Saby, Emil Salim, Palgunadi T. Setiawan, Shofwan Karim Elha, Sabam and Toenggoel Siagian, A'an Suryana, Dr. Sulastomo, Mely Tan, Will Tuchrello and Mestika Zed. This list cannot be comprehensive and I apologize for any inadvertent omissions. Despite all this help, there will have been errors of fact and interpretation, and they are entirely my responsibility.

The book was made possible by a generous grant from the Smith Richardson Foundation. The United States-Indonesia Society (USINDO) administered the grant, and, thanks to its rich array of visiting Indonesian speakers, was an ideal venue for keeping up with Indonesian affairs while in Washington. In addition, the talented staff of USINDO's Jakarta office headed by Tricia Iskandar saved me many hours of time and effort arranging appointments and paying bills. The Inter-Library Loan staff of the Alexandria (Virginia) Public Library system worked miracles prying rare volumes away from their homes so I could use them. Michael Anderson, old friend and Public Affairs Officer at the US Embassy, was an unstintingly generous host and advisor in Jakarta. My son Jamie provided indispensable technical advice and routinely exorcised computer demons. My wife, Barbara, who has shared my interest in Indonesia from the beginning, was, as ever, a wellspring of good judgement, moral support, and tireless, rigorous editing.

A Note on Terms and Spelling

Specialized writing on Islam in Indonesia is daunting for the uninitiated. Hardly anyone seems to use the same terms in the same way, and the terms themselves are often opaque and sometimes apparently senseless. My own non-favorite is "Islamist," meaning some sort of political radical and/or someone who believes in an Islamic state, a subject about which there is no clear agreement even among its advocates. The word is vaguely pejorative, suggesting a desire to throw bombs, but an absence of courage to do so. (People who do throw bombs are "terrorists.") The problem, of course, is the wretched ambiguity of that terminal "–ist," which suggests a desire to be or to do whatever the root implies, as in "anarchist," "hedonist" "extremist" and so on. But how can one be a reasonably devout Buddhist, and not be a Buddhismist? The same goes for "Islamist."

In the case of Indonesia, the term "Muslim" is also problematic. It usually means anyone whose faith is Islam, about 85% of the population. But it is also often used to mean someone who is politically a Muslim, as opposed to being a nationalist or a secularist, and votes for an Islamic political party. In this sense Muslims have always been a minority of the Indonesian population and remain so, despite the increase in Islamic religious observance in recent years.

The very diversity of Indonesian Islam, reflecting the complexity of the country itself, makes it hard to label. Until recently any serious discussion of the subject would have started with two terms, *abangan* and *santri*, popularized by anthropologist Clifford Geertz in his book *The Religion of Java*, published in 1960. By "*abangan*" Geertz meant the nominally Muslim peasantry of Java, whose religion, incorporating elements of ancestor worship and animism, centered around communal village feasts. By "*santri*" Geertz meant a pious or "observant" category of Muslims, mainly clerics, small merchants and landowners. A third Geertzian term, "*priyayi*," never as widely used, meant the mainly non-observant Javanese aristocracy, especially its lower ranks, which became the bureaucratic class of the Dutch East Indies. The *priyayi* were in large degree simply wealthier, higher-class *abangan*. Based on his own field work in East Java, Geertz used these terms to describe, not religion alone, but categories of lifestyle and economic class: broad in nature, shifting and evolving over time, varying from place to place and restricted to the ethnic Javanese of East and Central Java.

Educated foreigners and many Indonesians were delighted by the Geertzian categories, especially *abangan* and *santri*, because they provided respectable labels with a cachet of scholarship for a subject which up to then had typically been described with colonial pejoratives. Sir Stamford Raffles, for example, referred in 1817 to nominal Javanese Muslims as ignorant of their own religion, while those who knew more and took Islam seriously were "bigoted," or fanatical. (Raffles also noticed that even in the early 1800s Islam was intensifying as it continued to spread.) [1]

The Geertzian terms were soon distorted to denote religion only, and often applied to Indonesians in general, not just Javanese. The misuse was understandable because, as the Dutch understood, there was indeed an Indonesia-wide dichotomy between two styles of Islam, albeit more obvious in Java than in Outer Indonesia. This division was similar in its vagueness to the broad divide between "red" and "blue" political cultures in the USA, and, as in the American case, it has proved to be of enormous and enduring political significance. The distinction has been evident from the early days of Islamization, and its history on Java is now better understood thanks to the writings of historian Merle Ricklefs. While the underlying causes of this social and religious polarization are complex, they surely include geography (coastal versus inland), employment (commercial versus agrarian), social class, degree of education, and intensity (or absence) of Hindu-Buddhist penetration in the pre-Islamic era. Bipolarity has never implied lack of change, and neither end of the spectrum is today what it was half a century ago. One must grapple with this phenomenon, inexact as it is, to understand modern Indonesia, or Islam therein.

At the end of the day, some kind of label is still useful, if not necessary, to describe Indonesia's socio-religious bipolarity. I would have happily remained with *abangan* and *santri*, which had come to mean, rather usefully,

---

1   Thomas Stamford Raffles, *The History of Java*, London: John Murray, 1817, Vol. II, p. 2.

something more than Geertz had intended. This, however, would have invited loud cries of "Gotcha!" from some in the academic community, upon which I have depended heavily in writing this book. The problem, they have pointed out, is that the *abangan* category of nominal Muslim Javanese peasant practically no longer exists, at least not in a religious sense. It has been swept away, with a little help from the government, by the Islamic piety boom of the Suharto era. So I have resorted to the use of "Traditionalist" and "Reformist" to describe the two poles of Indonesian Islam. Others sometimes use "Modernist" to describe what I am calling "Reformist," but "Modernist" is increasingly confusing due to the fact that the Traditionalists, regarded in Geertz's days as political and religious has-beens, are today pulling ahead of their counterparts in accommodating to the challenges of modernity.

The terminological issues do not end with Traditionalist and Reformist. Within each broad category of Islam there are some who are more pious than others. Thus terms like "devout," "nominal" and "observant," inexact as they are, remain useful as indicators of the extent to which the practice of Islam is a core principle of personal life. Obviously this kind of distinction is found in all faiths, not just Islam.

The specialized writing on Islam is also replete with terms like Jihadist, Salafi, Salafi Jihadist, Neo-Sufi ("neo" can be attached to almost anything; e.g. neo-*santri*, even neo-Modernist), Wahabi and more. I have attempted to avoid such words wherever possible, but some of them are unavoidable. Partly for that reason an extensive glossary is included in this book.

Another problem arises with "conservative" and "radical," which can signify either political or religious attributes. Religious conservatives are doctrinally radical if their religious views diverge greatly from mainstream religious thought, but of course this a matter of judgment. Religious conservatives can also be politically radical if they are willing to support their religious conservatism through the use of force or intimidation, as was the case in the European Inquisition. The term "fundamentalist" is similarly familiar in western usage, connoting a return to the letter of scripture for guidance, often on politicized issues such as marriage and homosexuality. In Islam as in Christianity, fundamentalists can cite scripture for all kinds of ideologically divergent objectives.

"Orthodox" is occasionally used in discussions of Indonesian Islam. It is not a helpful term because it suggests a significant, uniform standard of religious doctrine which doesn't exist beyond Islam's most basic tenets. A scholarly argument can be made that Orthodox Islam, at least for Sunnis, is grounded in one or more of the classical legal schools or *mazhab*: Shafi'i, Maliki, Hanafi and Hanbali. But for many years the big debate in Islam has not been about the classical jurisprudence itself, but about whether it can be reinterpreted in the light of modern circumstances, and if so how. Thus to be "orthodox" or not is, in real-world terms, a purely theoretical distinction. John Esposito has usefully pointed out that in Islam what matters is not orthodoxy (correct doctrine) but orthopraxy (correct action).[2]

The words "terrorist" and "terrorism" have been debased in current usage to mean enemies who fight by irregular means. Friends and/or allies are almost never described as terrorists. On the whole I believe that "violent extremism" is preferable to "terrorism," but "terrorist" and "terrorism" are so embedded in current usage that not using these words entirely may convey an unintended political statement. I have used them sparingly and only to describe episodes of illegal violence against civilians carried out for the purpose of spreading fear or promoting a political agenda (e.g., the various bombings in Bali, Jakarta and elsewhere between 2002 and 2005, and again in 2009).

Finally, a note on spelling, especially of Arabic or Arabic-derived Indonesian words. T.E. Lawrence once said about Arabic spelling that "[t]here are some 'scientific systems' of transliteration, helpful to people who know enough Arabic not to need help, but a wash-out for the world. I spell my names anyhow, to show what rot the systems are."[3] My own system has been mainly to follow the spelling used in *Voices of Islam in Southeast Asia*[4] and to refer any questions to the authors of that invaluable work, compiled by experts on both religion and Arabic orthography.

---

2   John L. Esposito, *What Everyone Needs to Know about Islam*, Oxford: Oxford University Press, 2002, p. 140.
3   T. E. Lawrence, *Seven Pillars of Wisdom*, New York: Doubleday, 1935, p. 25.
4   Greg Fealy and Virginia Hooker, eds., *Voices of Islam in Southeast Asia: A Contemporary Sourcebook*, Singapore: Institute of Southeast Asian Studies, 2006.

INDONESIA

1

How Islam Arrived

Indonesia has about 205 million Muslim inhabitants, more than any other country. But Islam was Indonesia's second world religion, following Hindu-Buddhism, and conversion to Islam was both gradual and incomplete.

Think of cloves and pepper as the fifteenth-century equivalent of oil and natural gas, and you will be on the way to understanding why Islam came to Indonesia when it did. Demand for spices, both as medicines and as preservatives, helped to fuel the European Age of Exploration, Christopher Columbus towards the west, Vasco de Gama towards the east, both of them and many others looking for spices. The result was a boom in fiercely contested international trade, through the Red Sea and then by way of India to what would become Indonesia. At the beginning, when full-scale European colonialism did not yet exist, Muslim merchants proliferated along the trade routes in tempo with the trade itself. The growing Islamic presence was not, for the most part, some sort of jihad, although Southeast Asian rulers used Islam not only to resist the Portuguese intrusion, but also to expand their realms at the expense of an older, pre-Islamic ruling order. The resulting religious and social change was in some ways similar to that which accompanied the expansion of commerce and the Protestant Reformation in Europe.

The Terrain Where Islam Settled

Island Southeast Asia covers a vast area, roughly triangular in shape. It includes the modern Philippines at its northern apex, and the states of Malaysia and Singapore to the west. However, most of this great triangle of islands is today the Republic of Indonesia.

Indonesia is a blend of powerfully unifying and dividing elements which tend to come in pairs. Its flag is two horizontal bands, one red and one white, representing land and sea, suggesting that they are equally important. The sea divides the Indonesian islands but it also unites them. Until very recently the ocean was a highway, while mountainous interiors resisted travel and even habitation.

The island of Java occupies a central location. Java looks small on a map of modern Indonesia, but on it lives more than half of Indonesia's population of 240 million people. Indonesian Borneo – not counting Brunei and the Malaysian states of Sabah and Sarawak – is, by contrast, relatively huge, over four times the size of Java but with only one-twelfth of its inhabitants.[1] The reason is that Bornean soils, like most tropical soils without volcanic enrichment, are very poor – but paradoxically able to support some of the world's most spectacular (and rapidly disappearing) tropical forests. So another of Indonesia's paired contrasts is Java and the Rest, or Java and the Outer Islands; cramped but fecund versus spacious but infertile, mostly devoid of soil nutrients.

Indonesia has about 17,000 islands spread across more than 3,000 miles; the Dutch enjoyed comparing it to a girdle of emeralds around the equator. Only a handful of them are geographically obvious: Sumatra, larger than California; Kalimantan (or Indonesian Borneo), even bigger; Java, the densely settled hub of the nation; Sulawesi, with its contorted, ink-blot form, once known as "The Celebes," and the great expanse of Papua, Indonesia's half of the island of New Guinea. Some of the smaller islands are historically well known: Bali for its culture and tourism, and of course the Spice Islands, once "the Moluccas," today the Indonesian provinces of Maluku and North Maluku. These islands were the source of cloves and nutmeg, while pepper, a plant of Indian origin, was grown primarily in West Java and Sumatra.

As one might expect, insular geography spawned cultural and linguistic diversity, but once again there is an important unifying twist. Indonesia has hundreds of languages, but most of them are first cousins within the Austronesian (Malayo-Polynesian) language family, much as French, Italian and Spanish are closely related within the Romance language family. But this linguistic affinity stops short in portions of eastern Indonesia and above all

---

1   Indonesian population figures and land areas throughout are rounded from Thomas Brinkhoff, "City Population: Indonesia," constructed Jan. 20, 2008, using Badan Pusat Statistik figures accessed July 2008 at http://www.citypopulation.de/Indonesia.html.

on New Guinea, half of which belongs to Indonesia, where radically different Melanesian languages hold sway and diversity has run amok (*amok* being a good Indonesian word). There are only about ten million Melanesians, in and beyond Indonesia, but they speak roughly one-third of the world's languages, for reasons that scholars still cannot adequately explain.

That leaves the rest of Indonesia, plus Malaysia and the Philippines, speaking closely related languages, one of which, Malay, became the national language of both Indonesia and Malaysia. The reason for this relative linguistic unity lies in the timing of migration into the archipelago. "Java Man," a pre-human species of uncertain origin, lived in Indonesia as much as 1.5 million years ago.[2] Much later the first *Homo sapiens*, who were the ancestors of modern negrito and Australian aboriginal populations, migrated from the north into portions of the archipelago and beyond it to Australia. For our purposes, however, the big event in the peopling of Indonesia was the arrival of the Malayo-Polynesians, now renamed Austronesians just to confuse everyone. The Austronesian stage was important because it set the linguistic and social foundations for subsequent history. It began only about six thousand years ago, a short time in ethno-linguistic terms. The Austronesians probably came to Southeast Asia from Taiwan, where hill tribes still speak Austronesian languages.

The Austronesians brought with them metal tools, a distinctive artistic style and perhaps more advanced agriculture. They were above all skilled seafarers. They spread throughout the Indo-Pacific region, deep into the Pacific itself (Hawaii, New Zealand, and the rest of Polynesia) and even as far west as Madagascar, off the coast of East Africa. They formed enclaves in mainland Southeast Asia, including Austronesian hill tribes in Vietnam. The oldest inscription ever found, written in a language closely related to modern Indonesian, dating from the fourth century CE, comes from the lost Hindu-Buddhist kingdom of Champa, in what is now Vietnam.[3]

The Austronesians in time developed complex bronze-age communities across what is now Indonesia, with broad similarities, including house styles and other art forms like ceremonial axes and kettle drums, the "great bronze drums of Southeast Asia." These classic Austronesian styles are still visible in (for example) traditional house and textile design and are an important

---

2   The sketch of Indonesian prehistory here is based on Peter Bellwood, *Prehistory of the Indo-Malaysian Archipelago*, rev. ed., Honolulu: University of Hawai'i Press, 1997.
3   Georges Coedès, *Les états hindouisés de l'indochine et d'indonésie*, Paris: Editions E. de Boccard, 1964, p. 96.

element of Indonesia's cultural heritage. Early Austronesian religions blended animism, the worship of local spirits of earth and water, with cults of ancestor worship. Judging from surviving animist societies, these pre-Hindu-Buddhist Austronesians surely had extensive oral literatures, but if they possessed writing no evidence of it has survived. They engaged in long-distance, "international" trade, no surprise considering their foreign origins and proven sea-faring capacity. We know, for example, that some of the great bronze drums, superb examples of which can be seen in the National Museum in Jakarta, were made in what is now northern Vietnam; while others, probably more recent, were made locally. The Austronesians were ruled by high chiefs, some of whom, by two thousand years ago, were ready for a more sophisticated political system, one that could formally extend beyond village borders. That was probably the key factor in the coming of Indonesia's first world religion.

Indonesia's Hindu-Buddhist Era (Sixth to Sixteenth Centuries)

Scholars have long debated why Indian religion came to Indonesia. The first thing to bear in mind is that "India" did not yet exist as a state. Indian culture was, on the other hand, already a pan-Asian phenomenon. Indian Buddhism had arrived in China by the second century CE. Beginning in the fifth or sixth century every part of Southeast Asia became partially "Indianized" with two exceptions: Vietnam, which remained in neighboring China's cultural orbit, and the Philippines. While the much-debated causes of this conversion were no doubt multiple, and varied from place to place, the overriding motive was probably political.

Indian religion offered ambitious rulers the wholly new concept of religiously sanctioned universal kingship, limitless in geographic scope, as opposed to the parochial, kin-bounded world of the animist chief, no matter how wealthy or powerful. In many cases the primary agent of change was probably the high-caste Hindu (brahmin) advisor, who brought with him not only a new world of literacy, but also a variety of legal and technical skills, elaborated in written manuals, invaluable for an ambitious ruler striving to get ahead.

There was no significant Indian colonization or conquest. International trade with or by way of India facilitated the spread of Hinduism, but traders do not seem to have been agents of change, in contrast to the role of Muslim port officials a millennium later during the transition to Islam. In some cases, wandering Brahmins may have ingratiated themselves with

Bas reliefs on the ninth-century Borobudur temple show the kinds of ships that Indonesians were using at the time, centuries before Islam arrived. This one has been caught in a storm; terrified passengers huddle on deck while a crew member tries to furl the sail. | Pringle photo

local rulers and then promoted conversion. Or the initiative may have come mostly from local rulers. One historian suggests a hypothetical moment when a Southeast Asian ruler, eager to equip himself with the latest route to religious power and more effective governance, and aware that Indian religions were coming into vogue elsewhere, would summon a high priestly advisor to his court.[4]

As it developed, Indian religion in Indonesia included cults dedicated to major Hindu deities, such as Shiva and Vishnu, as well as Buddhism. To modern ears, the words "Hindu" and "Buddhist" suggest wholly different faiths, but that assumption is incorrect for this time and place. In Southeast Asian practice, the difference between Buddhism and Hinduism was often no more profound than the distinctions among the various cults dedicated to Hindu gods and goddesses. Either Hinduism or Buddhism could become the vehicle for royal cults. Kings identified with gods, deifying themselves in the process, and merged with them after death. Royal temples became royal tombs dedicated to royal ancestor worship.

Majapahit, in the fourteenth and fifteenth centuries, was indeed both

4   J.C. van Leur, *Indonesian Trade and Society*, The Hague: van Hoeve, 1955, p. 98.

Hindu and Buddhist. Its royal cult was the worship of "Shiva-Buddha," through which the ruler could assume the attributes of both deities, and modern Balinese Hinduism retains both Hindu and Buddhist aspects.

By the eighth century major Indianized states were established throughout Southeast Asia. In Indonesia they were of two types: inland-agricultural and coastal-commercial, another Indonesian duality that would survive into modern times. The early interior states, located in the rich, rice-growing plains of Central Java and elsewhere, produced some of the most magnificent "Indian" art anywhere. The most famous example is the ninth-century Borobudur, a Buddhist monument which, contrary to the general rule, was a pilgrimage site and not a royal cult monument. It portrays the life of the Buddha and symbolizes a religious progression toward enlightenment, and it is striking testimony to the sophistication of Indonesian culture at this early date.

The most noteworthy example of the coastal-commercial state model was Srivijaya (seventh to thirteenth centuries). Built like a wooden Venice over water in Palembang, South Sumatra, Srivijaya left no spectacular ruins; indeed its very existence had been forgotten until less than a century ago, when French historian Georges Coedès and his colleagues rediscovered it through extraordinary detective work among ancient inscriptions and Chinese records. Srivijaya was the first in a succession of states built to control and profit from the main sea route linking India with China through the Straits of Malacca. Its geopolitical descendants have included Malacca, which featured prominently in the Islamization of Indonesia, and the modern city-state of Singapore.

Java was the most thoroughly "Indianized" region of Indonesia. In time and for unknown reasons (earthquakes? political upheaval?) its political center would shift from central to eastern Java and then back again. However, the history of Javanese art strikingly illustrates how Indian religion became Javanized over time. It began in the eighth and ninth centuries with "pure" styles based on classical Indian prototypes. It evolved into forms in which Javanese folk elements, often dating to pre-Hindu times, resurfaced and became dominant, not long before the advent of Islam. The integration of Hindu and pre-Hindu culture created a strong, multi-layered foundation which in time would greatly influence the practice of Islam on Java.

The last powerful Hindu-Buddhist state, Majapahit, was based in eastern Java. Interestingly, its founding in the late thirteenth century coincided closely with the establishment of the first Muslim states in Indonesia, located about a thousand miles away in northern Sumatra. Majapahit endured until about 1510, leaving the island of Bali as Indonesia's only Hindu realm.

The Pioneers of Islam

There is a gap of about five hundred years between the earliest evidence of a foreign Muslim presence in Indonesia and the first indication that substantial conversion of Indonesians to Islam was taking place. A Muslim colony may have existed in Canton, China as early as the seventh century, not long after Prophet Muhammad's death.[5] From the tenth to the mid-twelfth centuries, envoys with Muslim-sounding names traveled to China from Srivijaya, the great entrepot port on the Straits of Malacca.[6] A tombstone with a Muslim date found in Leran, East Java, dates from 1082. Much more of this kind of scattered evidence exists, but it has limited meaning. Old grave markers were sometimes used as ships' ballast, thus could have originated elsewhere, and in any case there were no doubt colonies of Muslim traders resident in Indonesia's polyglot port communities well before any substantial religious change.

The first evidence of a Muslim ruler in Indonesia does not appear until 1211, at Lamreh in northern Sumatra. By 1292, Marco Polo, on his way back from China, reported that Perlak, across the Malacca Straits in what is now Malaysia, was Muslim, but two nearby states were still Hindu. At about the same time the ruler of Pasai, also in northern Sumatra, in what is now Aceh, became a Muslim. From this point onwards the pace quickens. Rulers elsewhere in the archipelago begin to convert, first in Sumatra and what is now Malaysia, then in the far eastern Spice Islands, by then the focus of international trade, and finally, in the fifteenth century, on Java itself. But the Hindu-Buddhist era did not end abruptly, and in most cases the old and new religions continued to co-exist. Among the earliest evidence on Java of Indonesian (as opposed to foreign) Muslims are tombstones dated in the Hindu calendar to 1368–1369 CE. This was at the height of the Majapahit empire, and the graves are located at Trowulan, the site of its Hindu-Buddhist court, south of modern Surabaya.

5   B. Schrieke, "Ruler and Realm in Early Java," *Indonesian Sociological Studies*, Part 2, The Hague: van Hoeve, 1957, p. 231.
6   M.C. Ricklefs, *A History of Modern Indonesia since c. 1200*, 4th ed., Stanford CA: Stanford University Press, 2008, pp. 3–5; absent other citation, this book has been my primary source for early Islamization.

Burgeoning Trade and Religious Globalization

The spread of Islam to Southeast Asia was a symptom of globalization, slower but not fundamentally different from the modern variety. Trade grew first and foremost as the result of increased demand for Indonesian spices and other luxury goods in China as well as in the West. Increased capital resulting from gold and silver discoveries in the New World played a role. So did the growing importance of a sea route to Asia which was increasingly in the hands of Muslim rulers, and the advance of Islam under the Mughal Empire in India, a critical intermediate stop, beginning in the early sixteenth century.

Until the end of the thirteenth century spices and other Indonesian exports to Europe followed a route from Asian ports (including those on the north coast of Java) via Indian ports to the Persian Gulf, thence by land to Baghdad, from there onward to the eastern Mediterranean coast, and then by sea to Venice and other European ports. Several things combined to change that: the Mongol conquest of Baghdad and the Abbasid caliphate in 1258; the end of the Crusader presence in the Mediterranean (Acre, the last Crusader stronghold, fell to Muslim forces in 1291), and the rise of the powerful Mameluke Sultanate in Egypt (1250–1517). Under Egyptian dominance, a new trade route developed, running from Indonesian ports to Cambay in Gujarat, north of modern Mumbai (Bombay); from there to Aden and other ports in Arabia, then across the Red Sea and down the Nile to Alexandria.

From India eastwards the shipping was mainly in the hands of the fervently Muslim Gujaratis. Egypt controlled the western end of the route and was a great beneficiary of it.[7] As the trade grew due to the European demand for spices, and with Muslims in control of both ends of the trade route, so did the importance of Indonesian ports and the presence in them of Muslim traders and entire Islamic communities.

By the fifteenth century, Srivijaya, the dominant port on the Straits of Malacca, had fallen into decline. Conquered by Majapahit in 1377, its ruling family fled elsewhere, and its old capital at Palembang on the Sumatran coast degenerated into a pirate lair. Then, sometime not long after 1400, a Hindu prince named Paramesvara, a descendant of the Srivijayan ruling

---

7   On the trade route shift, see esp. B. Schrieke, "The Shifts in Political and Economic Power in the Indonesian Archipelago in the Sixteenth and Seventeenth Century" in *Indonesian Sociological Studies*, Part 1, The Hague: van Hoeve, 1955, pp. 7–18.

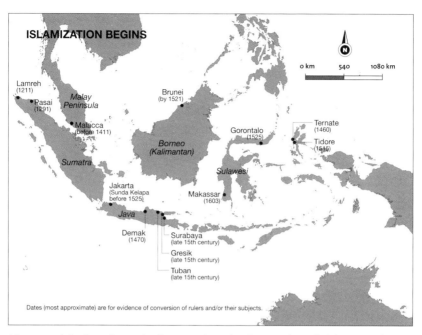

Islam spread slowly and sporadically across the archipelago. By the end of the sixteenth century the rulers of most major population centers had become Muslims.

family, founded a new port at Malacca, on what is now the Malaysian side of the straits. At first Paramesvara, aided according to tradition by warlike "Sea Gypsies," may have forced passing traders to visit his new city-state, but force would not have worked for long. To succeed and prosper, Malacca, like Srivijaya before it and Singapore after, had to be strong enough to eliminate rather than practice piracy, and well-governed enough to offer foreign traders a safe, congenial place to reprovision, exchange goods and store them. Most important, and the key factor in explaining the need for such a port, traders needed a place to await the seasonal change in monsoonal winds which determined what direction they could go at any given time of year, whether toward China and the Spice Islands or toward India.

Shortly before his death in about 1414, Malacca's founder converted to Islam and took the name Iskandar Shah. Under his successors Malacca quickly became the new Muslim Srivijaya. Javanese traders who had once shipped directly to India now stopped over in Malacca. It was a pure entrepôt port, living wholly on trade, without even growing its own food. Many foreigners lived there, including a large colony of Javanese.

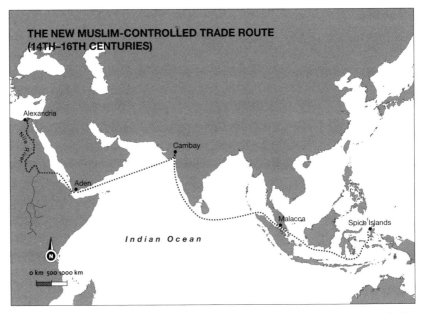

Muslim control of the western end of the spice trade route helped to stimulate the spread of Islam into what is now Indonesia.

Malacca maintained close ties with China. The famous Ming Dynasty Admiral Zheng He visited Malacca in 1409 on one of his epic "treasure fleet" voyages and bestowed a crown and robes of office on Iskandar Shah. Zheng He was a Muslim, but although his voyages were remembered in local folklore he is not, unlike some other Chinese, credited with having played a significant role in Islamic conversion.

As it prospered, Malacca's prestige stimulated the spread of Islam to smaller ports throughout the archipelago, including those on the north coast of Java. But in 1497 the Portuguese explorer Vasco de Gama reached India, and in 1511 Alphonse d'Albuquerque conquered Malacca. He built a new fortress there, in part with Islamic tombstones which he pillaged from its cemetery.

It might be assumed that the Portuguese conquest of Malacca inhibited the further spread of Islam. Instead it had the opposite effect. The Portuguese were not strong enough to monopolize the spice trade, as the Dutch later did. Not all Muslim traders ceased coming to Malacca, but, like fragments flying from a shattered rock, many of them, including the critically important Indian (Gujarati) element, scattered to other locations. Some went to Aceh, at the tip of Sumatra, already developing into a major pepper exporting port and center of Islamic learning. The rulers of Malacca, Iskandar Shah's descendants, eventually settled in Johore, at the tip of the Malay Peninsula, which also became a strong trading state in its own right. Others went back to the trading towns along the north coast of Java from which they had come to Malacca.

At first Malacca continued to prosper under Portuguese control and an astute Portuguese commentator, Tome Pires, could justifiably observe, "Whoever is lord of Malacca has his hand on the throat of Venice."[8] But by the end of the fifteenth century Muslim ports, most notably the new state of Demak on Java, were challenging the power of Majapahit, and before much longer Portuguese-controlled Malacca was also under Muslim siege.

Was There a Race with Christianity?

It is tempting to infer that the competition between Muslims and Christians for control of the spice trade was a race between religions, if not a clash of civilizations. One respected Dutch historian has written that the Portuguese expansion "must be viewed as a sequel to the Crusades."[9] The Christians had just reclaimed control of Spain from the Moors, and Portugal's aggressive campaign to capture the spice trade could have been seen by all concerned as an extension of that struggle.

The Portuguese were interested primarily in profit, not converts, but it was during their presence in the Spice Islands that St. Francis Xavier, a Spaniard and co-founder of the Jesuit order, appeared on the scene in 1546. He did not like the Portuguese, remarking that their knowledge was restricted to one verb, *rapio*, "to plunder," in which they showed "an amazing capacity for inventing new tenses and participles."[10] But Xavier founded a mission in the spice-producing east and his successors carried it on. It was to be the one area of Indonesia where Portuguese religious and cultural influence endured, in the form of musical styles, words in the modern Indonesian language, and a large Christian minority.

Elsewhere at the same period, in both the Philippines and Vietnam, Catholic missionaries were making much more significant gains for Christendom. Everywhere the rule held that once people converted to

---

8   Tome Pires, *The Suma Oriental of Tome Pires: An Account of the East, from the Red Sea to China, Written in Malacca and India in 1512–1515*, Armando Cortesao, ed., reprint ed., New Delhi: Asia Educational Services, 2005, Vol. 2, p. 287.
9   Schrieke, "Ruler and Realm," p. 233.
10   Quoted in D.G.E. Hall, *History of South-East Asia*, 3rd ed., London: Macmillan, 1968, p. 244.

either Islam or Christianity they rarely changed allegiance to the other new religion, implying that a race of sorts was indeed going on. The Spanish, hoping to get a portion of the spice trade, began to occupy what is now the Philippines in 1565. They found Islam already entrenched in the southern islands and beginning to spread north. Had they arrived even a decade or two later the Philippines might have ended up as a primarily Muslim country, not a Catholic country with a perennially restless Muslim minority in the south.

The Portuguese attacked the ships of Muslim traders, often killing Southeast Asian pilgrims enroute to Mecca. At one point the rulers of Gujarat and Yemen complained about this practice to the Sultan of Egypt, who sent an envoy to the Pope, who wrote a letter to the King of Portugal, who predictably did nothing.[11] Later, during the reign of Suleiman the Magnificent, the Acehnese sought and received military assistance from Turkey, probably in about 1540, against the pagan Batak people of the interior, and certainly in 1568, against the Portuguese.[12] On Java the Islamization of the north coast ports, already underway before the Portuguese captured Malacca, helped to prevent them from forming alliances with their potential allies, the remaining Hindu-Buddhist states in the interior.

While there is little doubt that Indonesian rulers sometimes used the banner of Islam as an ideological weapon, or that appeals to allies in the name of Islam could be effective, the struggle for the spice trade seems nonetheless to have been primarily a matter of power politics and commercial rivalry, not a religious race. Throughout the period under discussion, there were frequent conflicts among the new Muslim states in Indonesia and also among the Christian intruders, exemplified by the murderous early seventeenth century brawl between the Dutch and English for control of the Spice Islands, which happened despite the fact that the two countries were allies in Europe.[13]

Aceh was already a rising power when the Portuguese captured Malacca, and one expert on the subject believes that if the Portuguese had not captured Malacca, the Acehnese might well have tried to do so.

---

11 Schrieke, "Ruler and Realm," p. 234. He gives no date for this episode.
12 Anthony Reid, *Southeast Asia in the Age of Commerce 1450–1680*, Vol. 1: *The Lands Below the Winds*, New Haven and London: Yale University Press, 1988, pp. 146–47.
13 The most shocking event was the so-called "Amboina Massacre" of 1623: Hall, *History of South-East Asia*, p. 310.

Later a three-way conflict developed among the Catholic Portuguese, the rising Muslim state of Aceh, and Muslim Johore, where the former ruler of Malacca had established himself. After barely surviving constant attacks on Malacca, the Portuguese felt it necessary to form an alliance with Islamic Johore. At the end of the day they lost all interest in promoting Christianity. The Dutch arrived later with a similarly secular, mercenary perspective, but they were better financed, organized and equipped, hence were able to stay the course.

The Dynamics of Conversion

Why did Indonesians convert to Islam? Not all of them did, and certainly not right away. There is little evidence of exactly what happened, and the dynamics of conversion no doubt varied from place to place. We do know that people in small settlements or remote rural areas, far from the centers of trade, kept their blend of animism and ancestor worship. Elsewhere, while most Hindu-Buddhist rulers changed faiths, the speed of their followers' conversion was gradual and its intensity varied.

As had been the case with Hinduization eight centuries previously, Islamization presumably began at the top, among a diverse panoply of rulers. On Java these rulers were often heirs to a rich and complex civilization. Their ancestors had abandoned bronze-age religion because the Indian faiths offered literacy, technical skills and expanded political horizons. For their descendants, Islam offered no similar new and desirable features. Islam's major political distinction, the theoretical equality of all believers, probably did not appeal at all to the Indonesian aristocracy.

On the negative side, Islam did require practitioners to abandon alcohol and pork. Because pork was an important source of protein, forgoing it may have been a real problem for animists in remote, forested areas, but such populations were irrelevant in the initial stages of conversion focused on port cities. Conversion also required Hindu rulers to stop cremating and start burying their dead, which was likely to have offended the priestly class at first.

However, Islam was the religion of the booming trade routes, and it brought exciting new political as well as economic opportunities. As the ports expanded, a new class of officialdom, in which Muslims played key roles, was required to govern them. The most important was the *shahbandar*, or harbormaster. There were four of them in pre-Portuguese Malacca, each responsible for traders from different regions.[14]

With time, these officials gained status, and with status came the possibility of marriage with ruling families.[15] It seems likely that, despite an absence of documented examples, intermarriage would have required conversion to Islam. In some cases it may have been the familiar story of a threadbare aristocracy trading status for money. In other cases the rulers themselves received some of the profits of the trade and participated in it, directly or through royal agents. As rulers converted to Islam, and became sultans, and as word spread of powerful new Islamic realms in India and elsewhere, Islam itself gained status. When Europeans entered the region, Islam offered a unifying, international bond of partnership and some degree of protection against these dangerous, well-armed rivals.

Once converted, rulers might or might not try to convert their neighbors by force. If they did, in most cases political ambition rather than religion seems to have been the primary motive. The classic case was the north coast of Java. Tome Pires visited the area not long after 1511 and described a complex, multicultural society in the throes of change. There were animists and Muslims (including Chinese Muslims). Some Javanese leaders were Islamized, in varying degrees, while others remained entranced by the courtly prestige of the old Hindu-Buddhist order.[16] The Muslim rulers of the coastal ports could not compete with the old aristocracy in terms of pedigree, but they had money and ambition, and some of them used religion to help them topple what was left of Majapahit.

The first truly powerful of the new Islamic city-states on the north coast of Java was Demak, which may have been founded in about 1470 by a foreign, probably Chinese, Muslim. Demak and its offshoot states are credited with the extinction of Majapahit and the other remaining Hindu-Buddhist regimes in Central and West Java. One of the last to fall was Banten, a pepper port on the western end of the north coast. Banten's Hindu-Buddhist ruler, anticipating trouble at the hands of Demak, sought an alliance with the Portuguese in 1522. The agreement gave the Europeans permission to open a post at Sunda Kelapa, the site of modern Jakarta, but the Portuguese sailed away without acting. When they returned five years later, they found that Muslim Demak had conquered Hindu Banten in the intervening period, and they were not allowed to remain.

---

14   Pires, *Suma Oriental*, Vol. 2, p. 263.
15   Schrieke, "Shifts in Political and Economic Power," pp. 28–29.
16   See Pires' account of Java in his *Suma Oriental*, Vol. 2, pp. 166–200.

The new Muslim ruler of Banten was typically pragmatic about assimilating elements of the old religion where it would bolster his status, for example by using for his throne and city center a luminous rock which had been the meditation place of a famous Hindu holy man. It would be interesting to know if he was consciously emulating the Prophet's use of the Ka'bah in Mecca, also the site of a sacred rock revered in pre-Islamic times.[17]

Aside from Tome Pires' account, there is little first hand or documentary evidence about this period in Javanese history. Unlike their Hindu-Buddhist forbears, the new Muslim rulers did not leave inscriptions chiseled on stone, and records written on perishable material have rarely survived. Javanese chronicles or *babad*, all of them written in their current forms centuries later, were intended primarily to legitimize and enhance the prestige of later rulers. They are nonetheless rich in historical implications filtered through centuries of re-telling. Among the main actors are the nine *wali*, teachers and holy men (*wali* is short for *wali Allah*, meaning "friend of God"). Some of them were historical figures.

The stories about the *wali* include miraculous conversions to Islam and feats of derring-do. The *wali* created new characters for the *wayang* shadow puppet theatre, a pre-Islamic art form at the core of Javanese culture.[18] Some of the *wali*, like Sunan Giri of Gresik, proselytized in the name of Islam. He and his heirs are credited with converting the island of Madura and much of eastern Indonesia. The Dutch inaccurately referred to his descendants as "the Mohammedans' pope."[19]

As portrayed in the Javanese chronicles the *wali* always had illustrious ancestors, often from multiple sources, including China, Champa, the ancient, Austronesian-speaking Hindu kingdom in what is now Vietnam, and of course Majapahit. An American politician operating in such a mode would want to be descended from, among others, St. Peter, George Washington, Pocahontas and Booker T. Washington, and his creative genealogist would be able to arrange it for him, or her. The *wali* remain a vital component of Javanese Islam. Their tombs are still major pilgrimage sites, and books about them are still selling briskly.

---

17   Claude Guillot, "Banten in 1678," *Indonesia*, Vol. 57 (April 1994), pp. 90–91.

18   On the *Wali* tradition generally see "Wali: the First Preachers of Islam in Java," in James J. Fox, ed., *Religion and Ritual*, Indonesian Heritage Series, Vol. 9, Singapore: Didier Millet, 1998, pp. 18–19.

19   Schrieke, "Ruler and Realm," p. 239.

The early Javanese accommodation of Islam with older beliefs was quite striking, as can easily be understood by a visit to one of several ancient tomb complexes. One, that of Sunan Giri, *wali* and fervent crusading Muslim, is located in Gresik, near modern Surabaya on Java's north coast. It is a good example of traditional Javanese pagoda-style mosque architecture, derived from Hindu-Buddhist practice and richly decorated with Chinese-influenced carvings. To the west, in Cirebon, is the tomb of Putri Cina, the "Chinese Princess," who according to legend was the daughter of a Chinese emperor. As a convert to Islam, she features prominently in the life of another *wali*, Sunan Gunung Jati. In front of her grave in the Gunung Jati tomb complex are offering bowls with incense sticks, as in a Chinese temple, where women pray for enhanced fertility.

The Potent Role of Islamic Mysticism

Money and force might not have sufficed to convert the Javanese had Islam not been intellectually and aesthetically attractive to formerly Hindu-Buddhist Javanese rulers. Although the dynamics of conversion no doubt varied greatly from place to place, what might well have been most attractive to potential converts was the mystical content of contemporary Islam. Islamic mystics are called "Sufi" from the Arabic word for "wool," referring to the rough woolen garb often worn by monks and holy men in Islam as well as Christianity.

Sufism, like most mysticism, has less to do with religious doctrine than it does with the *methodology* of worship. Sufis believe, as do most other Muslims, that God is essentially unknowable, all-powerful and omnipresent. But Sufis also believe that if the proper devotional procedures are used, worshippers can more effectively approach God and achieve heightened awareness of Him.[20] Such a feat cannot be accomplished by anyone; it requires expert guidance from a master practitioner.

Sufism is not related to the division between Sunni and Shia Islam; it exists within both. However the vast majority of Indonesian Muslims have always been Sunni, with a small exception in modern times. Sufis have not always been tolerant or peaceful; they have also been violent jihadists, like the Sufi would-be Mahdi (a term roughly analogous to "messiah" in Judeo-Christian tradition) who massacred the British General "Chinese" Gordon

---

20 "Heightened awareness" is from the introduction to Martin van Bruinessen and Julia Day Howell, eds., *Sufism and the 'Modern' in Islam*, London: I.B. Tauris, 2006, p. 6.

at Khartoum in 1885, to cite one well-known example. In Indonesia, Sufis and their organizations participated in a number of uprisings against the Dutch in the late nineteenth and early twentieth centuries.[21]

A Sufi order or brotherhood (*tarekat*) is a group of devotees assembled under the guidance of a master primarily to conduct religious observances. Historically these masters have been more than just teachers; often they have assumed holy status and passed control of their organizations to their own descendants. Although the religious aspects of the *tarekat* are best known, brotherhoods could serve other social functions, including charitable work, health care, and as trade associations or guilds.[22]

Many Sufi orders were founded during the medieval period in the Middle East. It is likely that they arrived in Indonesia at an early date, certainly by the fifteenth century, although hard evidence of their presence is lacking.[23] Sufi holy men and brotherhoods would have been concentrated in the variegated, multi-national communities that developed in the expanding port cities.

Indonesian Sufis went to the Middle East to study and sometimes to live. Among the most famous was a sixteenth-century Sumatran poet and mystic named Hamzah Fansuri, who is among the first known poets in the Malay (Indonesian) language. There was another even earlier, possibly Sumatran Sufi scholar known to the Arabs as Mohammad al-Jawi, "Mohammed from Jawi," *Jawi* meaning somewhere in the Indonesian Archipelago, not necessarily Java.[24] Such scholars were active and sometimes prominent in centers of learning in southern Arabia, near the trade routes to the Far East, as early as the fourteenth century. Their presence is proof of an established Sufi intellectual connection between Indonesia and Arabia by that time.

There seems to be little doubt that prominent Sufi masters would have been able to meet leaders steeped in Hindu-Buddhist traditions on their own terms. As we have seen, Indonesia's Hindu-Buddhist rulers

21 Martin van Bruinessen, "The origins and development of the Sufi orders (tarekat) in Southeast Asia," *Studia Islamika-Indonesian Journal for Islamic Studies*, Vol. 1, No. 1 (1994) accessed July 2008 at http://www.let.uu.nl/~martin.vanbruinessen/personal/publications/Sufi%20orders%20in%201.

22 Fox, *Religion and Ritual*, p.16; on the likely role of Sufi trade guilds see A. Johns, "Muslim Mystics and Historical Writing" in D.G.E. Hall, ed., *Historians of South East Asia*, London: Oxford University Press, pp. 40–41.

23 Personal communication from Martin van Bruinessen; see also his "Origins and development of the Sufi orders."

24 R. Michael Feener and Michael Laffan, "Sufi Scents across the Indian Ocean: Yemeni Hagiography and the Earliest History of Southeast Asian Islam," *Archipel*, Vol. 70, 2005, pp. 185–208.

typically sought access to supernatural power through religious practices. As Islam gained strength, local rulers could have viewed Sufism as the latest and most politically advantageous method of acquiring such power. Sufism meshed neatly with the Indian tradition of holy men, hermits and esoteric paths to knowledge. The holy status and hereditary features of Sufi leadership, including reverence for deceased leaders, was compatible with the powerful strains of ancestor worship featured in most pre-Islamic religion in Indonesia. Sufism also coexisted easily with a Hindu philosophy which viewed all other religions as part of one infinite stream, a universalistic outlook broadly characteristic of mysticism in general. [25]

The transition from Hindu-Buddhism to mystical Islam might have been easier had it not been for the inherently controversial nature of Sufism within Islam itself. Then as now, Islam was a religion without universally agreed-upon doctrinal authority beyond the Koran. Except for fundamental core beliefs, including the Five Pillars of Islam, many teachings and traditions have been subject to debate and interpretation, much as they have been in other major faiths.

One complication for Sufism has always been that one of its main assumptions, that God is in all things, can slide easily into the conceit that man is personally divine and thereby collide with the central Islamic tenet that there is no God but Allah, which no Muslim accepts as open to re-interpretation. Thus the history of Sufism within Islam worldwide has been one of "thirteen centuries of controversies and polemics," to quote the title of one scholarly book on the subject.[26]

One famous Persian Sufi known as al-Hallaj, who announced that he had discovered "the truth" in himself, was executed as a heretic in 922 for claiming that it was possible to make a valid spiritual pilgrimage to Mecca without leaving home.[27] According to tradition, there was an Indonesian equivalent of al-Hallaj, a mystic and *wali* named Siti Jenar, who was put to death by his fellow *wali* for (among other things) equating himself with God.[28] He is nonetheless still revered by some Javanese mystics.

25 For a highly readable introduction to this subject, see Heinrich Zimmer, ed. Joseph Campbell, *Myths and Symbols in Indian Art and Civilization*, Princeton NJ: Princeton University Press, 1972.

26 Frederick de Jong and Bernd Radtke, eds., *Islamic Mysticism Contested: Thirteen Centuries of Controversies and Polemics*, Leiden: Brill, 1999.

27 Karen Armstrong, *Islam*, New York: Random House Modern Library, 2000, p. 75.

28 Azyumardi Azra, "Opposition to Sufism in the East Indies in the 17th and 18th Centuries" in de Jong and Radtke, *Islamic Mysticism Contested*, pp. 671–72.

The history of Islam in Indonesia has been one of fluctuation and tension between two broad religious styles: Sufi-influenced Islam, coexisting relatively easily with many older elements in local culture, and a less forgiving, more legalistic style emphasizing the requirements of doctrine as interpreted by the latest trends in global Islam. Historian Merle Ricklefs has described how Javanese Islam at first reflected the Sufi-influenced religious culture, a "mystic synthesis" which prevailed until the nineteenth century. After that a polarization gradually developed between Sufi-influenced Islam and more doctrinaire Islam.[29]

The contrast between two styles of Islam, more or less influenced by mysticism and local custom on one hand and by legalistic doctrine on the other, has never, if judged impartially, reflected a distinction between "good" and "bad" Islam. Nor have the two styles ever been static or exact. The differences between them have been stimulated and changed over time by many factors: constant waves of new thinking from the Middle East, the quest for modernity through education, the exigencies of the anti-colonial struggle, and the political impact of economic growth. We are talking about another Indonesian duality, hard to parse but obvious nonetheless, comparable to the equally imperfect distinction between "red" and "blue" political cultures in the United States, or the contrast between Protestant and Catholic political cultures in some regions of post-Medieval Europe. It is a duality that has had an enduring influence on Indonesia's political life, especially with regard to underlying assumptions about the role of Islam in human affairs.

Throughout the rest of this book I have used the terms "Traditionalist" to indicate the Sufi-influenced style and "Reformist" to refer to the more doctrinaire style. Although divisive to a degree, the Traditionalist-Reformist duality has also been positive and creative, a characteristic of Indonesia's broader diversity. Today it finds its most prominent expression in two great, mainstream Muslim organizations, Nahdlatul Ulama (Traditionalist) and Muhammadiyah (Reformist), both of them diverse within themselves. They will be frequently discussed in the pages ahead.

Today many Indonesians point out that Sufism meets the need for a religious "inner way," providing space for individual devotion and search

---

29 See M.C. Ricklefs, *Mystic Synthesis in Java: A History of Islamization from the Fourteenth to the Early Nineteenth Centuries*, Norwalk CT: Eastbridge, 2006, and, by the same author, *Polarizing Java: Islamic and Other Visions (c. 1830–1930)*, Singapore: National University of Singapore Press, 2007.

for truth, complementing the outward manifestation of Islamic piety expressed through formal worship. They use the words *batin* (inward) and *lahir* (outward) to express these contrasting but equally valid aspects of Islam, while the word for mysticism is *kebatinan* (innerness). Just as the Sufi style once aided conversion to Islam, so even today there are probably some, mainly Javanese, who would not be Muslims without it. Recently Sufism has taken on new forms and greatly strengthened Indonesia's modern Islamic revival.[30] But its humanistic appeal is nothing new; it is palpable in a sixteenth-century verse on the nature of God by Hamzah Fansuri, a good example of mysticism's lyrical side:

> He is the greatest of kings…
> He constantly conceals himself within a slave…
> He is both mother and father…
> Now He is a [merchant] traveler
> Now a comrade working in the fields
> Now His wealth is of no account
> Always sailing onto the reef[31]

(Ecological aside: Perhaps because Hamzah traveled a great deal, images of coral reefs occur frequently in his poetry, not for their aesthetic or environmental interest, but because they were a mortal threat to the sail-powered ships of the time.)

Indonesia on the Eve of Dutch Rule

One might have thought that with Islam in the ascendancy, Javanese power would have remained centered on the commercial north coast, where Islam had taken root. Instead a new Muslim state founded in the old Hindu-Buddhist heartland of Central Java became the first major Javanese power since the fall of Majaphit. It became known as Mataram, the same name used by a pre-Islamic kingdom in the same area seven centuries previously. Its most powerful ruler, Sultan Agung (reigned 1613–1646), began by eliminating Muslim rivals on the coast (the last one, Surabaya, fell in 1625), and then turned against the Dutch, who had planted their

---

30 Julia Day Howell, "Sufism and the Indonesian Islamic Revival," *Journal of Asian Studies*, Vol. 60, No. 3 (Aug. 2001), pp. 701–29.

31 Anthony Reid, *Southeast Asia in the Age of Commerce 1450–1680*, Vol. 2, *Expansion and Crisis*, New Haven and London: Yale University Press, 1993, p. 172.

headquarters at Batavia (Jakarta) in 1619 under a tough new commander, Jan Pieterszoon Coen.

Sultan Agung besieged Batavia twice, in 1628 and 1629, marching his elephant-equipped armies hundreds of kilometers across hilly, almost roadless terrain, and failed to achieve victory by only a narrow margin. It would take the Dutch the better part of two centuries to subdue Mataram and establish complete control over Java, and almost another century to complete the job beyond Java. Nevertheless, the failure of Agung's offensive marked the beginning of something approaching real colonialism in Indonesia.

Throughout Indonesia most of the old Hindu-Buddhist states were by then at least nominally Muslim. The last major shift from Hindu-Buddhism to Islam took place in 1605, when Makassar in South Sulawesi converted. The island of Bali remained Hindu and would not be completely controlled by the Dutch until early in the twentieth century, and there were still pockets of Hindu-Buddhism mingled with animism in East Java. In areas where Hindu-Buddhism had put down deep roots, mainly in East and Central Java, the older heritage remained strong and the resulting tension between religious styles would have political implications throughout the colonial period and beyond.

There were still important communities practicing animism and bronze-age lifestyles, mostly in remote interior regions little affected by either Hindu-Buddhism or Islam. These included the Bataks of Sumatra, the Toraja of South Sulawesi, most of the interior peoples of Borneo and many others. Many of them would remain untouched by world religion until the arrival of Christian missionaries in the nineteenth century. The western half of New Guinea was still virtual *terra incognita*, not even part of Dutch (hence eventually Indonesian) territory until 1848, and without a serious Dutch presence until the twentieth century.

At the beginning of the seventeenth century, Indonesia remained very thinly settled, perhaps four to five million people in Java and Bali, compared to 124 million today, and five million in the Outer Islands.[32] Beyond the settled areas, vast expanses remained forested, even on Java. Wars were still fought to gain control of population, which, unlike land, was a scarce commodity, a situation which seems unimaginable today.

Having bested the British (who, being preoccupied with India, were

---

32   Reid, *Southeast Asia in the Age of Commerce, 1450–1680*, Vol. 1, table 1, p. 14.

not really interested in Indonesia), the Dutch moved toward an effective monopoly of the spice trade, something the Portuguese had never achieved. In so doing they would resort to such draconian measures as forcibly restricting spice production in the eastern islands, but they soon discovered that they remained dependent on Indonesian middlemen and suppliers, usually Muslims. Except when rebels raised the banner of Islam against them, as they were to do fairly often, the Dutch cared little about Christian-Muslim distinctions. Always focused on profit, the Calvinist Protestant Hollanders thought it quite proper to ally themselves with Muslim Johore in 1641 in order to snatch Malacca from the Catholic Portuguese.

Other Muslim states within today's Indonesia, including Aceh and the emerging Buginese state in southern Sulawesi, were still independent international players. All this would change, but gradually. Only after the mid-nineteenth century would the Dutch see Islam as inherently dangerous, a cause of rebellion rather than simply the religion of most rebels, who were never in short supply. Meanwhile, the colonial rulers were creating economic conditions that nurtured the spread of Islam. The next chapter will explore these topics as well as the brief but critically important period of Japanese rule.

2

Islam Under Dutch and Japanese Rule (1629–1945)

One of the earliest Dutch expeditions to Indonesia made the mistake of visiting Aceh, then as now a place of intense Islamic fervency. Its leader, Frederick de Houtman, was captured after a fight broke out between his men and the Acehnese. After several months of detention he was told that the Sultan had decided to execute him unless he changed religions. His captors tried persuasion at first, but ended up brandishing a sword over his head, yelling "*Mau Islam*??" ("Accept Islam??") and threatening to trample him with elephants. The Hollander remained obdurate, but he survived because the Sultan apparently thought he would be more useful alive than dead.[1] The story had a happy ending: de Houtman spent his time in jail studying the Malay language – he compiled a word list which became the basis for later dictionaries and grammar books – and he was eventually released. On another occasion, in 1655, the Dutch were having trouble with the ruler of Palembang, in southern Sumatra. Members of their negotiating party were attacked and forced to undergo conversion by circumcision, a doctrinally dubious as well as painful method.[2]

While in general such episodes were rare, accounts of them no doubt grew in the telling, and they were common enough to encourage the stereotype of implacable, bloodthirsty Islam. But at the end of the day, the Dutch had to coexist and cooperate with Muslim subjects, and especially Muslim rulers, in order to achieve their commercial objectives, and they knew it.

1   Anthony Reid, "Islamization and Christianization in Southeast Asia: The Critical Phase, 1550–1650" in Anthony Reid, ed., *Southeast Asia in the Early Modern Era: Trade, Power and Belief*, Ithaca NY: Cornell University Press, 1993, pp. 173–74.
2   M.C. Ricklefs, *A History of Modern Indonesia since c. 1200*, 4th ed., Stanford CA: Stanford University Press, 2008, p. 81.

From Dutch Company to Dutch Colony

The Dutch presence in what would become Indonesia began as a semi-piratical enterprise operated by a quasi-private entity, the Dutch East India Company. Having achieved control of the spice trade, the Dutch discovered that even more money could be made from compelling the natives to grow cash crops, first coffee (not referred to as "Java" for nothing), then sugar and others.

But in addition to corruption and inefficiency, "Jan Compagnie" began to suffer from what in modern parlance would be called "mission creep": as it prospered, it expanded, and as it expanded it got embroiled with recalcitrant natives. Such embroilments led to warfare and growing need for military support. It was time for the state to take over, and the Indies became an official Dutch colony in 1800.

Shortly thereafter the Napoleonic Wars came to Indonesia. Bonaparte conquered the Netherlands, which led the British to occupy Java. Stamford Raffles, the glamorous, polymath British governor of Java (technically only a lieutenant governor under the Governor-General of India) wanted to keep the Dutch possession for Britain, but London, always concerned that the British Empire was getting too big, turned him down.

After the defeat of Napoleon the Dutch came back to Java. Armed with increasingly effective technology, they slowly spread into the Outer Islands, expanded their cash-crop agriculture, and gradually consolidated their control. By the time the twentieth century arrived they were beginning to be concerned, if only marginally, about the welfare of the Indonesians.

For the first two centuries of their presence in Indonesia the Dutch felt no need for a "Muslim policy." They remained focused on money and its corollary, achieving control, not converting the natives to Christianity. They began to worry about Islam only in the mid-nineteenth century, realizing that it could be a dangerous source of resistance to their imperial presence. But well before that, Islam was drawing strength from two factors: the growth of modern, international communications, including with the Middle East, and the unanticipated stimulus to Islamization which resulted from Dutch-sponsored economic development.

However, from the very beginning of Dutch rule there was constant warfare, highly various in nature, in which Muslim communities and leaders played important roles. These conflicts have been remembered in Indonesia, and that memory has helped to shape the relationship between Islam and nationalism.

Islam and Anti-colonial Warfare

During the seventeenth and eighteenth centuries, the Company slowly brought its rivals on Java under control, however imperfect by later standards. Cut off from the coast, and from direct involvement in international commerce, the Mataram kingdom lost the Islamic fervor which marked its high water mark under Sultan Agung, the great ruler who had nearly expelled the Dutch and had been a major architect of the "mystic synthesis" between Islam and traditional beliefs. Pre-Islamic religious currents enjoyed a renaissance, and Sultan Agung's son and successor, Amangkurat I (reigned 1646–1677), went so far as to massacre several thousand Muslim clerics.

Mataram was plagued by constant civil war, and in the eighteenth century it divided, with one court at Solo (Surakarta) and the other at Yogyakarta. Each of these later divided again, leaving the modern total of four royal houses in Central Java, two at each location. The Dutch took sides and influenced events, but they certainly did not govern the squabbling Javanese nobility. The first out-and-out military assault on a Javanese kingdom was not carried out until 1812 by Raffles, better known for his reputedly idealistic reforms.

In the Outer Islands the Company relied on Indonesian allies to achieve victories. The Dutch, as one historian has written, were simultaneously "ally and *kafir* [infidel], friend and foe" to the Indonesians.[3] In the Spice Islands, Sultan Saifuddin of Tidore allied with the Dutch to drive out the Spanish, who pulled back to Manila in 1663. The Dutch used Christian Ambonese with great war canoes to help achieve a spice monopoly, by uprooting clove and nutmeg trees in non-cooperating areas. In the conversion-by-circumcision episode mentioned earlier in this chapter, Muslim Jambi was helping the Christian Dutch against Muslim Palembang. Potent assistance from the Muslim Buginese of South Sulawesi helped the Dutch against the neighboring Makassarese. Religion never mattered much in these early colonial wars. The Dutch did not have the resources to attempt large-scale conversion of the natives to Christianity even had they been so inclined, although they did in time encourage or compel Roman Catholic communities which had been created by the Portuguese in the

---

3   Jean Gelman Taylor, *Indonesia: Peoples and Histories*, New Haven: Yale University Press, 2003, p. 141.

Spice Islands and elsewhere to become Protestants.[4]

Following the end of Company rule, and as the economic interests of the Dutch extended beyond spices to cash crops and minerals, they began to concentrate more on the expansion and consolidation of empire and the development of infrastructure. Conflict with Indonesians was constant, but the margin of military strength slowly shifted in favor of the Dutch. They no longer depended, at least not to the same degree, on native allies, although they often used colonial troops from Indonesia or their colonies elsewhere.

The causes of nineteenth and early twentieth century wars varied widely. In most of them, Indonesian rulers were still struggling to retain power, and the wealth and prestige that came with it. Rulers sometimes invoked Islam against encroaching infidels, but the idea of an Indonesian nation did not occur to them until the twentieth century. Sometimes resistance took on a desperate, emotional character, as newly subjected people invoked supernatural assistance in a hopeless effort to rid themselves of dimly understood taxes and regulations, or to restore a lost world of autonomous village communities. The Samin Movement in Java (1890–1917) was one classic example of such unrest; another was the suicidal reaction of Hindu Balinese monarchs against well-armed Dutch invaders in 1906–1908.

Three anti-colonial wars are worth mentioning at greater length:

The Padri War (1821–38) took place in the Minangkabau Highlands of West Sumatra from 1821 to 1838. The Padris were Muslim religious leaders, so named because they returned from the pilgrimage to Mecca via the port of Pedir in Aceh. The early nineteenth century was a time of turmoil in Minangkabau country. Gold, the traditional source of wealth, was running out and being replaced by cash crops, including coffee. This economic shift had produced a new class of merchants who traded directly with British and American traders in Penang, in what is now Malaysia. They chafed under the authority of local rulers whose wealth was based on gold and who were the product of old, pre-Islamic hierarchies (Minangkabau had once been a Hindu-Buddhist satellite of Majapahit).

The Padris had much in common with more recent Islamic fundamentalists. They preached religious reform and Wahabi-inspired

---

4   W. F. Wertheim, *Indonesian Society in Transition: A Study of Social Change*, 2nd rev. ed., The Hague: van Hoeve, 1969, p. 200.

purification. Adherents of Wahabi-style Islam, much later to become the state religion of Saudi Arabia, had temporarily taken control of the Holy Places in Arabia in 1803. Then as now, its followers campaigned against sin – alcohol, gambling and so on – and were offended by aspects of Minangkabau custom resulting from a matrilineal kinship system.[5] The merchant class supported the Padris because they believed they would get a better deal for their trading activities under Islamic law. In 1815 the Padri rebels murdered some members of the Minangkabau royal family. The old ruling class then asked for help from the Dutch, and signed a treaty ceding control to them in 1821.

The Islamic rebels were led by "Imam Bonjol," who was actually the Imam *of* Bonjol, a town in the Minangkabau Highlands. Like many anti-colonial rebel leaders, his name recognition today owes something to the fact that there is a major street named after him in modern Jakarta. He and his foes might have been allowed to fend for themselves, but the Acehnese, still a muscular power, had been expanding down the west coast of Sumatra, threatening Dutch interests. So the Dutch used troops against the Padris and eventually won.

In time the old ruling class of West Sumatra, like its counterpart on Java, was reduced to pliant, figurehead status. Imam Bonjol was arrested and exiled to Menado, a Christian area in northern Sulawesi, where he died. The Dutch saw the Padri conquest as a contest between Islam and *adat*, meaning custom or customary law, but always reserved in Dutch practice for non-Islamic customary law. It was soon to dawn on them that this apparent tension between custom and Islam could be the basis for an Indies-wide divide-and-rule strategy.

The Java War (1825–30) was at heart a reaction to a more interventionist style of colonial rule introduced by the British and continued by the restored Dutch government: new taxes, leasing of land to Europeans and Chinese for cash crop production, and growing assumption of administrative authority once exercised by Javanese rulers. Its leader, Diponegoro, is one of the more memorable figures in Indonesia's anti-colonial pantheon. He was a Javanese prince who for family reasons had been reared in a rural area,

---

5   Whether (or to what extent) the Padris were genuine Wahabis is subject to some dispute: see Jeffry Hadler, "A Historiography of Violence and the Secular State in Indonesia: Tuanku Imam Bonjol and the Uses of History," *Journal of Asian Studies*, Vol. 67, No. 3 (Aug 2008), esp. pp. 979–80.

*The Islamic rebel Diponegoro, known as the "*pesantren *prince" for his experience as a student of Islam, is depicted being arrested by the Dutch in 1830 when he accepted an invitation to negotiate with them. | Istana Palace Museum, Jakarta, Pringle photo*

where he studied at Islamic boarding schools (*pesantren*), consorted with their teachers, and became a devout Islamic mystic[6] – hence his reputation as "the *pesantren* prince." As a result he was atypically familiar with conditions in the countryside, beyond the isolation of the royal court.

With links to three worlds – rural Java, court circles and Islam – Diponegoro easily became a potent focal point for discontent. He then had a religious experience which convinced him that he was a future ruler of Java, the *ratu adil* (just king) of Javanese mythology. A poor harvest in 1821 was followed by a Dutch decision to abolish private leasing of lands, depriving aristocrats of revenue and obliging them to repay advances. The result was a simmering stew of popular and aristocratic discontents. In 1825 Diponegoro's men scuffled with those of a senior court official, and the Dutch, who by now recognized his vaulting ambition, tried to arrest

---

6   "Devout Islamic mystic" is slightly reworded from M.C. Ricklefs, *Polarizing Javanese Society: Islamic and Other Visions (c. 1830–1930)*, Singapore: National University of Singapore Press, 2007, p. 8.

him. The result was a major conflict which led to an estimated 200,000 Javanese casualties.

Diponegoro flaunted his Islamic identity, wearing white robes and a Turkish-style turban into battle, as he is depicted in a grand portrait in the entryway to the Indonesian Embassy in Washington. The religious community, led by Kiai Maja, rallied to support him. (Streets in modern Jakarta are named after both Diponegoro and Kiai Maja.) But by this time the Dutch were strong and they gradually wore the rebels down with superior military power. The turning point came when Diponegoro's religious supporters surrendered in 1827. Two years later, after he accepted a Dutch offer to negotiate, he was arrested and exiled to Makassar. The Java War is generally considered to have been a desperate effort to retain power by a dying aristocracy, despite its religious and populist overtones. Unlike the Padris, Diponegoro was not linked with Islamic reform, much less with Wahabism.

The Aceh War (1873–1912) began in 1873 and, arguably, never ended until (it is profoundly to be hoped) the twenty-first century. We are dealing here with an Indonesian state that fits the pattern of regional diversity within the Austronesian socio-linguistic family, but has always seemed somewhat more different than the rest. The most obvious explanation of Aceh's apparent contrariness is its long history as a regional power, poised in grand isolation at the tip of Sumatra. The Aceh Sultanate was a major beneficiary of the Islamic mercantile diaspora caused by the Portuguese capture of Malacca in 1511 and a jumping-off place for the pilgrimage to Mecca. Not surprisingly it soon became an established Islamic center.

The Aceh War was made possible by the Anglo-Dutch Sumatra Treaty of 1871, a classic example of imperialist deal-making designed to eliminate friction over rival claims to territory in Asia and Africa. By this time it was clear that Sumatra was loaded with natural resources. The treaty gave the Dutch Gold Coast (now Ghana, in West Africa) to Britain. In return the Dutch got a free hand in Sumatra, which meant they could do as they liked with Aceh, which was still extending its influence southward. Fighting began in 1873 after a rash US Consul in Singapore talked to Acehnese envoys about a possible US-Acehnese treaty. The Dutch reacted by sending a fleet to bombard Banda Aceh, the Acehnese capital. It was followed by an invasion force. The Acehnese retreated to the hills, sending appeals for help to all and sundry. The US Consul in Singapore recommended sympathetic consideration, but was overruled by his unimaginative superiors in Washington.

In 1881 the Dutch declared the war to be over, "one of the most fanciful pronouncements [in the history] of colonialism."[7] Fighting dragged on, year after year. Dutch stubbornness was reinforced by pressure from oil interests who thought there were interesting possibilities in affected areas. Finally the Dutch appointed a tough new military commander, assisted by their leading expert on Islamic affairs, Snouck Hurgronje. Increasingly modern weaponry was deployed. Resistance gradually tapered off, although some Muslim clerics were killed in battle as late as 1910–1912. But if the Acehnese were defeated militarily, for the time being, they were certainly not subdued politically, as later events would demonstrate.

Nineteenth-century anti-colonial warfare affected the future development of political Islam in several ways. It showed religious leaders that they could bolster their prestige and authority by allying with rulers in the fight against foreign oppression. The rulers discovered that Islam could bridge ethnic and territorial differences, as it had for the Prophet in ancient Arabia. Islam also restored a sense of individual worth to people disturbed and disoriented by waves of foreign-directed change and attendant disorder. Later, Islamic participation in these wars would ensure Islam a firm place in the foundation mythology of a new nation.

For the Dutch, from the Padri War onwards, anti-colonial warfare suggested an Indonesia-wide distinction between Islamic religious leaders and "customary" rulers whose authority was grounded in a pre-Islamic heritage – the so-called "*adat* community." If Islam could gain power by Islamizing and leading this community, the Dutch could maintain control by keeping it separate and explicitly non-Muslim.

The Sagacious Advisor: Snouck Hurgronje and Dutch Islamic Policy

The man who developed the strategy of opposing Islam to *adat* was Christiaan Snouck Hurgronje, Advisor on Native Affairs. By the standards of his times Snouck was a liberal and idealist, one of the founders of the Ethical Policy, which from 1901 onwards aimed to inject a new spirit of concern for Indonesian welfare into the hitherto mercenary ethos of Dutch colonialism. But he is most often remembered for his divide-and-rule *realpolitik*, first deployed to win the Aceh War.

Snouck's strategy was grounded in scholarship: he had visited Mecca

---

7   Ricklefs, *History of Modern Indonesia*, p.177.

and seen the large Indonesian community there; he spoke and read Arabic, and wrote copiously on Islam. His study of Islamic education is still regarded as "among the few essential works on the *pesantren* tradition."[8] He was more than mildly contemptuous of the Dutch colonial regime's ignorance of Islam. He pointed out, with good reason, that his compatriots both exaggerated and underestimated Islam's power. They fantasized that it was directed by a well-organized central authority similar to the papacy, a threatening inference for the largely Calvinist Dutch establishment. This authority supposedly operated through networks of Islamic "priests," some of them immigrant Arabs from Yemen The power of Islam was understood to be nurtured by the pilgrimage to Mecca and contact there with foreign Muslims. In fact, nothing like the papacy exists in Islam, and the absence of priestly authority between God and man is one of its defining characteristics.

At the same time, many Dutch believed that, despite this imagined Arabia-based conspiracy, Indonesian Islam remained watered down by local superstition, somehow not quite authentic, and therefore ripe for Christian missionary conversion.

Based on these assumptions the government tried to control Islamic activity and to place limits on the pilgrimage to restrict the flow of priestly subversives. But Snouck disagreed. He argued that the great majority of Muslims were not fanatically rebellious or anti-Dutch, that there were no priests or Pope, and that converting Muslims to Christianity would not be easy even in highly syncretic Java:

> Even in those parts of Java in which orthodox Islam has gained the least grip upon the population... the Hindu *pandit* [scholar, c.f. pundit] would experience as great difficulties in communicating with simple peasants as would the Christian missionary; yet the Muslim *kiyayi* or ... teacher, if he deigns to stoop to this lowly creature, is assured of a deferential hearing.[9]

---

8   Martin van Bruinessen, "Pesantren and Kitab Kuning: Maintenance and Continuation of a Tradition of Religious Learning," in Wolfgang Marschall, ed., *Texts from the Islands. Oral and Written Traditions of Indonesia and the Malay World*, Ethnologica Bernica 4, Berne: University of Berne, 1994, pp. 121–45, accessed at http://www.let.uu.nl/~martin.vanbruinessen/personal/publications/pesantren_and_kitab_kuning.htm.

9   Snouck Hurgronje, "Het Mohammedenism," Vol. 4, Part 2, p. 206, quoted in Harry J. Benda, *Continuity and Change in Southeast Asia: Collected Journal Articles of Harry J. Benda*, New Haven: Yale University Southeast Asia Studies, 1965, p. 86, n. 11.

Bureaucrat and scholar of Islam, Christiaan Snouck Hurgronje
was the principal author of late colonial Dutch Muslim policy.
Among other things, Snouck urged a clear distinction between
Islam as a religion (to be tolerated) and Islamic support for
anti-colonial violence (to be rigorously suppressed). | *Royal*
Netherlands Institute of Southeast Asian and Caribbean Studies

It followed, Snouck argued, that Islam *per se* was not the enemy. The real danger lay in Islamic extremism either in the hands of "local fanatics" or foreign agents of a pan-Islamic conspiracy. This distinction between pious observance and what today might be termed violent "Islamism" had first to be clearly recognized, Snouck asserted. After that the correct policy was to offer a *modus vivendi* to the majority of moderate Muslims, including lifting restrictions on the pilgrimage, while ruthlessly suppressing political fanatics promoting rebellion.

Tolerance of moderate Islam, Snouck said, was both a *sine qua non* for stability and a moral obligation on the part of a country which practiced religious tolerance at home, a clear reference to the Protestant-Catholic split within the Netherlands itself. Snouck was among the first to recognize the political utility of traditional pre-Islamic institutions and leaders, including the Javanese aristocracy and the customary leaders in the Outer Islands, as a force to counter expanding Islam.

With that in view, he helped establish a prestigious school of *adat* law at Leiden University in the Netherlands, which over the years produced a massive series of studies organized by region and covering the whole Indies. These volumes were supposedly no more than "guides" to *adat* law, which in theory cannot be codified because it is mostly oral and would lose a necessary element of flexibility if committed to writing. This notwithstanding, *adat* became a formal part of the Dutch colonial legal system, which featured different codes for Europeans, native Indonesians, and foreign minorities, such as the Chinese; and it remains an important element of Indonesian law today.

But despite his efforts to control political Islam, Snouck also deeply believed that Islam would inexorably gain ground unless the Dutch promoted Dutch values, and especially western education. He insisted that this was, in the long run, the only way to wean the Indonesian elites away from increasing Islamization. And he argued further that the Dutch government should provide jobs in the colonial civil service for the resulting new corps of western-educated Indonesians.

The Dutch eagerly accepted the divide-and-rule aspects of Snouck's advice. Playing on the distinction between Islam and *adat* became an enduring tenet of Dutch policy. In their ardor to bolster pre-Islamic custom, colonial administrators even tried to improve on what actually existed. On Hindu Bali, for example, they seized on the idea of a classical centralized state modeled on Indian norms with a full-blown caste system. In fact such a state had probably never existed on Bali, but, nothing daunted, the Dutch vigorously set about recreating one, at least superficially. "We shall, above all else," one official wrote in 1921, "have to uphold the caste system, otherwise the [Balinese Hindu] religion is done for, and there is a chance for the Muslims."[10]

In Aceh, as the forty-year war there dragged on, Snouck's *adat*-based policy meant trying to co-opt the territorial chiefs, the *uleebalang*, while attempting to crush the "fanatical" religious leaders, an effort in which Snouck himself was directly involved at the side of the Dutch military commander. It seemed to work, at least for a time, but when the Dutch returned to Indonesia after World War II, Aceh was the one place they did not try to reoccupy.

The Dutch never attempted widespread promotion of Christian missionary activity in Indonesia, although it is unclear whether Snouck's cautionary advice was the reason. The colonial government knew that any attempt to Christianize Muslim areas would probably be provocative and destabilizing, as well as fruitless. Therefore, and despite some pro-Christian

---

10   Henk Schulte Nordholt, *Bali: Colonial Conceptions and Political Change, 1700–1940*, Rotterdam: Erasmus University, 1986, p. 40.

*After the Dutch captured Teuku Umar, a famous Acehnese
leader, his widow Cut Nyat Dien continued to lead his troops in
guerrilla warfare against them until 1908, when she was finally
captured and exiled.* | EDM Archives

pressure from the Dutch parliament, missionaries were not allowed in most
Muslim areas, with the partial exception of Java, where both Protestants
and Jesuits made some headway among the aristocracy.[11] In any case, the
greatest opportunities were in those scattered but significant upland areas
where fertile soils had resulted in pockets of dense population so isolated
that they had been only lightly touched, if at all, by either Hinduism or
Islam. One such opportunity was in Dutch New Guinea (today referred to
as Papua), where in some areas there was no serious European presence
before World War II. Others were in Sulawesi and Borneo. The most
important was the highland interior of northern Sumatra, home of the
Batak peoples.

Lake Toba, the enormous volcanic caldera in the heart of Batak country,
was first seen by a European only in 1863. Before that, Muslim efforts to
convert the inhabitants had been mounted both by the Acehnese and by the

---

11   Ricklefs, *Polarizing Javanese Society*, pp. 105–25, 254–55.

Minangkabau of West Sumatra. The latter were successful in Islamizing the Mandailing Bataks in the south. The larger and more northerly population of Toba Bataks was converted by a vigorous German Protestant mission working well in advance of Dutch political control, beginning in the 1860s. It was hazardous work: a pair of early American missionaries had been killed and eaten by then-cannibalistic Toba Bataks.[12]

The result was one of the most numerous Christian populations in Indonesia, today numbering between three and four million people. Protestant missionaries also labored among isolated peoples in Sulawesi and Borneo, as did Roman Catholics on the island of Flores in Eastern Indonesia. As mentioned earlier, the Dutch had already converted to Protestantism the Catholic communities that had resulted from Portuguese efforts. All these conversions, plus the existence of many Christians among immigrant Chinese, assured the existence of an important, relatively well-educated Christian minority in Indonesia. Today it numbers more than nine percent of the population.[13]

On Java, Snouck's idea of an "Islamic New Deal" was partially implemented, and it was welcomed by many religious leaders. It apparently did reduce grassroots unrest. Restrictions on the pilgrimage to Mecca were lifted at least for a time and the number of pilgrims increased dramatically. In the mid-nineteenth century there were about 2,000 a year. By the turn of the century the annual numbers were up to over 7,000. They increased to over 50,000 in 1926/27, the largest contingent from any country in the world that year.[14] However the Dutch authorities continued to police the haj and set up an office in Jiddah to spy on the pilgrims.[15] After many appeals from the Muslim community, the Dutch even began to extend help to penniless hajis stranded in Mecca.[16]

The Dutch began to support a limited amount of education, government and private, the latter including both Christian and Islamic schools. Most important, they even supported a vigorous education effort by new Islamic organizations, although not without bouts of suspicion.

---

12 Frank L. Cooley, *Indonesia: Church and Society*, New York: Friendship Press, 1968, p. 67.

13 US Department of State, *Indonesia: International Freedom of Religion Report, 2005*, p. 1.

14 Harry J. Benda, *The Crescent and the Rising Sun: Indonesian Islam under the Japanese Occupation, 1942–1945*, The Hague: van Hoeve, 1958, p. 220, n. 34; p. 207, n. 30; also William R. Roff, "The Meccan Pilgrimage," in Raphael Israeli and Anthony H. Johns, eds., *Islam in Asia*, Boulder CO: Westview,1984, Vol. 2, p. 239.

15 Benedict Anderson, *Imagined Communities: Reflections on the Origins and Spread of Nationalism*, rev. ed., New York: Verso, 2002, p. 170.

16 Benda, *Crescent and Rising Sun*, p. 96.

But the more idealistic aspects of Snouck's agenda lost support as world depression pinched colonial revenues. Political unrest, often led by educated Indonesians, further dampened Dutch enthusiasm for education of all kinds.

Unintended Consequences of Sugar and Prosperity

Meanwhile the conditions created by colonialism in a context of international development had been strengthening Indonesian Islam in several ways. The expansion of the haj thanks to faster and less hazardous international travel was one such stimulus. Perhaps the most important was the unintentional impact of Dutch agricultural policy on the growth of an Islamic culture, especially in East Java, including a network of religious boarding schools, or *pesantren*.

Beginning in the nineteenth century, the Dutch began to open large expanses of uninhabited land in East Java for sugar cultivation. They made a momentous discovery: sugar could be grown in rotation with rice in irrigated fields, if they provided the irrigation systems. They then imported, from elsewhere in Java, villagers who grew rice on the new fields for their own consumption and were induced (or coerced) to supply labor for the sugar industry. They cultivated sugar between rice crops and manned the industrial-scale mills needed to refine it. The system was immensely profitable, and it soon became a renowned mainstay of the colonial economy.

The most famous writing on the Javanese sugar-rice-money nexus is a book by anthropologist Clifford Geertz entitled *Agricultural Involution*. With his customary brilliance, Geertz postulated that continuously refined agriculture on rich Javanese soils led not only to steady population growth, but also to what he described as "shared poverty" as, over time, additional inputs of labor were required to maintain increasing sugar production.[17] However, more recent scholarship has underlined that while the fecund peasantry certainly did not become wealthy, the new sugar-based economy stoked a development boom.[18] New towns like Jombang sprang up around the sugar mills, creating new employment. Commerce increased (much but not all of it run by ethnic Chinese), and Islam, always compatible with

---

17   Clifford Geertz, *Agricultural Involution: The Process of Ecological Change in Indonesia*, Berkeley CA: University of California Press, 1963, esp. p. 97.
18   R. E. Elson, "Clifford Geertz, 1926–2006: Meaning, Method and Indonesian Economic History," *Bulletin of Indonesian Economic Studies*, Vol. 43, No. 2, 2007, pp. 251–63.

trade, prospered in tandem. The *pesantren* system as it is known today dates mainly from this period, not, as once assumed, from the earliest days of Islam in Indonesia.[19] The boarding schools and their clerical owner-operators soon became the economic and institutional basis of Traditionalist Islam on Java.

The prosperity of Dutch Indonesia also attracted increasing numbers of Arab immigrants, resulting in the growth of an important economic, religious and political elite. Arab immigration peaked in the nineteenth century and by 1930 there were over 71,000 Arabs in Indonesia.[20] Most of them came from the Hadramaut, in modern Yemen. It was a poor, isolated place, wracked by drought and constant warfare, far from the mainstreams of Middle Eastern life. However, it had a surplus of *sayyid*, descendants of Prophet, including many who were well-educated clerics. Because of their religious prestige, some became professional mediators of tribal warfare, which was frequent in the Hadramaut of the time. Prominent among these hereditary diplomats was the al-Attas family.[21] Fast-forward to late twentieth-century Indonesia and, no coincidence, the highly respected Indonesian Foreign Minister was one Ali Alatas, of Hadrami Arab descent.

The Hadrami Arabs departed their arid homeland with little more than Islamic education and, in some cases, illustrious descent. Island Southeast Asia was a favored destination not only because it was prospering, but also because the inhabitants were more impressed by the Hadramis than would have been the case in Muslim areas of the Middle East. Even those who were not *sayyid* (did not claim descent from the Prophet) were regarded as exemplary Islamic role models. As for the *sayyid*, they could often parlay their titles into political leadership. As early as the late seventeenth century one of them married an Acehnese queen and eventually became the ruler of Aceh.[22] A Hadrami Arab became the Sultan of Pontianak, in what is

---

19 On nineteenth century establishment of *pesantren*, see Martin Van Bruinessen, "'Traditionalist' and 'Islamist' pesantren in contemporary Indonesia," in Farish A. Noor, Yoginder Sikand and Martin van Bruinessen eds., *The Madrasa in Asia: Political Activism and Transnational Linkages*. Amsterdam: Amsterdam University Press, 2008, accessed in July 2008 at http://www.let. uu.nl/~martin.vanbruinessen/personal/publications/pesantren_2.htm ; also interview with James J. Fox, 30 April 2007.

20 Giora Eliraz, *Islam in Indonesia: Radicalism and the Middle East Dimension*, Brighton: Sussex Academic Press, 2004, pp. 49–50.

21 Joseph Kostiner, "The Impact of the Hadrami Immigrants in the East Indies on Islamic Modernism and Social Change in the Hadramawt during the 20th Century," in Israeli and Johns, eds., *Islam in Asia*, Vol. 2, p. 207.

22 Taylor, *Indonesia: Peoples and Histories*, p. 213.

now the province of West Kalimantan.[23] Much more recently another, Mari Alkatiri, was the first prime minister of independent East Timor. In the colonial era Europeans typically saw the Hadrami *sayyid* as rivals, trouble-makers and purveyors of dangerously politicized Islam.

Arab migrants usually left their wives and families at home and married Indonesians. The *sayyid* title was transmitted to male descendants (female offspring are *sharifa*), resulting in a modern "Arab" population which is both highly identifiable and largely Indonesian by blood. Over time Arabs became traders (they were especially well known as batik cloth merchants), religious leaders, and politicians. They were mainstays of the old, moderate, westernized Socialist Party (Partai Sosialis Indonesia – PSI), banned under Sukarno and never revived. Today the most prominent are urbane, moderate, wealthy sophisticates like Ali Alatas, now deceased, and Mari'e Muhammad, recently Minister of Finance. However, other Indonesians of Arab descent have been violent extremists, including Abu Bakar Ba'asyir and Abdullah Sungkar of Jemaah Islamiyah, and Ja'afar Umar Thalib of Laskar Jihad,[24] important players in the violent events described in Chapter 6.

Nationalism and Reformist Islam

By the end of World War I, Indonesians were becoming aware of the international anti-colonial movement, the implications of Japan's defeat of Czarist Russia, communist sponsorship of anti-imperialism and other events which gradually changed their perception of the political future. But the danger of confronting Dutch power as opposed to hoping for improvement through cooperation remained obvious, especially to the tiny westernized elite who were at first the only ones with access to modern education. For dedicated Muslims, however, there was an alternative source of new ideas: the flow of new thinking from the Middle East.

The first stirrings of nationalism included the letters of Kartini, a progressive, western-educated Javanese aristocrat who promoted education for women and enjoyed close friendships with Dutch officials. Then in 1908 young, educated Javanese formed Budi Utomo, a cultural organization which developed mild political tendencies. Both Kartini's

---

23 Interview with Hamid Algadri in *Yemen Update*, accessed July 2008 at http://www.aiys.org/webdate/gadr.html.

24 For these names and more, see Eliraz, *Islam in Indonesia*, pp. 41–42.

pioneering feminism and Budi Utomo's vague nationalism were welcomed by Dutch authorities trying to implement the Ethical Policy, because they represented a degree of progress toward Indonesian political participation without appearing dangerous. But such early efforts, and there were others, were too harmless, Dutch and upper crust for the next generation of nationalists.

Throughout the interwar period, intellectual globalization continued to accelerate, constantly eroding the moral and political basis of colonial rule. New ideas arrived at an ever-faster pace, and they were picked up and amplified by a growing local press. By 1938 there were over 400 newspapers of all kinds and a modern literature was emerging in Indonesia.[25] Western-style education continued to expand, if very slowly, to include 88,233 primary, 1,786 secondary and 637 tertiary students by 1940.[26] A tiny but influential number of Indonesians went to study in Holland, where they were exposed to the thinking of communists, socialists and others quite unlike their stereotyped image of the condescending, colonial Dutch. But even in Indonesia the Dutch themselves could not help but contribute to the flood of anti-colonial thinking. They advertised the Indies as a paragon of progress and modernity, but western educated Indonesians knew better. They required Indonesian students to learn about the history of the Netherlands, which glorified Dutch resistance to foreign rule.

Indonesian Islam's awareness of the Holy Places, always strong, was now further stimulated by a kind of proto-CNN effect. It was big news in Indonesia when, in 1924, Ibn Saud, the then-youthful founder of modern Saudi Arabia, came out of the desert and recaptured Mecca and Medina, once ruled briefly by his ancestors. One result of this "Pax Wahabica" was an exodus of Traditionalist scholars, including many Indonesians, whose religion was seen as heretical by the fundamentalist Wahabis.[27] However, as mentioned above, the restoration of order which resulted from the Saudi conquest also contributed to a surge in pilgrims from Indonesia.

When Ibn Saud proposed a World Islamic Conference shortly after his triumph, many Indonesian Muslims were electrified. Several Indonesian would-be delegates left for Mecca to attend it – and the Dutch apparently

25 Ricklefs, *History of Modern Indonesia*, p. 221.
26 George McTurnan Kahin, *Nationalism and Revolution in Indonesia*, Ithaca NY: Cornell University Press, pp. 31–32.
27 James J. Fox, "Currents in Contemporary Islam in Indonesia," unpublished paper presented at Harvard Asia Vision 21, 29 April–1 May 2004, p. 4, courtesy of the author.

did nothing to stop them. However, only an incomplete congress was held in 1926, due to the opposition of Muslim rulers elsewhere.[28] They knew full well what Wahabism was, and did not care for it. But future President Sukarno, never known as a fervent Muslim, was so deeply impressed by Saud's triumph that when the Dutch exiled him to New Guinea and he had time to spare, he translated a biography of the Saudi ruler from English to Malay, soon to be renamed Indonesian.[29]

As nationalist sentiment developed and spread, the well-established dichotomy between Traditionalist and Reformist Islam emerged powerfully in modern dress. Influenced by the thinking of Muhammad Abduh in Egypt, the Reformists (known more generally as Modernists at the time) argued that the key to closing the gap with the secular West was to purge Islam of allegedly improper, locally derived practices. The Koran should be adhered to, but it should also be reinterpreted to provide for new requirements, especially modern, western-style education incorporating Islamic values and instruction in Arabic. In emphasizing a return to the fundamentals of Islam, this new iteration of Reformism was similar in methodology to Wahabism, but its modernizing, developmental objectives were at this time quite different from the puritan obsessions of the Wahabis.

In 1912 Muslim merchants who were disturbed by growing ethnic Chinese competition founded what was to become the Islamic Union or Sarekat Islam (SI). It was Indonesia's first mass political movement, the first political expression of Reformist Islam, the first to have "Islam" in its title, and the first to include leaders who were not western-trained. It soon developed wider objectives and a broader following, growing much faster than anyone expected to a claimed total of two million members by 1919.

Undiscriminating in its anti-colonial fervor, Sarekat Islam initially welcomed communists into its ranks. They had managed to persuade quite a few idealistic young Muslims that Marxism had much in common with Islamic values. Many Muslim intellectuals found Marxism appealing at first, in part because only a minority of them had any vested interest in capitalism, and also because the communists had been the first party in Holland to support independence for the Indies.[30] But in due course

28 Martin Kramer, *Islam Assembled: The Advent of Muslim Congresses*, New York: Colombia University Press, 1986, p 109. Benda is incorrect in saying that the congress was cancelled: *Crescent and Rising Sun*, p 52. H.O.S. Tjokroaminoto, the leader of Sarekat Islam led a Javanese delegation.

29 J.D. Legge, *Sukarno: a Political Biography*, New York: Praeger, 1972, p 138.

30 Kahin, *Nationalism and Revolution*, pp. 50–51.

there was a falling out, and the radical leftists departed in 1924 to form the Indonesian Communist Party (Partai Komunis Indonesia – PKI).

Muhammadiyah, which remains to this day Indonesia's preeminent mainstream Reformist organization, was also founded in 1912. Like SI, Muhammadiyah originated in Central Java, a province with both a heavy concentration of nominally Muslim Javanese officialdom and a large Islamic commercial class. Unlike SI, which remained politicized and distracted by its radical elements, Muhammadiyah developed a detailed reform program which appealed to a solid, middle class, mostly urban base, and which it has essentially followed ever since. It concentrated with great energy on an educational agenda. Its schools, including some taught in Dutch, soon included both standard western subjects as well as religious courses in Arabic.

With Muhammadiyah in the lead, Muslim schools soon created "a literate Muslim citizenry which numerically by far surpassed the few Indonesians versed in Western ways."[31] As in the case of the Padri reformers of West Sumatra a century earlier, Muhammadiyah's supporters included merchants who felt that their commerce was being disadvantaged by Dutch-supported reliance on local customary law. They believed their interests would be better served by a switch to Islamic law, especially in matters such as property rights and inheritance. Thus, Muhammadiyah both served and stimulated the growth of an educated Islamic middle class in Indonesia.

Leaders of the Traditionalist iteration of Indonesian Islam gradually became concerned about Muhammadiyah's Reformist teachings, which suggested, not too subtly, that Traditionalism was not up to the challenges of modernity, precisely because its religious philosophy was flawed. Although the growing tension between the two groups was cloaked in doctrinal terms, the underlying cleavage was political, pitting the urban, commercial Reformist elite, increasingly focused on anti-colonial politics, against an older, rural, land-owning clerical establishment rooted in the Islamic boarding schools (*pesantren*) of East and Central Java (a phenomenon discussed in Chapter 5). The Traditionalists were especially stung by Reformist charges that they were ill-educated country people who could not speak good Arabic and were unqualified for Islamic scholarship – a clear affront to Traditionalist legitimacy. A recent study has pointed out

---

31   Benda, *Crescent and Rising Sun*, p. 56.

that the wounds inflicted by this debate have continued to reverberate in Indonesian politics down to the present day.[32]

In 1926, the alarmed Traditionalist leadership founded the Nahdlatul Ulama, which means "Revival of the Religious Scholars," usually referred to as the NU. Like Muhammadiyah, the NU has always been a multifunctional organization: social, educational (with its great network of boarding schools, or *pesantren*), political and professional, but it has remained at heart an association of clerics, as its name implies. NU's venture into modernized education was modest in the beginning compared to that of Muhammadiyah, but would increase over time. Both organizations have remained a major force in Indonesian Islam's social and political life.

Islam and the Idea of Indonesia

Some Indonesian nationalists identified with Islam, either Reformist or Traditionalist, but others wanted to minimize religious distinctions and concentrate on forging national unity. These people were diverse in their backgrounds. Some were Muslims, but often educated in Dutch schools and influenced by secular western thought. Some were Javanese from the ranks of the mostly conservative, aristocrat-bureaucrat class. One of the latter was a young engineer named Sukarno, who in 1927 founded the Indonesian Nationalist Party (Partai Nasional Indonesia – PNI). Cutting across these categories was the youth of Indonesia, the *pemuda*, who would evolve into a quasi-institutionalized, quasi-permanent political force in their own right. They all knew that Indonesia was not a nation because the Dutch kept saying so; it would have to begin as an ideal.

Benedict Anderson, a noted student of Indonesia, has suggested that most national states created from diverse material, often from the wreckage of old empires (Hapsburg, Ottoman, *et al.*), are idealized, or, as he puts it, *imagined* communities.[33] To begin with an ideal and achieve reality can be a seemingly never-ending struggle, as it has been in the case of Indonesia. But the nationalists were lucky in having a talented assemblage of Founding Persons as well as a strenuous and imaginative corps of youthful cheerleaders. Equally valuable, they had the stereotypically *unimaginative* Dutch, who, by constantly repeating all the reasons why "Indonesia" could

---

32   Robin Bush, *Nahdlatul Ulama and the Struggle for Power within Islam and Politics in Indonesia*, Singapore: Institute of Southeast Asian Studies, 2009, pp. 29–33 and *passim*.
33   See his *Imagined Communities*.

never happen, usefully underlined what needed to be done.

The Dutch also helped by making one extraordinary tactical error: they gave the nationalists a national language, Malay, now known (in Indonesia but not in Malaysia, where the same language is spoken) as Indonesian. The gift was unintentional: the Dutch did not want the natives to learn Dutch, partly because they feared it would give them notions of equality,[34] but they needed an administrative language that could be used throughout the archipelago. Malay was the obvious choice: it had been the language of the ancient Srivijayan empire, whose inscriptions in Old Malay date from the seventh century, and had endured as a lingua franca of trade. Further developed and spread by the Dutch, Malay was also perfect for the nationalists, because it was widely spoken but was the native tongue of only a small minority in Sumatra, less than ten percent of Indonesians. As a result, Malay (unlike the Javanese language, for example) was politically neutral; all the nationalists had to do was to give it a new name.

So in 1926 the fired-up youth of Indonesia held a conference and pledged that they belonged to one fatherland, Indonesia; one nation, Indonesia, with one language, Indonesian[35] – all the things that skeptics, with the colonizers in the lead, were saying they lacked. Much more remained to be done in the realm of symbols: national flag, national philosophy, national anthem and so forth, not to mention such thorny practical issues as whether "Indonesia" should be based on the ancient Majapahit Empire – in which case it would arguably extend into British Malaya – or whether the more practical if less exciting foundation should be the existing Dutch East Indies.

One of the more interesting symbols would be approved later, in 1950: a national motto, Bhinneka Tunggal Ika, usually translated "Unity in Diversity" and often equated with the American E Pluribus Unum. A more literal and also more interesting translation of the Indonesian motto is "They are indeed different, but they are of the same kind, as there is no division in truth."[36] Bhinneka Tunggal Ika comes from an epic poem written in the Old Javanese language in the fourteenth century, at the time

---

34 Kahin, *Nationalism and Revolution*, p. 39.
35 S. Takdir Alisjahbana, *Indonesia: Social and Cultural Revolution*, Kuala Lumpur: Oxford in Asia, 1966, p. 64. Indonesian is often but redundantly referred to in English as *Bahasa Indonesia* – "*Bahasa*" simply means "language."
36 Quotations from Soewito Santosa, tr., *Sutasoma: a Study in Javanese Wajrayang*. New Delhi: International Academy of Indian Culture, 1975, p. 578. I am indebted to anthropologist John MacDougall for my interpretation of Indonesia's national motto.

of the Majapahit Empire. The stanza in question refers to the dual state religion of Majapahit, Shivaite and Buddhist. The poet was arguing that while Shivaism and Buddhism are different – much, one could argue, as Traditionalist and Reformist Islam are today – they are both truth, and thus are one. Seen in this context, Bhinneka Tunggal Ika implicitly acknowledges an element of tension between unity and diversity.

The Final Days of Dutch Rule

In 1926–27 the Indonesian communists launched small-scale insurrections on Java and Sumatra. The Dutch had no trouble suppressing them, and only two Europeans were killed. But the uprisings confirmed Dutch fears that the Ethical Policy had been coddling future rebels. Thirteen thousand people were arrested, some were shot, and the communists were put out of business until after the Japanese Occupation.[37] World depression soon made matters much worse. By 1936 the value of Indonesia's exports had dropped to one quarter of 1920 levels[38] and rural areas were hard hit by the impact of falling commodity prices. A new mass movement in central Java, led by a traditional Javanese leader admired with messianic fervor by many peasants, attracted a widespread rural following.[39] Then, in the early 1930's, a broad crackdown was launched against nationalist leaders of all kinds. Sukarno and many other leaders of the future Republic of Indonesia were arrested and exiled to remote areas. In May 1940, German troops invaded the Netherlands, and fears of a Japanese invasion of the Indies began to grow.

Despite the expansion of Islamic culture and influence under Dutch rule, Muslim political leaders were in a restless mood. Snouck's "New Deal" for Muslims had fallen by the wayside. Since the late 1920s the Dutch had been worrying more about controlling burgeoning Islamic education than supporting it. Their subsidies for Muslim and other private schools were far less than the amount given to Christian counterparts. Muslims were further upset by continuing use of only nominally Muslim Javanese officials to administer Islamic institutions, including courts and schools. The Dutch banned polygamy, although they later retracted the ban in the face of Muslim protest. Muslims wanted an Islamic university; the Dutch

---

37 Ricklefs, *History of Modern Indonesia*, p. 214.
38 See table in Kahin, *Nationalism and Revolution*, p. 56.
39 Ricklefs, *History of Modern Indonesia*, p. 225.

promised one but did little. It was left to the Japanese to complete and open it, a forerunner of the extensive Islamic tertiary educational system that exists today.[40]

When the Germans invaded Holland, the majority of Indonesia's nationalist leaders, perhaps hoping for concessions later, voiced their support for the Western Allies, while most of their disgruntled Muslim counterparts, already hopeful that the Japanese would be benevolent toward Islam, remained silent.[41]

Japan Sets the Stage for Independence

On the eve of the Japanese arrival the main elements of Indonesian political life as it would develop after independence were in place: political Islam, nationalism (supported by many Muslims who identified themselves primarily as nationalists) and minority parties supported by Christians and moderate socialists. Only communism was temporarily absent, its adherents driven into exile after the insurrections of the 1920s.

For two decades the major political organizations had been simultaneously competing with each other and striving for unity. But they had been playing a kind of game because, as the repression of the 1930s had proved, they had no hope of overcoming Dutch power. Now, thanks to the Japanese, everything would change and, as the war wound down, with independence suddenly and clearly in view, the stakes would become much higher.

The Japanese were well prepared to set about incorporating this vast, wealthy realm into their empire. But they ruled for only three and a half years, and after two of them they were already losing World War II. Japanese policy rapidly degenerated from empire building to plundering Indonesia for resources and forced labor. Dreams of Greater East Asia gave way to desperate improvisation, guided to no small degree by the outlook of various military commands and commanders, some of whom were nonetheless genuinely sympathetic to the Indonesians' aspirations for independence.

In general, Indonesians collaborated with the Japanese but they also pushed back on specific issues, especially in the waning years, always with awareness that they risked provoking extreme punishment if they

---

40 Benda, *Crescent and Rising Sun*, p. 187.
41 *Ibid.*, pp. 94–99.

miscalculated. The Japanese were well prepared, not least with regard to the Muslims, having since the mid-1930s worked at positioning themselves to pose as the protectors of Islam in Asia. They arrived with the notion that Indonesia's Muslims were potential allies who might welcome an Asian liberator, while the nationalists, more influenced by western education and having already voiced their support for the Allies, were clearly not to be trusted.

The Muslims welcomed this attention and recognition of their importance, an appreciation which they had found seriously absent during the later years of Dutch rule. In some parts of Sumatra they actually aided the Japanese landings. The Japanese anticipated good relations with them. Only a week after the fall of Jakarta, to the astonishment of the local citizenry, Japanese "Muslims" in army uniforms showed up in Jakarta mosques and participated in services.[42] But Muslim political organizations soon found themselves subject to the same ban on political activity as everyone else, while the Japanese pondered what to do next.

The occupation was a roller-coaster ride of positive and negative elements. Almost immediately a problem arose with the Japanese requirement that all attendees at public gatherings participate in a ceremonial bow to the emperor. To Muslims this looked alarmingly like the bow to Allah required for Islamic prayer. They objected and finally obtained an exemption, for religious services only. The Japanese allowed a new version of the *Volksraad*, the Indies legislative council, and while it was toothless even compared to its Dutch predecessor, it gave greater representation to Muslims. Muslim leaders were allowed to place representatives in the Office of Religious Affairs, where they were for all intents and purposes civil servants, a privilege allowed to no other group.

November 1943 saw the birth of the Masyumi (Majelis Syuro Muslimin Indonesia – Consultative Council of Indonesian Muslims), destined to be a powerhouse in Indonesian politics until its banning by Sukarno in 1960. Masyumi was initially a federation of Reformist Muhammadiyah and Traditionalist NU, sponsored by the Japanese military authorities and explicitly created to help the war effort, but it was also a real mass organization drawing on a genuine Islamic base.

An equally important benefit of Japanese rule was the opportunity to participate in military service. In early 1944 the Japanese created a national

---

42   *Ibid.*, p. 111.

militia, the PETA (Pembela Tanah Air – Defenders of the Fatherland) which was in many respects an ancestor of the Indonesian national army. Since the beginning of the occupation Muslim leaders had pressed for their own military force, arguing at one point that

> ... the history of Islam in modern times has been one of conflict with the evil machinations of England. Muslims all over the world should unite for a crusade to defeat the Americans and British who are the enemies of religion. It is very fortunate, indeed, that Java lives under protection of the Dai Nippon Army. Let us, therefore, set up a Muslim volunteer corps on Java, so that it may become the trailblazer in the effort to destroy America and England ...[43]

Although PETA was not specifically Islamic, Muslim religious leaders as well as rank-and-file served prominently in it. And the PETA flag was not the Indonesian red-and-white bicolor, but an Islamic crescent imposed on the rising sun of Japan. In December 1944, with the Allies on the offensive throughout the Pacific, the Japanese went a step further and allowed the formation of a specifically Islamic military wing of Masyumi, the Barisan Hizbullah (God's Forces).

Until near the end it appeared as if the Japanese were consistently favoring Islam and Islamic leaders. But as things fell apart for the occupiers, the nationalists began to get equal treatment, and the Japanese made it clear that they would not, in spite of what they had done for Islam, attempt to support an Islamic state. The result, especially in view of what was to follow, had a healthy unifying effect on hitherto contentious Indonesian politicians. One of the most prominent Islamic leaders, Wahid Hasyim, Masyumi Vice Chairman and father of future President Abdurrahman Wahid (Gus Dur), let fly with a purple passage straight from a textbook on nation building:

> Our past history has shown that we have not yet achieved unity. In the interests of this unity, which we most urgently require in our endeavor to establish our Indonesian State, in our minds the most important question is not, 'What ultimately should be the place of Islam [in that State]?' The important question should rather be,

---

43   *Djawa Baru*, I, 19, October 1, 1943, p. 1, quoted in Benda, *Crescent and Rising Sun*, p. 139.

'By what means shall we assure the place of [our] religion in Free Indonesia?' I therefore once again repeat: What we need most of all at this time is the indissoluble unity of the nation.[44]

The Japanese had declared their support for Indonesian independence in September, 1944. As their war effort disintegrated, they created additional paramilitary organizations to mobilize Indonesian support. The Japanese Navy had been the most oppressive agent of occupation, but now a genuinely enlightened Navy admiral, Maeda Tadashi, who was personally close to many Indonesian leaders, sponsored speaking tours for Sukarno and Hatta. The Japanese dropped any semblance of attempting to control Indonesian political activity. On August 17, 1945, two days after the Japanese surrender to the Allies, Sukarno proclaimed Indonesia's independence.

It is generally agreed that political Islam in Indonesia gained strength under the Japanese. For many reasons, however, it would be relegated to a weak position during the early decades of independence.

---

44 *"Agama dalam Indonesia Merdeka"* in *Indonesia Merdeka*, 1, 3, May 25, 1945, quoted in Benda, *Crescent and Rising Sun*, p. 189.

3

Sukarno and the Roots of Islamic Marginalization: 1945–1966

Six key episodes of the Sukarno era helped to shape the future of political Islam in Indonesia. Five of these events – the dispute over the Jakarta Charter (1945), the communist-led Madiun Affair (1948), the Darul Islam uprising (1948–62), the Outer Islands Rebellion (1957–58), and the attempted coup and communal killings of 1965–66 – continue to resonate with politically aware Indonesians. The sixth, the election of 1955, was the first democratic polling in Indonesia's history and remains an important indicator of political Islam's strength in the early days of the Republic.

Nationalism was the dominant political philosophy of the Sukarno Era, with President Sukarno as its chief priest. But political Islam, which had developed vigorously during the last years of Dutch rule and the Japanese interregnum, remained one powerful component of Indonesia's nationalism. As a general rule Muslim politicians saw no conflict between Islamic and nationalist goals, and they sometimes invoked Islam for nationalist ends. In October of 1945, for example, Nahdlatul Ulama and Masyumi declared that resistance against the returning Allied forces in defense of the new Indonesian Fatherland was a holy war.[1] However, when peace and independence arrived in 1949 most Indonesians were uncertain and divided about the place of political Islam in the new Republic.

Like similar contests elsewhere, Indonesia's anti-colonial revolution was more than just an effort to expel the colonial master: it also had elements of civil war and social upheaval. It was a time when the ideal of national unity was, for the first time, tested against the reality of Indonesia's diversity.

---

[1]   M.C. Ricklefs, *A History of Modern Indonesia since c. 1200*, 4th ed., Stanford CA: Stanford University Press, 2008, p. 253.

Indonesians were not yet sure who they really were. For many, regional or ethnic identity – Javanese, Sumatran or whatever – was as important and sometimes even more so than religion or ideology.

Sukarno, it may be argued, was ideally equipped to deal with Indonesia's rampaging diversity. He was born on Bali to a minor Javanese official in the Dutch colonial service, almost certainly a nominal Muslim, and his Hindu Balinese wife. Sukarno was not only brilliant; he also had a good formal education, much better than that of his successor, Suharto. From his time as an engineering student in the 1920s onward, his consuming passion was anti-colonial politics.

He seems to have read everything he could get his hands on, mining it all to master world religions and political theory. But, consciously or otherwise, his underlying philosophy was grounded in Hinduism, especially the assumption that all religions flow into one great spiritual sea. "I am a follower of Karl Marx," he once said, "but on the other hand, I am also a religious man, so I can grasp the entire gamut between Marxism and theism.... I know all the trends and understand them.... I have made myself the meeting place of all trends and ideologies. I have blended, blended and blended them until finally they become the present Sukarno."[2] He could without blinking attempt to reconcile Indonesia's competing political forces into one all-embracing concept, NASAKOM, an acronym derived from the Indonesian words for nationalism, religion and communism. For a time his passionate insistence on unity in diversity was indeed the glue that held the outgunned Republic of Indonesia together.

Into the Maelstrom

The victorious Allies knew almost nothing about Indonesia and its new nationalism. At first their role was to accept the Japanese surrender and wait for the Dutch to return and reclaim their possession. The Dutch, just emerging from German occupation, were eager to do so, but they needed help from the British and Americans. In October 1945, British Indian troops, charged with reoccupying Java, stumbled into a hornets' nest in the big East Javanese port city of Surabaya. Inspired in part by the Muslim declaration of Holy War mentioned earlier, Indonesian youth fought back hard under a charismatic Islamic leader, Sutomo, better known as Bung

---

2   Clifford Geertz, *Islam Observed: Religious Development in Indonesia and Morocco*, New Haven: Yale University Press, 1968, p. 85.

Tomo, and the British commander was killed. [3]

But by the middle of 1946 the Dutch had reoccupied most of Indonesia. As far as they were concerned, the nationalists had clearly collaborated with the Japanese and their preposterous demand for independence was intolerable. In the long, see-saw military struggle that ensued, the Indonesian forces were eventually beaten back to part of Central and East Java and a small area of Sumatra. The Dutch regained most economically important areas including the capital, Batavia (now Jakarta), and did their best to pretend that things were getting back to the way they were before World War II.

For all its problems, the infant Indonesian Republic had widespread popular support and growing military capacity. Colonialism had become an embarrassment to the West, and world opinion favored the Indonesians, who benefited from increasing diplomatic intervention by the United Nations and the United States. In December 1949 the Dutch formally ceded sovereignty to the Republic of Indonesia.

As the anti-colonial revolution drew to a close, Indonesia embarked on a period of parliamentary democracy marked by increasing regional and ideological stress. Parliamentary elections held in 1955 were to be the only free elections until 1999, and parties apparently favoring an Islamic state – primarily NU and Masyumi – won more than forty percent of the vote,[4] a result that is often cited as evidence of "Islamist" strength, but is somewhat misleading when looked at closely. The elections produced a stalemate among the four major parties, and hence led to no progress against economic chaos or political fragmentation. So in 1957 Sukarno ended Indonesia's brief parliamentary era and declared Guided Democracy, a non-system of personal, authoritarian rule. He assumed, and many Indonesians agreed, that he alone could achieve national unity.

However, as the goal of unity receded, economic conditions steadily worsened and Sukarno tried to stoke the fires of nationalism by invoking external crises. First, there was a long altercation with the Dutch over the western half of New Guinea, part of the former Dutch colony which had not been included in the 1949 transfer of sovereignty. Then Sukarno launched an unsuccessful campaign to "crush" the new Federation of

---

3   Benedict R. O'G. Anderson, *Java in a Time of Revolution: Occupation and Resistance, 1944–1946*, Ithaca NY: Cornell University Press, 1972, p. 157.

4   See discussion of the 1955 election later in this chapter.

Malaysia, which included territories in Borneo bordering Indonesia, leading to hostilities which peaked in 1963–64. By now, thanks in part to a burgeoning Communist Party, Indonesia was being swept up in Cold War competition between the great powers. The famous Year of Living Dangerously was just around the corner.

Seven Words that Won't Go Away: the Jakarta Charter

The first of the six formative episodes discussed in this chapter began in the closing days of the Japanese Occupation. By early 1945, the end of the war was at hand. Indonesian nationalists of all varieties saw the opportunity of the moment and were positioning themselves to make the most of it. The Japanese were understandably losing interest in Indonesia, but some of them remained sympathetic to the nationalist cause.

In March 1945, the Japanese established an Investigating Committee for Preparatory Work for Indonesian Independence to draft a constitution. The Japanese had vetted its membership, making sure that older and, from their standpoint, more responsible politicians dominated the proceedings. It was before this group that, on June 1, Sukarno first enunciated five principles or, in Sanskrit, *panca sila*, usually written as one word, which would be included in the preamble of the new republic's constitution and become its philosophical foundation.

The fifth principle (*sila*) of Pancasila as originally drafted was Belief in God (*Ketuhanan*), but there was no specific mention of Islam, the religion of the great majority of Indonesians. The representatives of Masyumi, the Muslim umbrella organization which at this point still included NU, argued that Islam was being treated as if it were no more important than any of Indonesia's other deist religions, meaning mainly Christianity. In response, the Committee produced a compromise henceforth known as the Jakarta Charter (Piagam Jakarta). It added a phrase after "Belief in God" which would become famous: "with the obligation for adherents of Islam to carry out Islamic law (*dengan kewajiban menjalankan syari'at Islam bagi pemuluk-pemulukanya*)."[5] Sukarno, future vice president Hatta and seven others, including the senior Muslim politicians on the committee, signed it on June 22, 1945.[6]

---

5   *Lengkap UUD 1945 (dalam Lintasan Amendemen) dan UUD (yang Pernah Berlaku) di Indonesia (sejak Tahun 1945)*, Jakarta: Lima Adi Sekawan, 2006.

6   For date: Nadirsyah Hosen, *Shari'a & Constitutional Reform in Indonesia*, Singapore: Institute of Southeast Asian Studies, 2007, p. 62.

It has never been clear exactly what the authors of the Jakarta Charter truly had in mind. It is most likely that they simply wanted Muslims obligated to follow the prescripts of their own religion on certain issues such as prayer, fasting, marriage, divorce and inheritance. The drafting Committee also called for a Muslim head of state and, influenced by the arguments of Muhammad Yamin, arch-apostle of a "Greater Indonesia," the inclusion in the new republic of British Malaya as well as Sarawak and Sabah (two British protectorates on Borneo).

However, the Japanese were not yet out of the picture. On August 9, 1945, the day that the second atomic bomb was dropped, they flew senior nationalist leaders, including Sukarno, to Vietnam to meet the supreme Japanese commander for the region, Field Marshall Terauchi Hisaichi. He proposed independence for the entire territory of the Netherlands Indies, but vetoed including the British territories. Japan surrendered to the Allies six days later, but of course the Japanese military remained in control of Indonesia. And as the Indonesians were getting ready to proclaim a constitution, the Japanese Navy intervened, claiming that Christians in its area of responsibility, Eastern Indonesia, would secede if the Jakarta Charter and the requirement that the head of state be a Muslim were retained, so both of these provisions were dropped as well.[7]

As a conciliatory gesture toward disappointed advocates of the Charter, the Indonesian leaders working on the constitution moved the principle of "Belief in God" from fifth to first place among the five principles of the preamble and changed the wording to belief in a singular God Almighty (*Ketuhanan yang Maha Esa*).[8] Independence along with the constitution was proclaimed on August 17, 1945, two days after the Japanese surrender.

But the Jakarta Charter refused to recede quietly into the mists of history. Instead, its seven words came to signify advocacy of an Islamic state – itself never defined. Yet as a leading scholar notes, "[The Charter] does not amount to the creation of a Negara Islam or Islamic state."[9] The 1945 Constitution, of which it would have been part, gave the president of

---

7 Ricklefs, *History of Modern Indonesia*, pp. 246 and 249; B.J.Boland, *The Struggle of Islam in Modern Indonesia*, The Hague: Martinus Nijhoff, 1982 rev. ed., pp. 17–41.

8 Boland, *The Struggle of Islam in Modern Indonesia*, pp. 21–22 (the original version of Pancasila in the preamble) and p. 36 (the revised version with Belief in One God moved from fifth to first place).

9 M.B. Hooker, "The State and Shari'a in Indonesia" in Arskal Salim and Azyumardi Azra, eds., *Shari'a and Politics in Modern Indonesia*, Singapore: Institute of Southeast Asian Studies, 2003, p. 38.

a *non*-Islamic state control over what would be included under the rubric of Islamic or sharia law. Moreover from independence onwards some elements of sharia pertaining to Muslim marriage, Muslim inheritance and Muslim education which had been incorporated in Dutch colonial law were included in the legal system of the new republic, leaving open to speculation what, if anything, the Jakarta Charter would mean in practice.

Debate over the Charter continued during the long-drawn effort to replace the 1945 Constitution, seen as temporary because it accommodated distasteful elements (such as a federal system) demanded by the Dutch during the peace negotiations leading up to independence. A provisional constitution was enacted in 1950, and during subsequent efforts to replace it there were more arguments about the Charter. Finally in 1959 Sukarno reinstated the original (1945) constitution by decree. In a bid to placate Muslims he argued that since the Jakarta Charter had inspired the entire 1945 constitution, its text did not need to be included. A decade later the Islamic parties pushed again for the Charter's revival. Once again they lost. By the early Suharto era, the NU was arguing that sharia law was required by Pancasila, even if an Islamic state was not. Another attempt in 2002 to adopt the Charter by constitutional amendment failed, as did a similar effort in 2004. More recently the Charter itself has become less fashionable as a symbol of fervently Islamic political goals, but advocacy of a yet-to-be defined Islamic state is still popular with a minority of Muslims.

Madiun: Betrayal from the Left (1948)

The Madiun Affair of September 1948 was a brief, bloody insurrection within the ranks of the Republican movement. It took place at the height of Indonesia's struggle for independence, reflecting factionalism within the Indonesian armed forces and divisions between devout and nominal Muslim elements, including the nominally Islamic peasantry who were to figure prominently in the bloodletting of 1965–66. This bitter interlude, redolent of national unity betrayed, helped set the stage for military rule and further Islamic marginalization in the decades ahead.

The insurrection began with a bid to seize control of the Indonesian Revolution by a left-of-center coalition which included the Communist Party. It came at a low point in the Revolution, when the Republican forces were besieged in Central Java, anticipating an attack by superior Dutch forces, which indeed came a short time later. The Indonesian army was still far from unified. It was suffering from friction between western-educated, relatively professional officers and a more numerous group who had served with Japanese-organized militias during the occupation, most of whom had little if any formal education.

In early 1948 tensions between these factions in Central Java grew when the army's Siliwangi Division was relocated there from West Java. The Siliwangi commander, Colonel Abdul Haris Nasution, was a leader of those who favored "rationalizing" the Republican army by reducing the number of untrained personnel and increasing the proportion of relative professionals. On the other side, favoring the unlettered militias, was a left-wing coalition, the People's Revolutionary Front. Conflict erupted between the two groups in the city of Surakarta (Solo), one of Central Java's two royal capitals.

Into this troubled situation, like a bolt from the red, came an enigmatic figure named Musso, a former leader of the Indonesian Communist Party. Musso had fled to the Soviet Union after failed communist uprisings against the Dutch in 1926–27, returning only once to Indonesia in the interim. The People's Front warmly welcomed this apostle of revolutionary *savoir faire* and made him their leader. But in September 1948, after unsuccessful skirmishes with the opposing faction, Musso and his followers were compelled to retreat from Surakarta to Madiun, a railroad town with a strong labor union presence and hence a center of left-wing sympathies. There they seized control of the city from Republican forces on September 18, 1948. The next day Sukarno reacted by denouncing the uprising as a traitorous plan by the communists to overthrow the infant Republic. In response, Musso called President Sukarno and Vice President Hatta slaves of the Japanese and Americans, and exhorted the "whole people" to take power.[10]

Musso's ignorance of Indonesian conditions was his undoing. Soviet models of class struggle gained little if any traction in the rural Java of 1948, certainly not enough to topple the Father of the Revolution. After President Sukarno denounced the uprising, Siliwangi troops moved against the pro-communist forces in Madiun, which the rebels-within-the-Revolution held for only 13 days. Within a day of the insurrection's beginning the Masyumi coalition (which at this time still included the Traditionalist Nahdlatul Ulama) called for a holy war against the communists. During

---

10   Ann Swift, *The Road to Madiun: The Indonesian Communist Uprising of 1948*, Ithaca NY: Cornell Modern Indonesian Project, Monograph Series, No. 69, 1989, esp. p. 75.

sporadic fighting which continued for over a month, Republican forces captured and executed Musso. Other communist leaders fled the country; they returned later and charged that Madiun had been a provocation instigated by the United States, a story which originated with the Dutch Communist Party.

To the Indonesian Army, the Madiun Affair became an enduring symbol of betrayal from the left. More generally, and together with the Darul Islam Rebellion which began at about the same time, Madiun helped make Indonesians aware that ideological extremism of all kinds was dangerous for a new nation trying to build itself on a diverse cultural foundation. Indeed Madiun stimulated minor outbreaks of communal violence between strongly Muslim groups and nominal Muslims who were politically pro-communist. These clashes, although they went largely unnoticed outside Indonesia, foreshadowed the much more serious sectarian violence of 1965–1966.[11]

The anticipated Dutch attack on Republican territory came on December 18, 1948. Sukarno and Hatta submitted to Dutch capture in their capital, Yogyakarta, in the hope that since the Dutch attack had violated a negotiated truce their plight would gain sympathy for the Republican cause. They were correct; international pressure for a settlement increased, and the Dutch ceded sovereignty to the Republic of Indonesia in December 1949.

Darul Islam: Betrayal from the Right (1948–62)

The transfer of the Siliwangi Division from West Java to Central Java, mentioned earlier in connection with the Madiun Affair, had major repercussions in both places. In West Java it left a power vacuum, filled by a charismatic leader named Kartosuwiryo, who had served as the West Java leader of the Japanese-sponsored Hizbullah militia. Kartosuwiryo soon launched his own rebellion with the express aim of creating an Islamic state, or Darul Islam (the abode of Islam), often abbreviated DI. The insurrection in West Java lasted until 1962, when Kartosuwiryo was finally captured and executed.

West Java, the hinterland of Jakarta and the home of the ethnic Sundanese, was less deeply Hinduized than Central and East Java, and partly for this reason had become more profoundly Islamic. But affiliates

---

11 *Ibid.*, p. 80, n. 144; Robert W. Hefner, *Civil Islam: Muslims and Democratization in Indonesia*, Princeton: Princeton University Press, pp. 50–51.

of Darul Islam claiming the same objective – creation of an Islamic state – were also active elsewhere, including Central Java, where fighting continued until 1955.[12] There an entire battalion from a brigade of the national army commanded by Lieutenant Colonel Suharto, later president of Indonesia, defected to Darul Islam in 1955. The future head of state then spent a formative period in his career pursuing DI rebels through the rugged terrain around two big volcanoes, Merapi and Merbabu, which loom north of Yogyakarta.[13]

Darul Islam proved to be contagious in two other important regions, and in a number of lesser cases not discussed here. In 1950 Lieutenant Colonel Kahar Muzakkar, whose hopes to be the commander in South Sulawesi had been denied by army headquarters, led 20,000 troops about to be demobilized under the government's military reform program into rebellion. In 1952, he allied formally with Kartosuwiryo's Darul Islam. The Sulawesi branch of the rebellion diminished after a number of defections and an attempt to join the 1958 Outer Islands rebellion, discussed below. Fighting in Sulawesi finally ended when the Indonesian Army captured and killed Kahar Muzakkar in 1965.

In 1953, perennially restless Aceh also joined Darul Islam. This case was typically different. The Acehnese had been strong supporters of the national revolution. As noted above, the Dutch, painfully aware of Acehnese hostility, never even attempted to reoccupy the province after World War II. It remains a matter of local pride that Aceh raised money to contribute a DC-3 to the fledgling Indonesian air force, a duplicate of which remains on display on the parade ground of the provincial capital, where it survived tsunami floodwaters in 2004.

But the Acehnese were soon offended by Sukarno's apparently irreligious lifestyle. They were also unhappy about the growing power of the communist party and their own loss of political control under the Republic. The central government had given Aceh autonomous status in 1949, but only a year later, Jakarta abolished the province and made it part of neighboring North Sumatra. The Acehnese reaction was predictable: in September 1953 its powerful leader, Daud Beureu'eh, announced that he was establishing a third front of the Darul Islam revolt. In an ironic

---

12   C. Van Dijk, *Rebellion Under the Banner of Islam: the Darul Islam in Indonesia*, The Hague: Martinus Nijhoff, 1981, p. 2.

13   *Ibid*, pp. 149 ff.

Indonesia's first president, Sukarno, argued that he could be simultaneously a Muslim, a nationalist, a communist and just about everything else, including a well-publicized aficionado of beautiful women, in this case Marilyn Monroe. His eclectic world view did not please religious conservatives. A copy of this photo hangs in the Hotel Indonesia, Jakarta's first modern hostelry. | Bettmann/Corbis

repetition of the colonial past, the national army then invaded Aceh, the Acehnese retreated to the hills, and stalemate ensued until 1959. That was not to be the end of problems between Aceh and Jakarta.

Had the various DI rebels not been highly motivated, their many-headed insurgency would not have lasted so long; in this respect the contrast between DI and the ephemeral 1958 Outer Islands Rebellion, described below, is striking. The causes of the DI insurgency were complex and variable from place to place; it was never simply, or even primarily, a matter of fighting for an Islamic state. Nevertheless, it had great impact on Islam as a political force in Indonesia.

Kartosuwiryo, the dominant personality of the DI movement, was intelligent and well-connected, one of the rare Indonesians admitted to a Dutch colonial medical school, and he had had a promising early political career in the nationalist movement.[14] After his rebellion got underway, he

---

14 *Ibid.*, pp. 20 ff.

became a prototypical messianic leader, a would-be Mahdi or, in pre-Islamic terms, a *ratu adil*, the all-powerful divine king of Indonesian tradition. But he had no shortage of real world grievances to exploit.

In West Java, and indeed everywhere except Aceh, friction arising from efforts to purge superabundant and ill-educated guerilla forces from the national army was the immediate cause of DI rebellion. Many of these guerillas, like Kartosuwirjo, were from the ranks of militias established by the Japanese, who had specifically encouraged Islamic participation. In many regions there was also social unrest directed against traditional leaders who had served the just-departed colonial power. Only in Aceh does DI seem to have been primarily a vehicle for separatism or pursuit of local autonomy.

An estimated 15,000 to 40,000 people died in the Darul Islam uprising on all fronts.[15] Darul Islam became synonymous with die-hard, Islamic extremism in Indonesia. It marked the failure of fervent Muslims to establish a new Islamic state or states within the Republic by armed struggle.[16] It left a lasting, highly negative impression on the Indonesian national army. But the heritage of DI, including its goal of Islamic statehood, has endured to the present. Researchers working on the origins of a later generation of violent extremists, including those associated with Jemaah Islamiyah, have often been able to track them back to quasi-hereditary networks established by the Darul Islam movement (see Chapter 6).

The Election of 1955

Indonesia's first national election was held in 1955. It was to be its only truly democratic election for more than four decades, and its results are often interpreted as a base line for measuring the subsequent strength of political Islam.

An important change in the party line-up had occurred three years previously, when the Traditionalist Nahdlatul Ulama (NU) withdrew from the Masyumi Muslim coalition dating from the Japanese occupation. The rupture resulted from ongoing friction between the largely rural, Java-

---

15 Greg Fealy, Virginia Hooker and Sally White, "Indonesia" in Fealy and Hooker, eds., *Voices of Islam in Southeast Asia: A Contemporary Sourcebook*, Institute of Southeast Asian Studies, Singapore: 2006, p. 49.

16 Taufik Abdullah, "The Formation of a New Paradigm? A Sketch on Contemporary Islamic Discourse" in Mark R. Woodward, ed., *Toward a New Paradigm: Recent Developments in Indonesian Islamic Thought*, Tempe AZ: Program for Southeast Asian Studies, Arizona State University, 1996, p. 51.

based clerics of the NU and the more urban, westernized, Outer Island-based leaders of the Reformist wing. The NU leaders once again felt as if they were being treated as country cousins and denied the recognition and positions which their influence warranted. Following the split, Masyumi became *the* Reformist political party, and the NU contested the 1955 election under its own name.[17]

More than two years elapsed between the passage of an electoral law in April 1953 and the election itself, guaranteeing a long and stressful campaign. The parties wanted to appear supportive of consensus, then as now a cherished ideal, but they could not avoid partisan behavior. Masyumi denied repeatedly that its support for an Islamic state conflicted with the state philosophy, Pancasila, with its emphasis on belief in a not-further-defined Almighty God, while the nationalist parties seemed bent on making Pancasila into an anti-Islamic slogan. The communists insisted, not too convincingly, that they were not anti-religious or anti-Pancasila, which they had elsewhere claimed to accept with never-defined "reservations." Masyumi attacked the communist PKI, recalling its role at Madiun and proposing to make the anniversary of the rebellion a day of national mourning.

The communists, desperate to cultivate an image of moderation, hit back at Masyumi by associating it with the Darul Islam rebellion. The parties in the ruling coalition, mainly Traditionalist Muslim NU and nationalist PNI, joined the communists in attacking Masyumi and the western-style socialist PSI as extremist and inimical to the shared central core of national values.[18] None of this would have appeared alarming to anyone accustomed to electoral rhetoric elsewhere, but Indonesians were still understandably uncertain about the boundary between political name-calling and resort to deadly force.

Despite wild predictions of supernatural events on voting day, the long-awaited polling was peaceful. The participation rate was 87.65% of registered voters. Many Indonesians saw voting as a solemn community obligation, so much so that women in advanced stages of pregnancy struggled to reach polling places, and in some cases babies were born there. Some villagers were probably influenced by their headmen to vote for certain parties, and others believed that voting was a legal requirement. But there seems to

---

17 Herbert Feith, *The Decline of Constitutional Democracy in Indonesia*, Ithaca NY: Cornell University Press, 1962, pp. 233–37.

18 Paraphrased from Feith, *Decline*, p. 359.

be no doubt that this pioneering election, held long before the days of international coaching and supervision, was on the whole free and fair.[19]

The results confirmed the strength of political Islam in Indonesia, but also suggested that party-based political competition was aggravating the social and sectarian cleavages in Indonesian society. Four parties received more than three-quarters of the vote: nationalist PNI (22.3%), Reformist Muslim Masyumi (20.9%), Traditionalist Muslim NU (18.4%) and communist PKI (16.4%). The largest of the minor parties, the old Islamic PSII (not to be confused with the socialist PSI), got only 2.9%.[20] The strong showing of the NU was a big surprise, portending the power and durability of Traditionalist Islam. The leading Muslim party, Masyumi, received fewer votes than many expected, but among the roughly one-third of Indonesians living in the Outer Islands it polled more than any other party.

The combined vote of NU, Masyumi and PSII, was slightly over 42% of the total. Since all of these parties supported the Jakarta Charter, this percentage is often seen as a measure of support for an Islamic state. But it is at best a dubious measure. For one thing neither the question of an Islamic state nor the Jakarta Charter itself appears to have been a major campaign issue. Both NU and Masyumi were internally diverse, especially the former. The NU, still finding its feet as a political actor, was already divided on the Jakarta Charter.[21] On the Masyumi side, former prime minister Mohammed Natsir, one of the most devout Islamic politicians in Indonesia, insisted during the campaign that a "state based on Islam" was compatible with Pancasila.[22] In short, there was in 1955 a widespread effort to paper over disagreement about an Islamic state which probably typified the thinking of many Muslim voters, although how many we cannot know.

The Outer Islands Rebellion (1958)

A talented British journalist who wrote the best eye-witness account of the Outer Islands Rebellion of 1958 called it "surely the politest, most ambiguous civil war in modern history."[23] Fighting was minimal and there was no serious communal strife. But it was arguably the greatest

---

19 This account of the elections is drawn largely from Feith, *Decline*, pp. 424-37.
20 Table in Feith, *Decline*, pp. 434-35.
21 Hefner, *Civil Islam*, p. 87, citing Allan A. Samson's 1972 Berkeley PhD dissertation, "Islam and Politics in Indonesia"; also *Civil Islam*, p. 241, n. 40.
22 Feith, *Decline*, p. 355.
23 James Mossman, *Rebels in Paradise: Indonesia's Civil War*, London: Jonathan Cape, 1961, addendum by the author, n.p.

challenge to national unity in the history of Indonesia up to present. The events of 1965–66 were far bloodier, but they never threatened the legal integrity of the state. More recently, threats of secession from Aceh and Papua have caused some foreign observers to speculate, incorrectly, that the country was falling apart. However, while the leaders of the 1958 rebellion disavowed any intention to break up Indonesia, their rebellion, if successful, might well have done so. Certainly such a result was foreseen by the rebellion's American backers, who believed that the division of Indonesia, while unfortunate, would be a price well worth paying to aid the struggle against communism.[24]

The communist PKI had recovered completely from the disgrace of Madiun. It had done so by strong organizational work, most particularly among the peasantry of East and Central Java. By 1955 it claimed one million members.[25] On the eve of the rebellion, it was strong enough to be attempting to infiltrate the Indonesian Army. One result was to further exacerbate the cleavage between nominally Muslim Javanese peasants and strongly Islamic landholders and merchants which had already surfaced during the Madiun affair.

Masyumi without NU was dominated by Outer Islanders who were devout Muslims but also western-educated and equipped with technocratic skills. Prominent among them were former prime minister Mohammed Natsir, of Minangkabau (West Sumatran) descent, and Sjafruddin Prawiranegara, a former central bank governor of mixed West Javanese and West Sumatran ancestry. Masyumi and the moderate-socialist PSI had been the mainstay of Indonesia's parliamentary democracy, which ended when Sukarno proclaimed Guided Democracy in 1957. Now the two parties were drawn closer together by shared resentment of Sukarno. His increasing resort to personal rule, his blithe disdain for sound economic management, his apparent drift toward communism – all these in combination were increasingly disturbing to both Islamic Reformists and their western-oriented socialist allies. Traditionalist NU opposed the rebellion and never broke with Sukarno, not surprising given its largely Javanese constituency and its generally pragmatic worldview.

---

24 Audrey R. and George McT. Kahin, *Subversion as Foreign Policy: The Secret Eisenhower and Dulles Debacle in Indonesia*, New York: The New Press, 1995, pp. 75, 87–91; Paul F. Gardner, *Shared Hopes, Separate Fears: Fifty Years of Indonesian-US Relations*, Boulder CO: Westview, 1997, esp. pp.133, 139.

25 Ricklefs, *History of Modern Indonesia*, p. 285.

Equally important was the growing conviction of the Outer Islanders that Jakarta's rule was not only ideologically offensive; it was also robbing them of their just due as the major producers of Indonesia's export earnings from oil, rubber and other cash crops. This economic grievance was increasingly relevant when export earnings dropped after the Korean War. Unwilling to fire civil servants or otherwise to cut expenses, the central government printed money, and the resulting runaway inflation, combined with exchange rates rigged to benefit the government, heavily penalized Outer Island producers. Another cause of the rebellion, as in the case of Darul Islam, was continuing factionalism in the military.

In December 1956 a number of army commanders on Sumatra set up regional councils and seized power in their areas. The leaders of these councils arrested members of the communist party and had meetings with representatives of Caltex, the US joint venture that operated the Sumatran oil fields, to reassure them that their assets would be safe.

A second arm of the insurgency was born when the military commander of Eastern Indonesia, including Sulawesi and all the islands east of Java, seized civil authority in March 1957 under the rubric of a "Universal Struggle Charter" or Permesta (Piagam Perjuangan Semesta Alam). The most important players in the Permesta wing of the rebellion were to be the Christians of North Sulawesi, giving the entire enterprise a strangely pluralistic cast, with Muslim and Christian elements separated by more than fifteen hundred miles of ocean.

In February 1958 the Sumatran rebels formed a government in West Sumatra, calling themselves the Revolutionary Government of the Republic of Indonesia (Pemerintah Revolusioner Republik Indonesia – PRRI). They formally allied with the Sulawesi dissidents not long after and even achieved a momentary link with what was left of Darul Islam in Aceh in 1959, too late to make any difference. Actual fighting was something of an anti-climax because the Indonesian army made short work of the rebels, bombing their capitals in Sulawesi and Sumatra, and then landing troops in rebel territory. The army captured Padang, the Sumatran insurgent capital, in May, although guerrilla resistance lingered on. Fighting was fiercer in North Sulawesi although major rebel activity had ended there as well by mid-1958.

The United States, with support from Malaya, briefly supported the uprising, badly misjudging both the resilience of Indonesian nationalism and the capability of the Indonesian Army. That the Americans were tempted toward intervention is hardly surprising given the Cold War environment. To the US, the western-trained, fervently anti-communist Muslims and technocrats of the PRRI seemed attractive potential partners, all the more so given their apparent control of oil and other Outer Island resources and Sukarno's alarming drift to the left. After all, in 1952 a Masyumi-led government had signed a short-lived confidential agreement with the US promising to support the "free world," resulting in the fall of the Indonesian cabinet when it became public knowledge.[26]

But the US intervention did not last long. On May 18, 1958, an American pilot carrying US military identification was shot down on a bombing raid over Ambon in Eastern Indonesia. The resulting publicity, including reports that the raid had damaged a church and killed civilians, was deeply embarrassing to the US, and in any case it was already clear that the rebels had lost. Two days later, attempting to limit the damage, the US Secretary of State, John Foster Dulles, publicly rejected intervention in the PRRI/Permesta uprising, saying it was a matter for the Indonesians to settle.[27] A shipment of arms bound for the Permesta rebels was redirected to the national army as a kind of peace offering.

Once again political Islam, this time its most westernized element, had been associated with treason, as was the genteel, Europeanized socialist party (PSI). The PRRI debacle gave Sukarno a good excuse to ban both the PSI and Masyumi, which he did in 1960, and neither was ever forgiven, even after his fall from power. Only one major rebel figure, economist Sumitro Djojohadikusumo of the PSI, ever held a senior official position again. Many of the Masyumi leaders, including western-trained technocrats and political moderates, were jailed. Their elimination from politics would help religious radicals to rise in the ranks of Reformist Islam from the late 1970s onwards. In the short term the Outer Islands rebellion strengthened the communists by seriously damaging their most influential opponents, the opposite of its intended effect.

Failed Coup and Bodies in Rivers: The Trauma of 1965–66

Ask any foreigner to name some episode from Indonesian history, and the most likely response will be either the Bali Bombing of 2002 or ... that film starring Sigourney Weaver, about "The Year of Living Dangerously." The

---

26 For the agreement's use of the term "free world," see Feith, *Decline*, p. 199.
27 Gardner, *Shared Hopes*, p. 180.

film title was based on a 1964 national day speech by Sukarno, who loved to salt his oratory with exotic references, in this case to an Italian phrase, *vivere pericoloso*, meaning "to live dangerously." Sukarno was never under any delusion about the peril of the times: his constant focus on achieving national unity was more than lust for power. If the 1958 rebellion was Indonesia's greatest constitutional test, it turned out in the end to be more comic opera than mortal peril. But the events of 1965–66 were massively traumatic, and remain so in the memories of many Indonesians.

The "attempted coup," as it is commonly called, was a bungled effort by left-wing, probably communist army officers to eliminate anti-communist generals who were allegedly plotting with the CIA to overthrow Sukarno. Had they succeeded, it is possible that the communists would have come to power, although a civil war might also have resulted. On September 30, 1965, the plotters killed six senior generals but somehow overlooked General (later President) Suharto, who commanded the army's strategic reserve, the most important military force in Jakarta.

The communist party prematurely applauded the plot, fatally attracting blame for the killings. But Suharto was able to neutralize the plotters, ease President Sukarno aside, and eventually establish a military government which he led for 32 years, until 1998. In the months that followed the attempted coup, there was massive violence in rural areas, particularly in East Java and Bali. On Java it was directed mainly against ethnic Javanese who were nominal Muslim members of the PKI and its mass organizations and carried out largely by Islamic youth groups, encouraged and facilitated by the army. (Some ethnic Chinese were also targeted, mainly in cities, but they were not, as is often thought, the primary targets of the violence.) The murky circumstances of the "coup" and the killings have stimulated controversy and speculation ever since.

To understand the violence it is essential to appreciate the context of growing crisis before the coup attempt. The communist party was well on its way to becoming, or so it seemed, the most powerful political force in Indonesia, and a showdown between it and the army was widely anticipated. External players, particularly communist China and the CIA, were said to be involved. Sukarno was rumored to be ill, perhaps fatally. But all this "wind news," the Indonesian term for rumor, was less important than what was actually going on in the countryside.

The PKI had been mobilizing support in rural areas by encouraging mass organizations, particularly its farmers' front (Barisan Tani Indonesia

– BTI) to enforce an existing but largely neglected land reform law. This law banned possession of more than five hectares of irrigated land per household. The communists initiated large-scale "unilateral action" to enforce it themselves. At a time of growing landlessness and population pressure, the land issue was extremely sensitive, and there was widespread doubt that anyone could implement the reform law impartially. But the communists saw the issue as a natural popularity-maker among the poor majority, and they apparently believed that no other organization, including the government, could or would challenge them.

Anthropologist Robert Hefner describes how the PKI campaign collided with vital Muslim interests in rural Central and East Java. The more prosperous elements in the countryside were usually observant Muslims; they included both relatively wealthy peasants and small merchants. The poorer peasants tended to be nominal Muslims, whose religion incorporated elements of Hindu-Buddhism, Islam, animism and ancestor worship. They were the foot soldiers of the PKI farmers' front. The numerous Islamic boarding schools (*pesantren*) depended on contributions from merchants and wealthier peasants, as well as produce from land owned by their clerical leaders. There was thus, as Hefner puts it, "a circulation of wealth from economic to religious elites."[28]

In a time of high political uncertainty, it was hardly surprising that the relatively prosperous Muslims should see the PKI's efforts as a direct threat to their way of life. The threat was particularly powerful in East Java where *pesantren* dominated the social landscape and were the foundation of the NU party. The communists made a fatal error in assuming that they had a monopoly on organizational strength in the countryside. Indeed, the NU youth organization, Ansor, played a major role in the killing, with military encouragement. Here is how Harold Crouch, a leading student of the Indonesian army, describes what happened in East Java in late 1965:

> Although the Army usually had control of operations in the towns, religious leaders in the villages were encouraged to take their own measures. Most commonly the lead was taken by the *kiyai* (religious teachers) and *ulama* (religious scholars) affiliated with the NU, who mobilized students from their *pesantren* (religious schools) to drag communists, members of pro-PKI organizations, and suspects from

28   Hefner, *Civil Islam*, p. 53.

their homes and take them to river banks where their throats were cut and their bodies thrown into the river. Members of the Ansor youth organization moved from area to area inciting Muslims to exterminate "atheists," and by the middle of November killings had taken place in almost all parts of the province. In some villages the massacre even extended to children, while in others only party activists were killed. Often the Army stood by, sometimes supplying trucks to cart off the victims, although it was not uncommon for soldiers to participate more actively. [29]

Only on the Hindu island of Bali, adjacent to Java and even more densely populated, was there a similar pattern of massacre, and there as well the core issue behind the violence was friction aroused by PKI efforts to seize and redistribute land in accordance with previously ignored national legislation.[30] There were, of course, very few Muslims on Bali. There the opposing factions were the communists on one side and their Hindu opponents affiliated with the Nationalist Party (PNI) on the other, the latter again supported by the army. The preexisting antagonism between poor and medium-to-wealthy peasants was broadly similar. It seems clear that the entire phenomenon was more class-based than religious in nature, despite the fact that both Muslim authorities on Java and their Hindu counterparts on Bali proclaimed the violence to be part of a holy war against atheism.[31]

The extent of the killings was never documented by hard evidence. Estimates of the numbers killed throughout Indonesia range from under 100,000 to over one million.[32] Eyewitness accounts are scattered and anecdotal. There seems to have been a pattern of villagers describing terrible things which happened in another village, but not in their own, where, they explained, everyone got along with everyone else. There is a suspicious absence of relevant photography or mass graves in areas where large rivers were not at hand.

---

29 Harold Crouch, *The Army and Politics in Indonesia*, Ithaca NY: Cornell University Press, 1978, p. 152. More recent accounts include John Roosa, *Pretext for Mass Murder: The September 30th Movement and Suharto's Coup d'Etat in Indonesia*, Madison WI: University of Wisconsin Press, 2006.

30 Geoffrey Robinson, *The Dark Side of Paradise: Political Violence in Bali*, Ithaca NY: Cornell University Press, 1995, Ch. 10.

31 For Java, Hefner, *Civil Islam*, p. 108; for Bali, Robert Pringle, *A Short History of Bali: Indonesia's Hindu Realm*, Sydney: Allen and Unwin, 2004, p.177.

32 For a review of estimates of numbers killed, see Crouch, *Army and Politics*, p. 155.

But no one denies that horrific events of the kind described above did take place, on whatever scale, or that the killings have profoundly troubled Indonesians down to this day. Many people would still rather not talk about it. In 2007 a newly revised, government-approved school history text appeared which attempted to describe the events of 1965–66 along the lines described above, noting the leading role played by the NU's Ansor youth organization in East Java. Leaders of the NU intervened because they felt that the text was too even handed, suggesting as it did some degree of moral parity between the NU and the communists.[33] The book was withdrawn for revision. This happened at a time when the Indonesian press and publishing industry had become, with rare exceptions, completely free by international standards.

Summing up the Sukarno Era

The events of 1965–66, which included massive detentions of communists and communist front members in addition to the events outlined above, destroyed the PKI as a political force, leaving the political Muslims, the nationalists, and a collection of minorities to share whatever power the army was willing to grant – and it was often quite a bit, especially at first.

Political Islam certainly experienced ups and downs under Sukarno. It was hurt by the Darul Islam rebellion, which proved that some Muslims put religion before national unity. It was damaged further by the Outer Islands uprising, in which respected Reformist Muslims collaborated with disgruntled military officers, liberal socialists and foreign intelligence operatives in an adventure which risked breaking up the country. But the Muslim parties had surprised everyone by their strong showing in the 1955 parliamentary elections. After the events of 1965–66 and the elimination of communism, organized Islam, without which things could well have turned out differently, might have been expected to enjoy favored status under Suharto's new regime. But it was not to be so, at least not for more than two decades.

---

33 Personal information from several informants; for a partial account see Paige Johnson Tan, "Teaching and Remembering: The Legacy of the Suharto Era lingers in school history books," *Inside Indonesia* No. 92, April–June, 2008, accessed July 2008 at http://www.insideindonesia.org/content/view/1077/47.

4

The Suharto Era: Islam Repressed, Islam Resurgent

There must be no *chaos*.

– Suharto, *Pikiran* ("Thoughts") [1]

G eneral Suharto ruled Indonesia for 32 years, from 1966 to 1998, almost twice as long as Sukarno. He regarded his fundamental duty in terms ironically reminiscent of the Dutch, who loved to talk about peace and order (*rust en ordre*). He saw Indonesia's diversity more as a series of threats than as a national asset. Especially in his early days the Communist Party, despite its destruction in 1965–1966, was Threat Number One, but political Islam of the Reformist variety remained solidly in second place, thanks largely to memories of Darul Islam and the Outer Islands Rebellion. Towards the end of his rule, increasingly desperate to maintain himself in power, Suharto began to court hard-line Reformist proponents of Islamic fundamentalism in order to divide and defeat a growing pro-democracy movement which included new, politically liberal Muslim elements.

Suharto's greatest accomplishment was to promote successfully Indonesia's economic development, most notably in small towns and rural areas. But just as economic development under the Dutch had stimulated Islam, so it did under Suharto, and the long-term results of economic stimulus once again far outweighed sporadic attempts at repression.

---

1   Quoted in R. E. Elson, *Suharto: A Political Biography*, Cambridge: Cambridge University Press, 2001, p. 130, from Suharto's autobiography, *Pikiran*, published in English as *My thoughts, words and deeds: an autobiography as told to G. Dwipayana and Ramadhan K.H. Trans. Sumadi; Muti'ah Lestiono, ed.*, Jakarta: Citra Lamtoro Gung Persada, 1991.

The Man and his Methods

Born in 1921, Suharto passed a troubled childhood in a Central Javanese village. He was proud of his humble origins, which were useful to him politically, and hotly denied rumors of aristocratic origins. Following a brief enlistment in the Dutch colonial army, his real start came in a Japanese-sponsored militia during World War II. After that, he moved naturally into the new Indonesian Army, mostly in Central Java, where he continued to serve after the end of the anti-Dutch struggle in 1949.

Suharto's experience fighting Darul Islam rebels in Central Java, and its probable influence on his unsympathetic attitude toward political Islam, was mentioned earlier. He became commander of the important Diponegoro Division before moving on to head the army's strategic reserve in Jakarta, two years before the attempted coup of September 30, 1965. At that point he proved to be the right man in the right place at the right time to go much further. He had no formal education beyond secondary school, not counting military training, and no experience outside Indonesia. He was a Muslim but, typically of many Javanese, Islam was not a dominant element in his worldview.

In trying to parse Suharto's rather opaque personality, many commentators have stressed his Javanese cultural attributes, sometimes overemphasizing his fondness for religious mysticism and the occult.

Sukarno, destroyed politically by the events of 1965-66, is shown turning over power to General Suharto (at left) on March 11, 1966. Sukarno died in 1970, leaving Suharto to rule Indonesia for almost three more decades. | Beryl Bernay/Getty Images

However that may be, he was certainly influenced by the world of Javanese shadow puppet theater (*wayang kulit*). In the early days of his presidency he regularly staged *wayang* performances at the presidential palace, the same building formerly occupied by Dutch governors-general. It was the springtime of his rule, there were no serious security concerns, and even the most junior of diplomats serving in Jakarta were invited to attend. Not many of them did, but the president's cabinet, closest advisors and family would always be there, sitting in overstuffed sofas in the front row, and it was easy to meet and mingle with them. Of course only the best puppet masters performed. For guests who stayed until dawn, breakfast was served.

Most of the plays were from the Indian Mahabharata cycle, which takes dozens of all-night sessions to complete. In this epic of conflict between two families, there is no good and evil, only left and right. There is every conceivable kind of political behavior, from brute force to cunning and indirection. Things are often not what they seem: the most powerful characters are not the sleek aristocrats or the brawny warriors, but the grotesque, apparently low-born clowns who actually represent the gods of pre-Hindu Java, a purely Javanese injection into the Indian narrative. Anyone steeped in this tradition would not be without a strong grounding in functional political science, and so it was with Suharto. According to one scholar, the *wayang* philosophy envisions "a stable world based on conflict,"[2] which pretty well sums up Suharto's own political vision. He was anything but a simple soldier.

The core of the *wayang* world is pre-Muslim, not anti-Muslim. As we have already seen, many Javanese are adept at assimilating what others may see as divergent religious beliefs. Suharto's periodic hostility to Islam had everything to do with his preoccupation with avoiding chaos and his instincts as an army officer, and little to do with religion. Two decades into his rule, when he began to court some Muslims and even stress his own hitherto well-concealed Islamic beliefs, he was as always motivated primarily by the need for control – which by that time he equated with maintaining himself in power.

It is wrong to see Suharto as an all-powerful military dictator. Even if he might have aspired to such a role, he did not have the tools to do the

2   Claire Holt quoted in Benedict. R. O'G. Anderson, *Mythology and the Tolerance of the Javanese*, Ithaca NY: Cornell Modern Indonesia Project, Monograph Series, 1965, p 5.

job in the face of massive historic and cultural obstacles. The president never hesitated to use force, including clandestine dirty tricks. There were plenty of political prisoners, mostly suspected communists arrested after the 1965–1966 upheaval. The Indonesian armed forces were no longer riven by factionalism, and Suharto strongly supported the doctrine of a "dual function" (*dwifungsi*) for the army, giving it equal roles in defense and government, especially at the local level. Army officers increasingly became governors and district heads. But Suharto never achieved anything approaching totalitarian-style control. His 1984 effort to make Pancasila into a credo of conformity was not a success. He probably sensed that total control was not a practical option given the diversity of Indonesian society.

Indeed Indonesian politics and politicking remained lively in spite of Suharto's sporadic repression. During his reign Indonesia held eight legislative elections for the Peoples' Consultative Assembly (Majelis Permusyawaratan Rakyat – MPR), which then elected him, more or less dutifully. These elections were certainly neither free nor fair, but especially in the early years they were always contested, *inter alia* by Muslim politicians. Despite constant effort and considerable shutting down of newspapers, Suharto never managed to stifle embarrassing expressions of political opinion. The rumor mill was irrepressible. The press self-censored as necessary, but was adept at innuendo. Ploys such as headlines reading "Evil Dictator with Corrupt Family Overthrown in Popular Uprising" – one had to read further to learn that all this was taking place in South America – were much beloved by editors and the reading public alike, as were satirical "corner columns" peddling political gossip.

Suharto's preferred *modus operandi* was to control Indonesia's disparate political forces by organizing and manipulating them, dividing or replacing recalcitrant leaders and creating new organizations where necessary. Looking at the totality of his three decades in office, it is hard to discern any ideological pattern beyond waving the bloody shirt of anti-communism, a tactic which over time became ritualistic. As the credibility of the communist menace faded, political Islam became a favorite but hardly the sole target. Worried by a resurgence of Islam in the late 1970s, Suharto reconstituted the moribund Nationalist Party, formerly Sukarno's PNI, threw in the Christian parties to add further anti-Muslim leavening, and renamed it the Indonesian Democracy Party (PDI), although there was nothing democratic about it. But two decades later he went after the PDI when it seemed to be getting too powerful. In the 1990s, he turned against the burgeoning and genuinely pro-democracy movement brought to life by the excesses of his later years.

As he grew older Suharto increasingly made use of force: sending in the army to quell campus unrest in 1978, a campaign of disappearances and murder against alleged criminals beginning in 1983, a harsh crackdown on Muslim rioters in Tanjung Priok in 1984, to cite three examples out of many. The army resorted to ill-concealed clandestine operations from Aceh to East Timor, which Indonesia occupied in 1975. This bad habit grew into a pathology which would linger beyond the end of the New Order.

Early Days: The Repression of Reformist Islam

One of Suharto's first challenges on taking office was what to do about Reformist Islam. In 1960 his predecessor, Sukarno, had banned the major Reformist party, Masyumi, for complicity in the Outer Islands Rebellion. After Sukarno's fall there was much pressure from Masyumi's numerous adherents to allow it to reclaim its rightful place as a major political actor. A related problem involved virtually all Muslim politicians, whether Traditionalist (NU) or Reformist (mainly ex-Masyumi), who agreed that it was wrong to keep on treating them with such suspicion given their strong anti-communism and their role (especially the NU) in obliterating the Communist Party – and thereby bringing Suharto himself to power.

Finally in 1968 Suharto allowed the Reformists to reconstitute themselves as the Indonesian Muslim Party (Partai Muslimin Indonesia – Pamusi) under a new name and a cooperative leader, but he refused to allow the old Masyumi leaders – Mohammed Roem, Sjafruddin Prawiranegara, and, most importantly, due to his religious prestige, Mohammad Natsir – to hold office. Interestingly, the most prominent non-Masyumi supporter of the 1958 rebellion, economist Sumitro Djojohadikusumo, from the also-banned, secular Socialist Party (PSI), was allowed to resume a prominent public role as a major architect of Suharto's economic policy. Masyumi followers were not happy with this one-sided "compromise" and continued to agitate, so in 1971 Suharto's operatives installed a second, even more pliant new leadership for the Reformist party they had created. It was no more acceptable to Natsir and his colleagues, who remained sidelined, although not physically persecuted.[3]

---

3   Personal experience. I was assigned to the US Embassy in Jakarta from 1970 to 1974.

This decapitation of Reformist Islam came at a price. When, in 1973, Suharto forced the creation of a new, unified Muslim political party (Partai Persatuan Pembangunan – PPP, or Unity and Development Party), so cosseted that it did not even have a reference to Islam in its title, the most senior Reformists were excluded from it as well. Thus barred from formal politics, Mohammed Natsir, a man who is revered to this day by many Indonesian Muslims, turned his attention to proselytization (*dakwah*), a grass-roots effort to promote Islamic revival and thwart conversion to other religions, especially Christianity. The key organization behind this effort was the Indonesian Islamic Mission Council (Dewan Dakwah Islamiyah Indonesia – DDII), which Natsir had created in 1967. It is worth noting that Christian proselytization has remained an irritant to many pious Indonesian Muslims, even more so in recent years as foreign missionaries have extended their efforts into strongly Muslim (as opposed to animist) areas of the country, such as West Sumatra.

Reformist Islam had long been more immediately beholden to contemporary Middle Eastern inspiration than its mainly NU, Traditionalist counterpart. Not surprisingly, then, the Reformists took the lead in renewing and enhancing ties with well-funded foreign Muslims, primarily in the Middle East. This effort continued and in 1987 they created another organization, the Indonesian Committee for the Solidarity of the Muslim World (Komite Indonesia untuk Solidaritas Dunia Islam – KISDI), which energetically imported and disseminated radical conspiracy theories. KISDI blamed the troubles of Islam in general, and Indonesia in particular, on Jews, Israel, the domestic Chinese (who were prospering under Suharto), and foreign-supported organizations like the Ford Foundation.

The old Masyumi style, which combined western (usually Dutch) education and pro-western sympathies with fervent Islam and devout anti-communism, almost vanished from politics. Reformism, partly due to the influence of militant Middle Eastern thinking, became increasingly, although never entirely, fundamentalist, puritanical and anti-western in its orientation. The Reformists' reoriented fundamentalism, deprived of its original anti-colonial motivation, led to "one of the greatest tensions and ironies" of Indonesian Islam: the development of a hard-line "legalistic stream" within Reformism.[4]

---

4   Modified from Robin Bush, *Nahdlatul Ulama and the Struggle for Power within Islam and Politics in Indonesia*, Singapore: Institute of Southeast Asian Studies, 2009, p. 31.

The Hindu-Buddhist Revival

Mohammed Natsir's preoccupation with missionary work among his fellow Indonesians was stimulated in part by the conversion of many former Communist Party (PKI) members to religions other than Islam. As we have seen, the basic issue behind the sectarian killings of 1965–66 on Java was conflict between nominally Muslim communists, mainly peasants, and the commercial, landholding supporters of the Islamic boarding schools (*pesantren*) represented by the NU. Suharto's New Order required the now powerless PKI constituency to "have a religion" (*beragama*), which meant adopting a monotheistic faith as mandated by the state philosophy of "Belief in One Supreme God." For many of the recently bloodied peasantry, formal Islam was not yet an attractive option, and by the early 1970s a widespread Hindu revival was underway in significant areas of Java.

Two other religions took advantage of this opportunity. Christian missionaries rapidly converted an estimated three percent of the Javanese population[5] and boasted about it. Non-Islamic Javanese mysticism (*kepercayaan, kebatinan*) also appeared on the upsurge, with initial government support. Mysticism was not just a religious phenomenon; it had a long record of serving as a vehicle for regional chauvinism and occasional rebellion, demonstrated by Diponegoro's mysticism and frequent episodes of peasant unrest during the colonial period.

In 1972 a Javanese mystical sect headquartered in the royal capital of Solo affiliated itself with the newly created government party, Golkar (an acronym for "*golongan karya*," meaning "functional groups"), and Jakarta buzzed with rumors that the government was about to recognize mysticism as an official religion. But Suharto recognized the danger of appearing to sponsor an anti-Islamic religious revival, and before long certain of the Javanese sects were under investigation, allegedly because of concern that old links between mystics and communists should not be re-established. Mysticism was later recognized as a belief, but never given equal status with Indonesia's official religions.

As memories of the 1966 bloodletting faded, Islam would more than offset earlier losses to mysticism and Christianity on Java, to the point where the communal rituals associated with nominal Muslim peasant culture were

---

5   Robert W. Hefner, *Civil Islam: Muslims and Democratization in Indonesia*, Princeton: Princeton University Press, 2000, p. 108.

vanishing by the late 1980s.[6] The Muslim conversion campaigns of Natsir's movement and its allies had something to with this. But the success of the government's efforts to fund rural development, sometimes locally managed and already under way by the early 1970s, was a boon to rural Islamic leaders and institutions and more important in the long run.

The saga of the Hindu-mystic revival and its aftermath well illustrates the extent to which Suharto's Muslim policy came to resemble that of the Dutch. Consciously or otherwise, the president followed the guidelines laid down by Snouck Hurgronje, the famous Dutch advisor on Islamic affairs: distinguish between religious observance and religiously inspired subversion. Support observance or you will feed the flames of subversion. But do not hesitate to use force against subversion when it does occur.

Economic Growth and Islamic Expansion

The greatest accomplishment of the Suharto regime was widely distributed economic development, which bolstered the growth of an educated middle class as well as the growth of Islam, not least in rural areas. From 1965, shortly before Suharto took office, to 1997, when Indonesia was hammered by a regional economic crash, per capita GDP corrected for inflation rose at an average of about 4.8 percent annually, a rate higher than that of Malaysia and only slightly lower than that of Thailand.

Beginning in 1986, roughly the final decade of Suharto's rule, Indonesia's per capita growth was even higher – about six percent.[7] During the same period the number of Indonesians living below the official poverty line dropped by approximately three-quarters, although economic inequality also increased.[8] Literacy more than doubled to about ninety percent (where it has remained ever since) [9] and the number of years of schooling per capita quadrupled.[10] In addition, the government supported a highly effective program of family planning. Between 1965 and 1997,

---

6   Hefner, Civil Islam, p. 84.
7   Thee Kian Wee, "Reflections on the New Order 'Miracle'," in Grayson Lloyd and Shannon Smith, eds,, Indonesia Today: Challenges of History, p. 166; Hal Hill, "The Indonesian Economy, Growth, Crisis and Recovery," The Singapore Economic Review, Vol. 52, No. 2, 2007, p. 5.
8   Ann Booth, "Poverty and Inequality in the Soeharto Era: An Assessment," Bulletin of Indonesian Economic Studies, Vol. 36, No. 1, April 2000, table 3, p. 78, also p. 86.
9   Hefner, Civil Islam, p. 119. The rate in 2007 was still 90.4% according to UNDP figures: Novia D. Rulistia, "Focus on Adult Illiteracy in Indonesia: Improving or Relapse?" Jakarta Post, April 21, 2009.
10 Pierre van der Eng, "Indonesia's Economy and Standard of Living in the 20th Century" in Lloyd and Smith, eds., Indonesia Today, p. 192.

Muslim prayer rooms or small buildings (musholla) at filling stations, such as the one visible in the left background of this photo, were once rare but are now ubiquitous, another symptom of increasing Islamic observance. | Pringle photo

the population growth rate slowed to approximately two percent, among the lowest for any developing country.[11]

With economic development came rapid social change, which, combined with globalization – an important factor since the very arrival of Islam – resulted in unprecedented intellectual ferment and an upsurge in Islamic observance already visible by the late 1970s. By the end of the New Order in 1998, Islamic styles and practices had proliferated and changed among both Traditionalists and Reformists, to the point where this distinction became increasingly blurred, although never eliminated.

This was not what Suharto had intended. He wanted to see development, especially in rural areas, because he knew that a contented peasantry was one vital element in a secure state. He did not anticipate that rural prosperity would, as it had under the Dutch, stimulate further growth in the depth and breadth of Islam.

At the macro level, Suharto supported western-style economic rationality, expressed through a series of five-year plans. They were created and carried

11   Thee Kian Wie, "Reflections on the New Order 'Miracle'," p. 165.

out by economists many of whom were funded by the Ford Foundation and trained at the University of California, famous in Indonesia as the "Berkeley Mafia." This policy encouraged foreign investment and better economic management, but stopped well short of eliminating economic nationalism, much less corruption.

At the micro level, Suharto used some of the profits from Indonesia's oil boom to fund small development projects in the countryside. He gave equally enthusiastic support to increasing rice production by means of new "miracle" varieties, which required more use of fertilizer and pesticides, but greatly increased yields. As a result, Indonesia achieved rice self-sufficiency in 1984. The moral high point of Suharto's career came the next year when Indonesia was able to send food to starving people in Ethiopia, and he received a gold medal from the United Nations Food and Agricultural Organization.

Anthropologist Clifford Geertz returned to Indonesia in 1986, two decades after he had written his famous book on Javanese religion and society, and was amazed at the results:

> For someone who had known it before the storm, [a reference to the killings of 1965–66] the place seemed to have exchanged the gathered-up energies of politics for the scattered-out ones of trade. The conjunction of the Green Revolution… and the settling in of military rule… led to a commercialization of town life at least as pervasive, and nearly as obsessive, as its politicization once had been. Buying and selling – diverse, intricate, virtually continuous buying and selling, reaching into all levels and corners of society and operating on all sorts of scale and degrees of extension – replaced getting ready for doomsday as the dominant preoccupation of just about everyone.[12]

Suharto's gifts to Islam went well beyond support for village-level development. In 1983 he appointed a talented diplomat and Islamic scholar from a *pesantren* background, Munawar Sjadzali, to be his Minister of Religion. Sjadzali was an outstanding, widely respected Muslim progressive. He did things like initiating debate on whether certain verses in

---

12   Clifford Geertz, *After the Fact: Two Countries, Four Decades, One Anthropologist*, Cambridge: Harvard University Press, 1995, p 11.

the Koran relating to slavery had lost their relevance and suggesting that the country needed its own Indonesia-based system of Islamic jurisprudence (*fikh*). In 1990, under Sjadzali's tenure, an important law was passed putting Indonesia's Islamic court system on an equal basis with its civil and military courts.[13] In the late 1970s the government began to expand the state-operated, multi-level Islamic university system. Enrollment at these institutions almost quadrupled between 1979 and 1991. Today they educate about 18% of Indonesia's tertiary students[14] and have become a bulwark not only of Islamic scholarship, but of moderate, mainstream Islamic doctrine.

Using the same oil revenues that supported local development programs, Suharto also funded construction of mosques, prayer halls and Islamic day schools (*madrasah*), especially in areas seen as insufficiently Islamic. In East Java the number of mosques increased from 15,574 in 1973 to 25,655 in 1990. There was a similar program in Central Java, and more was done by one of the president's private foundations.[15]

Indonesia's president was by no means the only one who did not fully understand the religious implications of his largesse. Western experts working in Indonesia in the early 1970s certainly did not. They were much more focused on concerns that "miracle" high-yielding rice varieties, which eliminated much of the need for rural labor, would cause social unrest to recur on overpopulated Java.[16] To oversimplify, they feared that the old nominally Muslim peasantry, which had been a mainstay of the Communist Party, would be pitched into a new radical reaction, this time due to loss of employment. It did not happen; instead, after their initial flirtation with the Hindu revival, many Javanese villagers set up shops, bought radios and motor scooters, and became observant Muslims.

The growing connection between commercial development and Islam which began under Suharto has continued apace down to the present. Islamic goods and services have proliferated into fields such as tourism, publishing, fashion, and lifestyle counseling. Clerics routinely peddle advice via television, the internet and radio, which can reach customers

---

13 Martin van Bruinessen, "Islamic state or state Islam? Fifty years of state-Islam relations in Indonesia," in Ingrid Wessel (Hrsg.), *Indonesien am Ende des 20. Jahrhunderts*, Hamburg: Abera-Verlag, 1996, pp. 19–34, accessed July, 2008, at http://www.let.uu.nl/~martin.vanbruinessen/personal/publications/State-Islam.htm.
14 Hefner, *Civil Islam*, p. 120.
15 *Ibid.*, p. 121.
16 Personal experience.

mired in Indonesia's notorious traffic jams. One entrepreneur offers Islamic guidance to the lovelorn, noting that one of the Prophet's favorite pleasures was bathing with His wife, with details on how to emulate Him available to subscribers.[17] On a more serious note, there has been a significant growth in Islamic banking, which complies with sharia-based prohibitions by, for example, replacing interest earnings with dividend-sharing. The first sharia bank in Indonesia was established in 1991. Islamic banking now includes rural and microfinance operations as well as conventional urban banking, although it still amounts to only about two percent of Indonesia's financial sector.[18]

Reformist Islam Radicalized
The expanding, diversified Muslim intelligentsia of the New Order was overwhelmingly moderate, often with impeccable religious credentials. But it also included proponents of an Islamic radicalism which drew strength from both new and old sources.

By the late 1970s the politically restricted Reformist leaders' new concentration on religious propagation and revival included a sometimes clandestine, campus-based Islamic education (*tarbiyah*) movement which built on Indonesia's well established tradition of youth activism. Try as the regime might, through infiltration and cooptation, it could not control such activity, much less eliminate it. Students were exposed to radical thinking, frequently inspired by Reformism's new links with the Middle East. Some campus groups adopted the cell-based (*usroh*) organizational style of the Egyptian Muslim Brotherhood, including the founders of the Justice Party (Partai Keadilan – PK).[19] This party, now the PKS (Partai Keadilan Sejahtera), is today widely regarded as Indonesia's most sophisticated and potentially dangerous radical Islamic political organization (see Chapter 7).

There was also a benign aspect of campus activism, including efforts to meld pious Islam with middle class life styles, relaxed dress, pop music

---

17 Greg Fealy, "Consuming Islam: Commodified Religion and Aspirational Pietism in Contemporary Indonesia," in Greg Fealy and Sally White, eds., *Expressing Islam: Religious Life and Politics in Indonesia*, Singapore: Institute of Southeast Asian Studies, 2008, p. 29 especially the reproduced advertisement (photo no. 2).

18 *Ibid.*, p. 19, chart on p. 232; see also chapters by Umar Juoro, Muhammad Syafii Antonio and Minako Sakai.

19 Greg Fealy, Virginia Hooker and Sally White, "Indonesia," in Greg Fealy and Virginia Hooker, eds., *Voices of Islam in Southeast Asia: A Contemporary Sourcebook*, Singapore: Institute of Southeast Asian Studies, 2006, pp. 48–9.

and seminars on religion and development.[20] One of the best-known venues for such activities was the Salman Mosque at the Bandung Institute of Technology. Its designer, Achmad Noe'man, produced a stylish, airy building without a dome, designed to emphasize the connection between the precepts of modern Islam and modern aesthetics generally.[21]

The most important new doctrine entering Indonesia at this time was Salafism, fundamentalist Islam similar in spirit to the Wahabism of Saudi Arabia. Wahabi doctrine had been much talked about in pre-independence Indonesia (see Chapter 2) but rarely experienced except, arguably, during the early nineteenth-century Padri War. The Islamic Reformism of the 1920s and 1930s had emphasized return to scripture as a path that would lead simultaneously to religious reformation and secular progress, enabling colonized peoples to compete with their colonizers. In contrast, the main current of Salafism tends to be uncompromisingly puritanical. It rejects association with the secular west or compromise with religious pluralism. The most religiously conservative variants of Salafism condemn political activity altogether, because it detracts from religious study. However some Salafis, often referred to as Salafi Jihadists, favor violent as opposed to peaceful jihad (or struggle).[22]

Partly as a result of Saudi and other foreign funding, Salafism was well represented in the expansion of Islamic education which took place during the Suharto regime, although much less in the state Islamic schools mentioned earlier than in the increasingly numerous and diverse private religious schools. The best-known "radical" Salafi school, the *pesantren* al-Mukmin at Ngruki, near Solo, was founded in 1972, and it is often seen as the flagship school of violent Islamic extremism in Indonesia (see Chapter 5).

Salafism thrived on Suharto's repression, which had at least as much impact on Muslim opinion as his mosque-building activities or his

---

20   Hefner, *Civil Islam*, p. 123.
21   Agus S. Ekomadyo, "Architectural Representation of Islamic Modernism and Neo-Modernism in Indonesia: Between Internationalism and Regionalism: Case Study: Architecture of Achmad Noe'man. Paper submitted to Regional Architecture and Identity in the Age of Globalization CSAAR 2007, accessed September 2009 at www.ar.itb.ac.id/ekomadyo/.../ASEModernismNoemanCSAAR.pdf.
22   On the terminology, see Martin van Bruinessen,"'Traditionalist' and 'Islamist' pesantren in Indonesia," in Farish A. Noor, Yoginder Sikand and Martin van Bruinessen, eds., *The Madrasa in Asia: Political Activism and Transnational Linkages*. Amsterdam: Amsterdam University Press, 2008, accessed July 2008 at http://www.let.uu.nl/~martin.vanbruinessen/personal/publications/pesantren_2.htm.

development programs. The new radicalism was also appealing to members of the old Darul Islam (DI) networks. They were demonized by the Suharto regime, which, after the obliteration of communism, needed a new and more credible threat. Perhaps the best example of this process was the murky relationship between Suharto's operatives and "Komando Jihad," a network (or networks) based largely on old DI adherents. "Komando Jihad" was blamed for various incidents from the late 1970s onwards, including the hijacking of an Indonesian airliner in 1981, a bombing of the (Buddhist) Borobudur in 1985, and an unsuccessful effort to stage a bombing on Bali a short time later, a bungled precursor of the Bali bombings of 2002 and 2005.

"Komando Jihad" seems to have had genuine terrorist objectives. Yet it was also manipulated if not created by Suharto's foremost architect of clandestine dirty tricks, his close friend General Ali Murtopo. He used it against allegedly communist enemies and at the same time employed it as a "useful scarecrow,"[23] evidence of the new Muslim menace. Murtopo may even have named it; the term "Komando Jihad" was apparently never used by its members.[24]

By the mid-1980s Suharto's repression and Muslim reaction to it, combined with a worsening international climate, had created a pool of potential Muslim recruits for service in Afghanistan. These were the people who would carry out the far more serious violence of the next two decades.

Radical Islam was greatly aided by the new connections to the Middle East established by the politically frustrated Reformists. In 1980 former Masyumi leader Mohammed Natsir helped establish in Jakarta the Institute for Islamic and Arabic Studies (Lembaga Ilmu Pengetahuan Islam dan Arab – LIPIA), a branch of the Saudi Arabian Muhammad bin Saud University.[25] Over the next two decades LIPIA would produce at least 5,000 graduates, including many who became Salafi leaders.

23 "Useful scarecrow" is from Martin van Bruinessen, "Genealogies of Islamic Radicalism in post-Suharto Indonesia," *Southeast Asia Research*, Vol. 10, No. 2, July, 2002, pp. 117–54, accessed July 2008 at http://www.let.uu.nl/~martin.vanbruinessen/personal/publications/genealogies_islamic_radicalism.htm.
24 International Crisis Group (hereafter cited as ICG), *Al-Qaeda in Southeast Asia: The case of the "Ngruki Network" in Indonesia (Corrected on 10 January 2003)*, Asia Briefing No. 20, 8 Aug. 2003, p. 5. All International Crisis Group reports are available on the ICG website; see listing for International Crisis Group in the Further Reading list.
25 ICG, *Indonesia Backgrounder: Why Salafism and Terrorism Mostly Don't Mix*, Asia Report No. 83, 13 September 2004, pp. 7–8; Giora Eliraz, *Islam in Indonesia; Modernism, Radicalism, and the Middle East Dimension*, Brighton: Sussex Academic Press, 2004, p. 38.

A division soon developed between purists bent on religious study and followers of a politically oriented style modeled on the Muslim Brotherhood As a result many "pure" Salafis left LIPIA and joined or founded new Salafi-oriented schools elsewhere. A scattering of Salafi schools were already in existence, including Ngruki, mentioned earlier; another *pesantren* operated by the Islamic Association (Persis), a puritanical organization which had existed since 1923 and practiced a home-grown philosophy similar to but unconnected with Saudi Wahabism; and schools founded by al-Irsyad, an organization founded by the Indonesian Arab community in 1914.[26] But the majority of the Suharto-era Salafist schools, numbering in the hundreds, were new.[27]

It is important to bear in mind that these fundamentalist schools amounted to less than one percent of Indonesian Muslim schools, which were themselves only about one-fifth of Indonesia's total school system, a subject discussed further in the following chapter.

The new influx of foreign money and propaganda in the Suharto era was impressive and unprecedented in volume and influence. One Saudi foundation alone has given away one million books in Indonesia since its founding in 1992.[28] Such efforts both fed on and stimulated awareness of the Arab-Israeli conflict and other Middle Eastern issues. By the mid-1970s student demonstrations against Israel and its US supporters had already become commonplace.[29] One of the more interesting examples of Indonesian Islam's growing sensitivity to external events occurred when the Iranian Revolution of 1979 sent a frisson of excitement through the Islamic intelligentsia, resulting in a few converts to Shiism.[30]

Reformist Muslims and Democracy

It would be wrong to leave the impression that Reformist Islam in the waning days of Suharto's rule was wholly in the thrall of reaction, religious radicalism, or collaboration with the president, discussed below. Reformism was becoming increasingly diverse and, like Indonesian Islam in

---

26 On the origin of al-Irsyad, see Natalie Mobini-Kesheh, *The Hadrami Awakening: Community and Identity in the Netherlands East Indies, 1900–1942*, Ithaca NY: Southeast Asia Program, Cornell University, 1999, esp. Ch. 4 (pp. 71–90).

27 ICG, *Why Salafism and Terrorism*, p. 10.

28 *Ibid.*, p. 6.

29 Personal experience: as a junior diplomat in a less security-conscious age I was told to meet with student demonstrators in front of the US embassy in Jakarta and answer their questions at the time of the 1973 Yom Kippur War.

30 Van Bruinessen, "Genealogies of Islamic Radicalism."

general, divided largely along generational lines. Some younger Reformist intellectuals and politicians made common cause with Traditionalists and others in leading opposition to Suharto and promoting democracy. This group included NU Chairman Abdurrahman Wahid (Traditionalist), Muhammadiyah Chairman Amien Rais (Reformist) and the foremost Indonesian intellectual and Muslim scholar of the time, Nurcholish Madjid, who drew on both Traditionalism and Modernism.

The movement led by these men made possible Indonesia's transition to democracy. While it was pluralistic in composition, including all of Indonesia's major socio-religious categories, there is no question that political Islam, despite the varied views of Muslim leaders on other issues, was a critically important force. Islam's role in creating Indonesia's new democracy is among the most important aspects of its historic heritage, with few parallels elsewhere. It has not been forgotten by Indonesians.

The Urbanization of Traditionalist Styles

The Traditionalists of the NU suffered far less from New Order repression than their Reformist, ex-Masyumi co-religionists. From Suharto's point of view most of them were, after all, comfortably Javanese, and very few of them had been implicated in either Darul Islam or the Outer Islands Rebellion. But if the NU suffered less than the Reformists, it nonetheless found life under Suharto vexing. Its leaders remained irked about not getting sufficient credit for helping to destroy communism in 1966. Javanese Traditionalists were still wrestling with whether they wanted to stay directly involved in politics at all, or withdraw to their *pesantren* and bury themselves in religious study and behind-the-scenes advocacy.

In 1971, following the first New Order election, the NU lost control of the Ministry of Religious Affairs. It was a severe blow because this ministry is in charge of funds dispensed in support of Islamic education. The ministry was also, then as now, a major source of patronage, largely because it held the key to control of sharia-based institutions within the Indonesian legal system, such as Islamic courts, the operation of the pilgrimage (haj) and the administration of Islamic charities.

In 1973 the NU allowed itself to be herded into the New Order's umbrella party for Muslims, the PPP. There, owing to the demoralized and fragmented state of the Reformists, it assumed a dominant role and helped the PPP to achieve a credible showing in the 1977 and 1982 elections (which, like most elections under Suharto, were manipulated but not consistently controlled).

But in 1984, offended by Suharto's growing anti-Muslim campaign, the NU pulled out of the PPP and abandoned formal politics. Without it the PPP made a miserable showing in the 1987 elections.[31]

In other words, the NU proved politically resilient under daunting circumstances, the only Islamic party to survive the 1970s more or less intact. But it was the social and religious evolution of Traditionalist Islam that was most surprising, and most significant in the long run. The Sufi-influenced religion of the Traditionalists began to gain a constituency among the new urban Muslim middle classes created by the New Order's economic policies and especially among women. Sufism's emphasis on inner religious experience and personal closeness to God appealed to many Indonesians who were not attracted by the puritanical side of Reformism, or by its positions on such issues as polygamy and female subordination.

The NU's theology, which made room for the study of tradition and multi-sourced precedent, turned out to be more flexible than the scriptural preoccupation of the Reformists. As a result, the Traditionalists, far from fading away as had seemed likely only a few decades previously, re-emerged as a dynamic element on the religious scene, linked to a global revival of Sufism. Moreover, they did so without losing their original, largely rural base.[32]

Indonesia's modern Sufism found expression through radio preachers, life-style publications, popular music and urban discussion groups. Muslim intellectuals began to develop "this-worldly ethical and devotional" Sufism beyond the Sufi orders.[33] The term "neo-Sufism" was coined to cover a wide variety of new styles, and neo-Sufi books were best sellers from the 1970s onwards.[34]

Faces of Suharto-Era Islam: Four New Players

Four Muslims who came to prominence in the Suharto years illustrate the variety and vitality of Islamic intellectual life in New Order Indonesia. All were born on Java between 1936 and 1944. One, Nurcholish Madjid, came from a mixed Reformist-Traditionalist background, but was born and raised in the Traditionalist heartland of East Java. The second, Abdurrahman

31 Hefner, Civil Islam, p. 168.
32 See the introductory essay by the editors in Martin van Bruinessen and Julia Day Howell, eds., Sufism and the 'Modern' in Islam, London: I.B.Tauris, 2007, pp. 3–18.
33 Van Bruinessen and Howell, Sufism and the 'Modern', p. 11.
34 Julia Day Howell, "Sufism and the Indonesian Islamic Revival," Journal of Asian Studies, Vol. 60, No. 3, 2001, p. 710.

Wahid, from the same town as Madjid, is the son and grandson of senior NU leaders. The third, Amien Rais, is a Javanese with strong ties to Muhammadiyah, the Reformist mass organization. The fourth, Abu Bakar Ba'asyir, was born in Solo, Central Java, of Indonesian "Arab" ancestry. All four were influenced in varying degrees by intellectual currents emanating from both the Middle East and the West. Wahid would become Indonesia's fourth president. Madjid, an apostle of tolerance and pluralism, was the best-known public intellectual of his generation. Amien Rais, who with Madjid and Wahid was a leader of the pro-democracy movement, represented the new face of Reformist Islam, beginning to recover from its trauma under Suharto. Ba'asyir, representing the politically radical face of Indonesian Islam, has come to epitomize the threat of Islamic extremism in Indonesia, a role he plays with gusto.

Nurcholish Madjid was born in Jombang, East Java. He came to prominence as a two-term leader of the Islamic Students' Association (Himpunan Mahasiswa Islam – HMI), which initially supported the New Order. A prolific speaker, writer and scholar, he sought a middle ground between Islamic piety and the exigencies of modern life. He felt it could be found through new interpretations of the Koran and classical Islamic sources, and he consistently applied his formidable intellectual capacity to this end. One of his most famous speeches, delivered in January 1970, resonated with the youth of Indonesia's rising middle class by asserting that intellectual freedom and liberal values were fully compatible with Islam.[35]

At the University of Chicago, Madjid wrote his PhD thesis on Ibn Taymiyyah, a medieval philosopher popular with both the conservative elders of Reformist Islam and modern Salafist radicals, arguing that even in Taymiyyah's teaching a justification for Islamic pluralism, based on the application of reason to scripture, could be found.[36] When, in 1986, Madjid began a discussion group (today a university) he called it "Paramadina," a reference to the multi-religious governance (often called a "charter" or "constitution") which the Prophet and his followers installed in Medina after his flight there from Mecca.

---

35 "The Necessity of Reform of Islamic Thought and the Problem of the Integrity of the Umat," excerpted in Fealy and Hooker, eds., *Voices of Islam*, p. 221; full text in English in Charles Kurzman, ed., *Liberal Islam: a Sourcebook*, Oxford: Oxford University Press, 1998, pp. 284–89.
36 On Taymiyyah, see Karen Armstrong, *Islam: A Short History*, New York: Random House, Modern Library, 2000, p. 104.

Nurcholish Madjid, shown with his wife, was probably the most famous Islamic intellectual of the Suharto era. | Hendra Suhara/TEMPO

Madjid, who died in 2005, was convinced that the record of political Islam in Indonesia had been a disaster, leading to sectarian strife and the Outer Islands Rebellion, as well as the destruction of Masyumi and the liberal-intellectual Socialist Party (PSI). He offended old-school Reformists by telling them in no uncertain terms that their pursuit of an Islamic state was a dead end. Instead, he said, Islamic objectives could best be realized by separating piety from formal, party-based politics, and concentrating on teaching and reform. But he personally engaged on a regular basis with political leaders up to and including the President and provided critical intellectual support for the pro-democracy movement.

Unlike Wahid, he did not shy away from participating in Suharto's attempt, late in his rule, to sponsor ICMI, a new organization for Muslim intellectuals (broadly defined). He favored the idea of a distinctively Indonesian style of Islam, anathema to those Reformists who insist on the universality of Islam. He argued that all the major religions of Indonesia should be considered as "equal citizens" of the country, but that Islam had a special role as a binding force and provider of an "overarching civilizational unity."[37] Conservative critics accused him of "bourgeois pluralism."[38] He deeply resented what he understood as occasional Christian efforts to use his arguments to promote the spread of Christianity.

---

37 Martin van Bruinessen, "Nurcholish Madjid, Indonesian Muslim Intellectual," ISIM Review No, 17. Spring 2006, pp. 22-3, expanded version accessed July 2008 at http://www.let.uu.nl/~martin.vanbruinessen/personal/publications/nurcholish_madjid.htm.
38 *Ibid*.

Abu Bakar Ba'asyr, was co-founder of the violent extremist organization Jemaah Islamyah and remains an indefatigable spokesman for extremist causes. He is shown here burning an Israeli flag in 2002. | Dimas Ardian/Getty Images

Abu Bakar Ba'asyir is at the opposite end of the Islamic political spectrum from Nurcholish Madjid. He is an Arab, meaning that some of his ancestors were immigrants from the Hadramaut region of Yemen. Ba'asyir's theology is Salafi Jihadist, stressing strict observance of scriptural Islam, rejecting any meaningful collaboration with non-Muslims, and glorifying martyrdom in defense of Islamic values as he sees them. He has become a widely recognized standard bearer for Islamic extremism in Indonesia. He attended Gontor *pesantren* in East Java, then al-Irsyad, an Arab-founded university in Solo, became active in an Islamic youth group, and, in 1972, with Abdullah Sungkar, also an Arab, founded the al-Mukmin Pesantren at Ngruki, Central Java, as a reaction to what he regarded as the paucity of sufficiently radical thinking in other *pesantren*.[39] Both men were active in the residual Darul Islam movement in the 1980s.

In 1982 both Ba'asyir and Sungkar were tried and convicted of subversion. They were released in 1985, and fled to Malaysia to escape further charges, returning to Ngruki in 1999 after the advent of democracy.

---

39   Van Bruinessen, "'Traditionalist' and 'Islamist' pesantren."

When Sungkar died in 1999, Ba'asyir replaced him as the leader of the radical regional organization Jemaah Islamiyah. Although Ba'asyir openly voices support for Osama bin Laden, he has never been convicted of direct involvement in terrorism.[40]

Abdurrahman Wahid (Gus Dur) is both a leading scion of the Nahdlatul Ulama's tradition-encrusted, hereditary leadership, and a liberal apostle of democracy and pluralism – an apparent paradox which, once understood, goes far to explain important aspects of Indonesian Islam.[41] His grandfather, Hasyim Asy'ari, was a senior cleric behind the founding of the NU and his father, Wahid Hasyim, led it during the tumultuous times of the Japanese Occupation and early independence. He was born and initially educated in the *pesantren* center of Jombang, East Java. As a child he was exceedingly bright, a precocious reader, and an avid soccer fan (not player). He studied abroad at Al-Azhar in Cairo (where he was bored) and then in more secular Baghdad (which he thoroughly enjoyed) for a total of about seven years. He returned to Indonesia in the early 1970s and gravitated naturally into a position of leadership in the NU, eventually serving as its national chairman from 1984 to 1999.[42]

As a rising politician he astonished foreigners by the strength of his pro-democracy convictions and his liberal views on issues such as normalizing relations with Israel. Wahid's opinions offended some among the NU's varied membership, but his equally unorthodox religious and other habits were, for them, a good deal more controversial, sometimes crossing the boundary between the normal Traditionalist penchant for ancestor worship and Islamic mysticism into behavior that struck some as out-and-out paganism (e.g., participating in a Javanese rite propitiating the Queen of the Southern Ocean). Wahid was not, however, unprecedented: in the early 1970s one of the NU's leaders was Z.E. Subchan, "...the kind of

---

40 For more on Ba'asyir and Sungkar, see Fealy and Hooker, eds., *Voices of Islam*, p. 442; John T. Sidel, *Riots, Pogroms, Jihad: Religious Violence in Indonesia*, Ithaca NY: Cornell University Press, pp. 202-08; and ICG, *Al-Qaeda in Southeast Asia*, esp. pp. 6–7.

41 For Wahid's background see Greg Barton, *Abdurrahman Wahid, Muslim Democrat, Indonesian President: a View from the Inside*, Sydney: University of New South Wales Press, 2002 and Martin van Bruinessen's "Back to Situbondo? Nahdlatul Ulama Attitudes toward Abdurrahman's Presidency and his Fall" in Henk Schulte Nordholt and Irwan Abdullah, eds., *Indonesia: in Search of Transition*, Yogyakarta: Pustaka Pelajar, 2002, pp. 15–46; accessed July 2008 at http://www.let.uu.nl/~martin.vanbruinessen/personal/publications/back_to_situbondo.htm.

42 Martin van Bruinessen,"Saints, Politicians and Sufi Bureaucrats" in van Bruinessen and Howell, *Sufism and the 'Modern,'* p. 104.

President Wahid's daughter, Yenny, assists him in signing a document at an OPEC summit in 2000. Hugo Chavez of Venezuela is at left. | REUTERS/Juan Carlos Ulate

brilliant eccentric only imaginable in the NU… remembered for his taste for alcohol, dance and nightclubs."[43]

Wahid was an early leader of the pro-democracy movement and was its most prominent figure until 1997. His presidency (1999–2001) was plagued primarily by his failing health and increasingly erratic behavior, not by others' rejection of his religious behavior, his bouts of opportunism, or his liberal political beliefs. He is often referred to as "Gus Dur", not a nickname, but an indicator of high rank within the NU hierarchy – "Gus" is an abbreviated title, Si Bagus, while "Dur" is a short version of his name, Abdurrahman.

Amien Rais was born in 1944 in Solo, Central Java, to parents both of whom were active in Muhammadiyah. He rose to head the organization himself before assuming leadership of the anti-Suharto, pro-democracy movement after Wahid suffered a stroke in late 1997. As a young student Rais wanted to be a diplomat and studied international relations at Gadjah Mada University, where he was later appointed a professor. His higher education included a fellowship at Al-Azhar in Cairo, an MA from Notre Dame (Indiana) (research topic: the foreign policy of Egypt's President Anwar Sadat) and a PhD from the University of Chicago (topic: the Muslim Brotherhood, the influential mass movement founded in Egypt in 1928

---

43 Hefner, *Civil Islam*, p. 90.

Amien Rais, a prominent Reformist leader of the Suharto era and a major figure in the pro-democracy movement. | Paula Bronstein/Getty Images

which emphasizes both political activism *and* religion).

From his leadership of Muhammadiyah, Rais, like Wahid, moved easily into national politics. He was one of the "reform activists"[44] at ICMI in its early days, until he crossed the increasingly irascible Suharto, who had him fired in 1998, thereby enhancing his political appeal.[45] In the same year Rais founded the National Mandate Party (Partai Amanat Nasional – PAN) and, by 2002, was chair of Indonesia's reformed and democratized People's Consultative Assembly (MPR). Rais became keenly interested in social issues and scathingly critical of US Foreign Policy. PAN, a secular nationalist party with a Muslim constituency, received six percent of the vote in the 2009 parliamentary election.

Interesting note: Nurcholish Madjid, Amien Rais, and Ahmad Syafi'i Ma'arif, who succeeded Rais as head of Muhammadiyah, all studied at the University of Chicago, partly due to the presence there of noted Muslim theologian Fazlur Rahman, from Pakistan.

Suharto and Pancasila

As conceived during the independence movement, Pancasila was a credo of pluralism, designed to enhance national unity by celebrating Indonesia's diversity, however vaguely. But in 1984 Suharto tried to stand Pancasila on

---

44 Term in quotes is from *Ibid.*, p. 149.
45 *Ibid.*, p.199.

its head by converting it into a uniform ideology which, he thought, would help eliminate opposition to him personally and prevent further descent into chaos. It had the opposite effect.

His vehicle was legislation requiring all mass organizations to have Pancasila as as their "sole basis" (*asas tunggal*). To many Muslims this formula went too far towards explicitly excluding Islam, and in September 1984 their unhappiness led to rioting at Jakarta's port city, Tanjung Priok, which the army harshly repressed with many casualties. The law was passed anyway the next year. The Tanjung Priok violence was followed by the Komando Jihad bombing of the Borobudur and other evidence of Muslim unrest. In response the regime accelerated its ideological campaign. It required civil servants and the military to take courses on the practice of Pancasila. In the words of his biographer it was

> ... Suharto's supreme effort at building a new and comprehensive sense of what it meant to be Indonesian, which included a rejection of sectional interests based on religion (read: Islam) and ethnicity, the annihilation of leftist and liberal thinking... and the embracing of an enforced collegiality to overturn the old culture of conflict and disharmony."[46]

In the months that followed there was more banning of newspapers, long-delayed executions of communist leaders (including Syam, an architect of the 1965 coup attempt), and more efficient political control by the domestic policing apparatus of the armed forces.

Suharto's effort to eliminate diversity by fiat had no lasting results and served mainly to demonstrate that he was losing his touch. Pancasila, despite having been thus misused, was not discredited for long, and today has largely resumed its original meaning as a broad expression of pluralism.

Suharto's "Greening": ICMI and the Military

By the late 1980s the Suharto regime was showing multiple symptoms of decadence. His was the familiar story of an aging strong man unwilling to relinquish power and unable to cope with changing circumstances. Suharto allowed his grasping family to get out of control, offending practically everyone, including some in the military, where he could no longer rely

---

46 Elson, *Suharto*, p. 241.

on personal friends from his youth. East Timor, occupied by Indonesian troops in 1975, had become an endless migraine.

Suharto's behavior was increasingly distasteful to Indonesia's rising, educated middle classes, especially to youth conscious of their historic role as the vanguard of political reform and revolution. Most important of all, perhaps, Indonesians were becoming bored to distraction by their aging, corrupt, out-of-touch leader.

Sensing that things were not going well, the ruler became more selective about his oppression of activist Muslims and began to court some of them publicly. Already in 1988 he had eased into retirement his old friend General Benny Murdani, the Catholic commander of the armed forces, in part for speaking truth to him about his parasitic family. Two key events followed: First, in late 1990, Suharto blessed the formation of a proposed Muslim Intellectuals Association (Ikatan Cendekiawan Muslim Indonesia – ICMI) being put together by prominent Muslim intellectuals, including religious moderates like Nurcholish Madjid. Second, Abdurrahman Wahid, the rising star of the NU, which by this time was formally out of politics, refused to join ICMI. Instead he allied with others in 1991 to formalize the merging pro-democracy movement by creating the Democracy Forum.[47]

Suharto soon realized that the new pro-democracy movement was getting out of hand. His reaction was to form an alliance with religiously conservative Muslims from the older generation of Masyumi adherents, some of the same people he had spent two decades oppressing. Many of them were associated with DDII and KISDI, the hard-line Islamic propagation and global solidarity movements established after Masyumi was excluded from formal politics.

Suharto's motives for embracing his old enemies were probably mixed. On the one hand, he instinctively gravitated to the manipulative tactics which had always been his stock response to opposition; on the other, his turn toward Islam may have reflected to some degree the increasing religiosity typical of many aging people. Tactically his new Islamic posture proved to be futile. Whatever it really was, it appeared blatantly opportunistic, and the anti-Suharto democracy movement would only grow in strength as the New Order stumbled toward breakdown.

Suharto's sponsorship of ICMI, which was supposedly a new vehicle for all Muslim intellectuals, is more difficult to explain than his courtship

---

47   Hefner, *Civil Islam*, p.162.

of the ex-Masyumi religious conservatives. He seems to have genuinely desired a more constructive relationship with Muslims who were suitably willing to work with him, especially those from the business community. To head ICMI he chose B. J. Habibie, later to serve as his vice president and to succeed him as president. Habibie was a personal protégé of Suharto's, well known for his brilliant career in Germany as an aeronautical engineer, primarily with the Messerschmitt company.

At first ICMI attracted a heterogeneous mixture of Islamic intellectuals and reform activists. In the end, under Suharto's pressure, it was increasingly dominated by bureaucrats and regime supporters drawn from the ranks of the hard-line Reformists now allied with the President. But especially in its early days ICMI was not Suharto's puppet. Indeed one of its initial leaders, Sri Bintang Pamungkas, a Muslim intellectual and parliamentarian, was forced off ICMI's board and sentenced to three years in prison, but never silenced, for insulting the President in a 1995 lecture.[48]

ICMI never wholly lost the respect of the Islamic community, and it is still in existence. It served its immediate purpose of demonstrating that Suharto was turning a new page with regard to Islam, and is credited with sponsoring some important initiatives such as the establishment of an Islamic bank (today they have proliferated). More broadly, ICMI made it possible for government bureaucrats – once firmly rooted in a non-observant lifestyle – to become visibly pious Muslims.[49]

Suharto's rapprochement with Islam also included an apparent effort to Islamize, or "green," the military. Up to this time Christian officers, who tended to be above average in wealth and education, had been favored out of proportion to their numbers in the Indonesian population and had dominated the most senior positions. But for several years following the removal of Murdani in 1988 they found themselves being passed over for promotion, and they were naturally upset.

Widespread reports of rivalry between "green" (Islamic) and "red and white" (nationalist) factions in the military offended those who cherished its reputation for being blind to sectarian differences. Some officers began to see the flaunting of Islam as a key to career advancement.

The most notorious example was Suharto's ambitious, fast-rising son-in-law, General Prabowo Subianto. Prabowo's father was Sumitro

---

48   Elson, *Suharto*, p. 285.
49   Hefner, *Civil Islam*, pp. 154–55.

Djojohadikusumo, the western-trained economist who had been a leader of the Outer Islands Rebellion. The family was a classic example of the nominally observant Muslim Javanese aristocracy. But as times changed, Prabowo became a prominently observant Muslim and was influential within the new "green" element in the military. More recently he has entered politics at the head of his own political party, Gerindra (Partai Gerakan Indonesia Raya – Great Indonesia Movement Party) which received 4.5% of the vote in the 2009 election.

Leaving aside Suharto's motives of the moment, there was a legitimate need to redress the Muslim deficit in the military, especially given the more general increase in Muslim piety and observance in Indonesia. Although the "greening" episode was controversial at the time, it does not seem to have permanently altered the military's predominantly nationalist, non-sectarian ideology, and at this writing there is no evidence of a significant politically Islamic bloc in the ranks of the military.[50]

The End of the New Order: Chaos and the Transition to Democracy

During his last decade in office Suharto lost control of the state. One defining episode took place in July of 1996 when government-organized thugs attacked the office of the divided Nationalist Party (PDI), headed by Megawati Sukarnoputri, the daughter of the late president. She had popular appeal, she had joined the burgeoning democracy movement, and she had survived Suharto's effort to create a rival PDI leadership. So he unleashed brute force against her and against the party whose political philosophy was probably closest to his own, notwithstanding his newfound Islamic piety. Of course such behavior further stimulated the pro-democracy opposition, which now included two prominent Muslim political leaders, Gus Dur and Amien Rais, as well as Megawati herself.

The president might have survived longer had it not been for the Asian financial crisis, which hit Indonesia in August 1997. Within a few months it destroyed much of the economic progress achieved by the New Order. In March 1998 the People's Consultative Assembly (MPR) unanimously

---

50 For an overview of military greening see Hefner, *Civil Islam*, pp.151–52; also Marcus Mietzner, "Godly Men in Green," *Inside Indonesia* No. 53, Jan.–March 1998, accessed at http://www. insideindonesia.org/edit53/mietzn.htm; comments on the current situation are based partly on interviews with Harold Crouch, author of *The Army and Politics in Indonesia* and an emeritus professor at the Australian National University, and with Colonel Don McFetridge, former US Defense Attache in Jakarta.

Indonesia's descent into violent unrest from 1998 to 2005 resulted from the misrule of the late Suharto years combined with the devastating financial crisis of 1997. Here crowds remove cars destroyed by the May 1998 riots in Jakarta's Chinese district, which killed an estimated 1300 people. | Antara/Hadiyanto.

accorded Suharto an eighth six-year term, but by this time it was clear to everyone except the President and his family that the Indonesian center was not holding. The breaking point came on May 13–14, when the "worst urban riots in Indonesia's history"[51] erupted in Jakarta's ethnic Chinese district, killing an estimated 1300 people and causing as many as 150,000 Chinese[52] to flee the country. It was widely rumored, but never proved, that the President's "green" son-in-law, General Prabowo, who at this time commanded the same strategic reserve force (KOSTRAD) that Suharto himself had led in 1965–66, stood by and allowed the mayhem to proceed. Perhaps he hoped to prove a continuing need for Suharto at the helm. Instead, widespread reaction, including the advice of his army chief, General Wiranto, compelled the president to resign a few days later.

---

51 "Worst urban riots in Indonesia's history" is from M.C. Ricklefs, A *History of Modern Indonesia since c. 1200*, 4th ed., Stanford CA: Stanford University Press, p. 380.
52 Figures on deaths/refugees are from Hefner, *Civil Islam*, p. 206.

Vice President Habibie immediately succeeded Suharto as interim president, and then presided over a transition to democracy which for speed and productivity bears comparison with any parallel event in world history. Habibie's accomplishments during his 17 months in office included legislation leading to democratic elections in June 1999, the abolition of Suharto's controls on political parties, and the enactment of radical decentralization which devolved significant powers to local governments. Habibie was also responsible for the release of all political prisoners, the establishment of press freedom, the separation of the police from the army (a reform which proved to be important in the forthcoming battle against violent Islamic extremism), and the approval of a referendum in embattled East Timor.

It is still something of a mystery how this brilliant engineer with no apparent talent for politics managed to do so much in such a short time. But then, much to Habibie's disappointment, the new People's Consultative Congress turned him down as President and elected Gus Dur (Abdurrahman Wahid) instead.

The same parliamentary elections of June 1999 that led to Habibie's departure and brought Wahid to power were Indonesia's first fair elections in almost 45 years. Comparison with the 1955 elections suggests that despite the Islamic boom of the late New Order, the percentage of Indonesians voting for a party favoring the Jakarta Charter, code words for an Islamic state, had actually declined, a subject that will be analyzed at greater length in Chapter 7.

While the elections of 1999 were surprisingly orderly, conditions in Indonesia by this time were anything but. The multiple consequences of Suharto's misrule, compounded by an Asia-wide financial crisis, had led his country into the very chaos which he so much feared. The anti-Chinese riots that preceded his downfall, above all the major outbreak in Jakarta, did as much to damage Indonesia's image as anything since the killings of 1965–1966. Equally ominous, in February of 1997, Christian Dayaks native to the provinces of Central and West Kalimantan attacked Muslim immigrants from Madura. These episodes were among the first in what would become an epidemic of religious and ethnic violence sufficiently serious to call the future of the nation into question. Increasing turmoil was primarily the result of Suharto's terminal behavior, and cannot be blamed on the liberating impact of political reform. Indeed democracy would turn out to be part of a solution, but that was less than clear in 1999.

5

Islam Organized

The preceding chapters of this book have outlined the history which influenced Islam's role in Indonesia today. The final chapters will shift away from history, and look at two current issues that preoccupy many foreign observers: the causes of recent violent extremism and the possibility that the country may be drifting toward Islamic authoritarianism or even state failure due to political intimidation exercised by a radical minority.

Before that, however, it may be useful to discuss the Islamic institutions that underlie Islamic society and politics in modern Indonesia. What is still special about the two umbrella organizations, Traditionalist Nahdlatul Ulama and Reformist Muhammadiyah? What is important about Islamic education? What is a *pesantren*, and how does it differ from a *madrasah* or from a state-run school? What is "sharia law" and who defines it? What do proponents of an Islamic State really want? What about Islam and the status of women?

Islamic Institutions – the Two Big Ones:
Muhammadiyah and Nahdlatul Ulama

Nahdlatul Ulama and Muhammadiyah remain the organizational giants of Indonesian Islam. They are alive and well, not about to depart from the Indonesian political, educational or cultural scene any time soon. Accurate figures on membership do not seem to exist, but NU is apparently somewhat the larger of the two with more than 30 million members.[1]

---

1   One recent overview estimates 25–30 million for Muhammadiyah and 35–40 million for NU. See Greg Fealy, Virginia Hooker and Sally White, "Indonesia," in Greg Fealy and Virginia Hooker, eds., *Voices of Islam in Southeast Asia*, Singapore: Institute of Southeast Asian Studies, 2006, pp. 40–41, but contrast this with polling data cited later in this section.

Their total following is about one quarter of the Indonesian population; somewhat more, as a proportion of the Indonesian population, than the percentage which has voted consistently for Islamic political parties since 1955 (see Chapter 7).

Both organizations are national in scope, headed by a general chairman, with offices at various lower levels of government, from province to district. Together they operate hundreds of universities and other post-secondary schools, myriad educational programs, thousands of high schools, numerous medical facilities from hospitals to family planning clinics, and major affiliates for youth and women.[2]

Muhammadiyah and NU represent what is often called "mainstream Islam." This term has two implications: first, that the two organizations, although far from homogeneous themselves, represent collectively the view of most Indonesian Muslims, and second, that their views are predominantly middle-of-the-road in both religious doctrine and politics. Both have condemned the illegal violence that has plagued Indonesia since the fall of Suharto. They are not and never have been fronts for violent extremist activities, in the manner of some cultural or humanitarian organizations elsewhere in the Muslim world. Having said that, it is also true that elements of the great Muhammadiyah family still yearn for an Islamic state, while the NU, also true to its past, is seen by its friends as more tolerant of religious pluralism and by its critics as soft on heresy. In polling conducted in 2004, 42 percent of respondents identified themselves with the NU "community," suggesting approval of its political-religious outlook, while only 12 percent identified with Muhammadiyah.[3]

Both organizations have always been politically powerful. At times in the past, they have been reluctant or unable to participate directly in politics, but neither has ever ceased trying to influence government. As noted earlier in this book, Muhammadiyah, founded in 1912, was a new variant

---

2   For more detailed figures see Suzaina Kadir, "Contested Visions of State and Society in Indonesian Islam: The Nahdlatul Ulama in Perspective," in Chris Manning and Peter van Dierman, eds., *Indonesia in Transition: Social Aspects of Reformasi and Crisis*, Singapore: Institute of Southeast Asian Studies, 2000, p. 335, n. 5; also James J. Fox, ed., *Religion and Ritual*, Indonesian Heritage Series, Vol. 9, Singapore: Didier Millet, 1998, esp. p. 28.

3   Analysis is based on Martin van Bruinessen, "Traditionalist and Islamist pesantren in contemporary Indonesia," in Farish A. Noor, Yoginder Sikand and Martin van Bruinessen, eds., *The Madrasa in Asia: Political Activism and Transnational Linkages.* Amsterdam: Amsterdam University Press, 2008, accessed July 2008 at http://www.let.uu.nl/~martin.vanbruinessen/personal/publications/pesantren_2.htm ; the figures are from R. William Liddle and Saiful Mujani. "Indonesia's Approaching Elections: Politics, Islam and Public Opinion," *Journal of Democracy*, Vol. 15, No. 1, Jan. 2004, p. 121.

of Reformist Islam with an agenda emphasizing modern education, partly as an anti-colonial strategy. The NU was then created in 1926 primarily as a reaction to the growing strength of Muhammadiyah, which appeared to challenge both the Islamic doctrine and the socio-economic status of the Traditionalist elite. Both Muhammadiyah and NU were included in the Masyumi umbrella organization created under Japanese auspices in 1943. The NU withdrew from Masyumi in 1952, which then became a primarily Reformist party.[4] But after Sukarno banned Masyumi in 1960, Reformism lost its bearings politically, and, thanks in no small part to the effect of political repression under Suharto, it became divided along both political and religious lines.

The NU began as and still is primarily an organization of Traditionalist clerics or *kiai*. This independent-minded clerical constituency, scattered among rural *pesantren*, has historically been fractious and distrustful of its own Jakarta-based leadership. There was great distress among the *kiai*, for example, when in the 1960s the NU leadership decided to support Sukarno's effort to blend nationalism, communism and religion (including Islam) into a national ideology, NASAKOM. The *kiai* did not like being thus associated with godless communism, and the episode left a residue of ill feeling which helps to explain the ardent local-level NU support for the anti-communist mayhem of 1965–66.[5] At the same time, however, the NU has always wanted to remain on good terms with national leadership because it is vitally interested in government-controlled jobs in the Ministry of Religious Affairs, as well as, more broadly, in maintaining a government compatible with Islam. Recurring tension between the NU's religious agenda and the exigencies of practical politics goes a long way to explain the organization's inconsistency and ambivalence toward central authority over the years.

Abdurrahman Wahid (Gus Dur) became General Chairman of the NU in 1984 and subsequently a leader of the pro-democracy movement which helped to unseat Suharto. He then formed a new National Awakening Party (Partai Kebangkitan Bangsa – PKB) which contested the 1999 elections, one of at least four political parties competing for NU support at this time. Wahid became president in 1999, replacing Habibie, as part of a coalition including Reformist as well as Traditionalist Islamic parties. Despite his

---

4   Some Traditionalists from Jakarta and West Java remained in Masyumi due to fear of ethnic Javanese dominance of the NU – personal communication from Martin van Bruinessen.

5   Suzaina Kadir, "Contested Visions," p. 323.

NU credentials, Wahid's presidency (1999–2001) was controversial among the NU's *kiai* establishment primarily because of his unorthodox religious behavior, not his liberal politics.[6] Since his presidency, NU voters have continued to divide their support among several political parties despite the fact that the social force of the NU's underlying credo, Traditionalist, Sufi-influenced Islam in increasingly modern dress, has never been greater.

Muhammadiyah, like Reformist Islam generally, remains strained by tension between its moderate roots and the tug of religious fundamentalism and anti-western radicalism introduced in the Suharto era. The varied political character of its recent general chairmen – Amien Rais (1995–1998), Ahmad Syafi'i Ma'arif (2000–2005), and Din Syamsuddin (2005–) has reflected the organization's ideological ambivalence, as well as some drift toward a more conservative, fundamentalist-influenced stance. This trend notwithstanding, Muhammadiyah has not lost its historic commitment to health, education and civic affairs generally, as indicated by its strong role in preparing voters for Indonesia's post-Suharto local elections.

The two giants remain noteworthy for many reasons. "No Muslim society [elsewhere] has Islamic welfare organizations as large or as well established," according to a recent study of Islamic education around the world.[7] They also differ from their counterparts in other countries in having consistently supported the developmental goals and policies of Indonesia's pluralist leadership, rather than viewing them as antithetical to Islam. Because of their strong community ties nationwide and their support for development, they have undercut the appeal of Islamic radicalism in Indonesia.[8]

Both organizations can trace their intellectual and religious roots to Middle Eastern precedent: Islamic schools and fifteenth to sixteenth century Sufi networks in the case of the NU, and the teachings of the nineteenth-century Egyptian reformer Muhammad 'Abduh in the case of Muhammadiyah. 'Abduh had many individual and organizational

---

6   See the sketch of Wahid in Chapter 4, which draws on Martin van Bruinessen's "Back to Situbondo? Nahdlatul Ulama Attitudes toward Abdurrahman's Presidency and his Fall" in Henk Schulte Nordholt and Irwan Abdullah, eds., *Indonesia: in Search of Transition*, Yogyakarta: Pustaka Pelajar, 2002, pp. 15–46; accessed July 2008 at http://www.let.uu.nl/~martin. vanbruinessen/personal/publications/back_to_situbondo.htm.
7   Azyumardi Azra, Dina Afrianty and Robert W. Hefner, "Pesantren and Madrasa: Muslim Schools and National Ideals in Indonesia," in Robert W. Hefner and Muhammad Qasim Zaman, eds., *Schooling Islam: The Culture and Politics of Modern Muslim Education*, Princeton: Princeton University Press, 2007, p. 193.
8   Giora Eliraz, *Islam in Indonesia: Modern Radicalism and the Middle East Dimension*, Brighton: Sussex Academic Press, 2004, p. 87.

followers around the world, but what made Muhammadiyah different from those in the Middle East was that it took 'Abduh's religious ideas "far beyond their original boundaries,"[9] incorporating them in a broader social program which has been further developed in the last three decades by a new generation of Islamic modernizers like Nurcholish Madjid.

With the restoration of democracy in Indonesia after 1999, Muslim political parties re-emerged in confusing array. Almost all of them have formal or informal ties to either Muhammadiyah or Nahdlatul Ulama. As of 2008, 161 politicians from Muhammadiyah backgrounds were serving in the 550-member parliament in various parties.[10] The number of parliamentarians similarly influenced by NU affiliation is probably as high or higher.

Since 1999 both Muhammadiyah and NU have provided major support for Indonesia's new, decentralized democracy. They cooperate on social issues such as the fight against HIV/AIDS.[11] Together they operate a nation-wide election monitoring and voter education program which reaches millions of voters. This effort has contributed greatly to the success of Indonesia's numerous local elections, 73 of them in 2006 alone. One expert notes that the program is "a remarkable story, unknown outside Indonesia, and unprecedented for a Muslim majority country."[12]

In recent decades the NU has allowed female *pesantren* students to study the ancient religious texts which are the basis of its religious practice. Because of this, and because Middle Eastern-style puritanical fundamentalism is antithetical to most of its followers, the NU has been able to embark on a significant reinterpretation of these texts in the light of modern norms and requirements, especially as they apply to the status of women. This is another remarkable story, which is related briefly at the conclusion of this chapter.

The explosion of Indonesian Islamic organizational life in recent years, and especially the well-publicized presence of sometimes radical, foreign-based Islamic mass organizations, raises the possibility that the days of

---

9   *Ibid.*, p. 21.
10   Remarks by Dr. Din Syamsuddin, President of Muhammadiyah, before the United States-Indonesia Society, 31 July 2008.
11   "NU and Mummadiyah Fight HIV/AIDS," translated from the newspaper *Republika*, 9 July 2008.
12   Douglas E. Ramage, "Indonesia: Democracy First, Good Governance Later" in Daljit Singh and Lorraine Carlos Salazar, eds., *Southeast Asian Affairs 2007*, Singapore: Institute of Southeast Asian Studies, 2007, p.149.

bipolar NU-Muhammadiyah domination may be numbered. Sometimes cited in this connection are the Hizbut Tahrir, or Party of Liberation, which advocates restoration of a global caliphate, and the Tablighi Jumaat, a group founded in British India which today energetically promotes its puritanical message world-wide. These groups, both of which now have substantial followings in Indonesia, are among those pushing Muhammadiyah in particular towards a more religiously conservative stance. The broader question, which cannot be answered at this time, is whether the spread of non-mainstream Islam in Indonesia will in time eclipse the two old giants, or simply continue to complement and complicate Indonesia's repertory of Islamic styles.

The Muslim Educational System in Outline

Many foreigners suspect that Muslim schools everywhere are hotbeds of proto-terrorism. Thus, in early 2007, at the beginning of the American presidential campaign, someone in the US leaked a report claiming that Barack Obama had attended a "radical Muslim *madrasah*" during his childhood years in Indonesia. Reporters immediately fanned out in search of this school, and they found it in Menteng, the toniest district of pre-World War II Jakarta, once the home of the Dutch colonial elite and now populated by diplomats and wealthy, far-from-radical Indonesians.

The school, a state-run (not Islamic) primary school, or Sekolah Dasar Negri, reacted calmly to its sudden fame. Teachers managed to unearth a photo of the impish Obama, age about five, and told the press that he was remembered as a very active student. When a wide-eyed foreign reporter asked whether there had been many Muslims at the school, the headmaster responded affirmatively, explaining that Indonesia was, after all, a country with a majority Muslim population. (The school continued to bask in media attention as Obama's popularity in Indonesia surged throughout his 2008 election campaign and its students celebrated when he won.)

Indonesia's educational system is as huge and complicated as the country itself. It includes both government schools (the great majority) and private (including religious) schools. Indonesia is not a secular state – it is a multi-religious state, based on the principle of Belief in One (unspecified) Supreme God. Islamic schools exist at all levels of education from pre-school to university, as do Christian schools, although in much smaller numbers.

At the secondary level, the most widely used and misunderstood terms are *pesantren* and *madrasah*. A *pesantren* is an Islamic boarding school, usually rural. *Pesantren* were once almost entirely Javanese and devoted exclusively to religious subjects, but that is no longer the case. The term *madrasah* can be applied to any Muslim school, most often below university level, that is not a boarding school. Just to confuse matters, many *pesantren* operate a *madrasah* on the side, sometimes as a vehicle for non-religious instruction.[13] There are about 14,000 *pesantren* and 38,000 *madrasah* in Indonesia, with about ten million students, or approximately one-fifth of Indonesia's secondary enrollment.[14]

In 1975 the government began a process of integrating Islamic schools into the state system, eventually requiring them to accept a loosely regulated state curriculum (jointly developed by the Ministries of Education and Religious Affairs) as a condition of financial support.[15] Most Muslim schools accepted these terms, although some of the radical, privately operated minority did not. It is no longer true that girls are a minority in Indonesia's *madrasah*; by 2002 they outnumbered boys at the most senior level.[16]

The expansion of Islamic state universities under Suharto, mentioned in the previous chapter, has continued. It has benefited significantly from foreign assistance, most notably a long-standing relationship with McGill University in Montreal. This program, dating to the mid-1970s, has trained about 150 Indonesians to the MA and PhD level, and surely ranks among the most effective long-term aid efforts ever undertaken in Indonesia. The McGill program originally focused on religious subjects, through its well-known Department of Islamic Studies; more recently, and in response to Indonesian wishes, it has shifted toward preparing future Islamic University faculty to teach non-religious subjects as well.[17] Its graduates are today an important force for pluralism and moderation in the Islamic university system.

---

13 Azra *et al.*, "Pesantren and Madrasa" in Hefner and Zaman, eds., *Schooling Islam*, p. 197, n. 6.
14 *Ibid.*, p. 173; see also Robert W. Hefner, "Islamic Schools, Social Movements and Democracy in Indonesia," in Hefner, ed, *Making Modern Muslims: The Politics of Islamic Education in Indonesia*, Honolulu: University of Hawaii Press, 2009, pp. 57, 69. The figures on numbers of *pesantren* and *madrasah* are rounded and courtesy of Bahrissalim of the Asia Foundation, compiled from Indonesian Department of Religion statistics.
15 *Ibid.*, p. 65; Azra *et al.*, "Pesantren and Madrasa," p. 187; personal communication from Julia Howell; interview with Harris Iskandar, Education and Cultural Attache, Embassy of Indonesia, July 2008.
16 Azra *et al.*, "Pesantren and Madrasa," table, p.181.
17 Interview with Professor R. Philip Buckley, Principal Investigator, IAIN Indonesia Social Equity Project, McGill University, April 2, 2009.

Barack Obama attended this primary school on Besuki Street in Menteng, an upscale neighborhood of Jakarta. It is a state school, not a Muslim school, much less a "radical madrasah" as rumor in the United States had it when the school suddenly became famous in January 2006. | Pringle photo

At the top of the system, there are four State Islamic Universities (Universitas Islam Negeri – UIN), followed by 14 State Islamic Institutes (Institut Agama Islam Negeri – IAIN) and 34 second-tier tertiary Islamic institutions with fewer departments (Sekolah Tinggi Agama Islam Negeri – STAIN). The UINs offer a full range of departments (such as education, medicine, social sciences) and often-impressive facilities. They emphasize general education and require a course on democracy, including women's rights. These reforms have inevitably disturbed a few religious conservatives who have accused the UINs of fostering apostasy,[18] but most Indonesians seem to regard them as a resounding success. Because the Islamic universities provide most of the teachers for *pesantren* and *madrasah*, their moderate policies are feeding back into the secondary system.

The Pesantren System

Indonesia's Islamic boarding schools have attracted attention from anti-terrorist specialists since one of them, the al-Mukmin *pesantren* at Ngruki, near Yogyakarta, was identified as the alma mater of more than its share of the terrorists linked with the Jemaah Islamiyah organization. Most accounts

18 Azra *et al.*, "Pesantren and Madrasa", p 191, 198 n. 9.

do not mention that the Ngukri *pesantren* (as it is generally called) was founded in 1972 precisely as a reaction to the politically moderate nature of the vast majority of *pesantren*. At least one leading scholar believes that Ngruki's links to terrorism have been exaggerated.[19] Nonetheless it seems clear that a small number of *pesantren*, perhaps 50 out of the roughly 14,000 total, have encouraged violent extremism, and perhaps served in more specific ways to facilitate the operations of terrorist networks.[20]

The word "*pesantren*" means literally "place of the *santri*," or religious scholars, which pretty well sums up what a *pesantren* was and in many cases still is. The earliest *pesantren* were once thought to have been established at the beginning of Islamization on Java, but it now seems that there were very few until the nineteenth century.[21] The heyday of *pesantren* building began when the Dutch colonial government developed hitherto vacant lands, especially in East Java, for sugar cultivation, thereby stimulating commerce, population growth and attendant religious activity (see Chapter 2).

A traditional *pesantren* includes a mosque, space for teaching, and some facilities, however informal, for housing and feeding its students. The head of a *pesantren* is a *kiai*, a Javanese term meaning the same thing as the better-known Arabic term *alim* (plural *ulama*). In the past *pesantren* were often referred to as *pondok pesantren* or just *pondok*, a word meaning a hut built of bamboo or other light materials. This usage reflected a heritage of humble origins and scholars wandering in search of knowledge, but today many *pesantren* are well endowed with permanent buildings. Until recently students did the cooking, laundry and even tilled the fields belonging to their *pesantren*. As will be obvious by now, the *pesantren* tradition has a good deal in common with the monastic tradition in Christianity, without the obligation of celibacy or a life-long commitment.

Within this tradition, dominant until very recently and still influential, the *kiai* is a man of learning, deriving stature from his reputation for scholarship and the success of his *pesantren*. To become a *kiai*, it helps greatly to be born into a *kiai* family, but the fundamental requirement is religious scholarship, acquired by studying under recognized religious scholars, beginning in Indonesia and later (if possible) in the Middle East.

---

19 Personal communication with Martin van Bruinessen; see also his "'Traditionalist' and 'Islamist' pesantren in contemporary Indonesia."

20 International Crisis Group (hereafter cited as ICG), *Indonesia: The Hotel Bombings,* Area Briefing No. 94, 24 July 2009, esp. p.7, For the number of extremist *pesantren* see ICG, *Indonesia: Noordin Top's Support Base,* Asia Briefing No. 95, p. 13.

21 *Ibid.*; see also Azra *et al.,* "Pesantren and Madrasa," p. 97, n. 2.

Martin van Bruinessen notes that:

> There is something paradoxical in the *pesantren* tradtion. It is firmly rooted in the Indonesian soil; the *pondok* and *pesantren* may be called typical Indonesian institutions, in several respects unlike traditional schools elsewhere in the Muslim world. But at the same time this tradition is self-consciously international in orientation and continues to see not some place in the Archipelago but Mecca as its focus or orientation.[22]

Study in Mecca, once a favored destination, became more difficult in the 1920s when the Saudi (Wahabi) conquest of the Holy Places ended Traditionalist-style instruction in the religious schools there. That led to an exodus of many Indonesian Traditionalist scholars, but since then they have continued to study in other prestigious Middle Eastern locations such as Cairo's Al-Azhar University, once attended by President Abdurrahman Wahid.

To be securely established, a *kiai* must have an intellectual genealogy or *silsilah*, linking him backwards in time with other scholars, the more famous the better. ("I studied under so-and-so, who studied under so and so,…" and so on, sometimes for centuries.) The underlying concept of establishing a sacred, legitimizing linkage with past authority is not unlike the laying on of hands rite for the ordination of bishops in some Christian denominations. The religious curriculum of a traditional *pesantren* centers on the reading of sacred texts: the Koran, the Traditions of the Prophet (Hadith), and Islamic jurisprudence (*fikh*) found primarily in a specific corpus of old teachings and commentaries, the so-called "yellow books" or *kitab kuning*. Once upon a time, and still in the more homely, rural *pesantren*, such instruction often consisted entirely of the rote memorization of Arabic texts, but a leading *kiai* must understand his texts, not just memorize them. As noted above, most *pesantren* and *madrasah* are today integrated into a national educational system, and their curricula usually include general education as well as religious instruction.

---

22 Martin van Bruinessen, "Pesantren and Kitab Kuning: Maintenance and Continuation of a Tradition of Religious Learning," in Wolfgang Marschall, ed., *Texts from the Islands. Oral and Written Traditions of Indonesia and the Malay World*, Ethnologica Bernica 4, Berne: University of Berne, 1994, pp. 121–45, accessed at http://www.let.uu.nl/~martin.vanbruinessen/personal/publications/pesantren_and_kitab_kuning.htm

At least until recently, the *kiai* was the absolute master of his *pesantren*, and his mastery extended to all fields – administration, education and religious observance in the *pesantren's* mosque. The *kiai's* mastery may be somewhat less absolute since religious schools have been required to follow the national curriculum if they want to receive government funding, but otherwise things do not seem to have changed much in many *pesantren*. The *kiai* often owns the *pesantren* buildings and associated agricultural lands. He is expected to be rich, not too many questions asked. He is required to be a man of the world, not just a cleric. The use of "he" in this context is deliberate. There are still no female *pesantren* heads in Indonesia, although in general the Traditionalists have become notably more flexible on gender issues than their Reformist counterparts (see the final section of this chapter). Women students were rare in *pesantren* until the 1950s, and they are still segregated, with their own classes.[23]

Exerting political influence where necessary is definitely expected of senior *kiai*, individually or, as in the case of both the founding and the current operation of the NU, collectively. Since the succession to *pesantren* leadership is often hereditary, it is assumed that a *kiai* will give special treatment to his own children, grooming the men for future *pesantren* leadership and senior status within the *kiai* network and seeking to arrange marriages to his most promising male students for his female children. One can now understand how and why President Wahid was the son and grandson of very senior *kiai*; indeed his grandfather, Hasyim Asy'ari, was the senior religious advisor to the founders of the NU.

But however impressive his lineage, the son of a prestigious *kiai* might not himself become one, if, for example, he is not a good scholar, or he prefers to go into business in Surabaya, or to work for the Ministry of Religious Affairs in Jakarta. On the other hand, as Martin van Bruinessen puts it, "A man of common origin may be very learned but will never be recognized as a kyai, whereas a kyai's son will always enjoy respect even if he is an idiot."[24]

For a variety of reasons, including leadership failures, *pesantren* often fade from prominence after two or three generations, to be replaced by other *pesantren*. So to preserve the system as a whole, its leaders, much like

---

23   Pieternella van Doorn-Harder, *Women Shaping Islam: Reading the Qur'an in Indonesia*, Urbana and Chicago: University of Illinois Press, 2006, pp. 172–73.
24   Martin van Bruinessen, "Back to Situbondo?" pp. 15–46.

the aristocratic families of Western tradition, have constructed networks of marriage alliances with each other. An ambitious *kiai* marries his children to those of other *kiai*, and there are usually plenty of them, given the prevalence of polygamy.[25]

A Garland of Pesantren

The *pesantren* system described above was once a largely but not entirely ethnic Javanese, NU-affiliated, rural phenomenon, with its heartland in Central and especially East Java. There have always been some regional variations of *pesantren*, known by different names, (e.g. *surau* in West Sumatra, *dayah* in Aceh). In recent decades *pesantren* have become much more varied as they reacted to government regulation, shifting currents of Islamic doctrine, and the demands of modernity. Many of the more prestigious *pesantren* have added college faculties offering advanced vocational training to broaden employment opportunities for their graduates.[26] A glance at several noteworthy *pesantren* illustrates that they are today no less diverse than Indonesian Islam itself.[27]

Gontor, the "Modern Pesantren" In 1926 three brothers in Ponorogo, East Java, founded a different kind of *pesantren* in order to produce a new generation of modern Muslims destined for secular as well as religious leadership. The curriculum was designed to inculcate an independent, entrepreneurial spirit and to enable Gontor's graduates to interact on terms of equality with their fellow Muslims everywhere.

Students had to pass an entrance exam, unheard of in traditional *pesantren*. They were also required to master Arabic, so they could read and understand religious texts without translation. They were forbidden to speak Indonesian at the school. An Australian scholar who visited Gontor in the early 1960s and wrote a classic account of it[28] said the tone of the place reminded him of an Australian/British public school.

---

25 See the classic account of the *pesantren* system in Zamakhsyari Dhofier, *The Pesantren Tradition: The Role of the Kyai in the Maintenance of Traditional Islam in Java*, Program for Southeast Asian Studies, Monograph Series Press, Tempe AZ: Arizona State University, 1999 (originally published in Indonesian in 1982), pp. 42–45.

26 Hefner, "Islamic Schools, Social Movements and Democracy," p. 66.

27 For a useful categorization of *pesantren* in modern Indonesia, see "The Four Types of Pesantren" in James J. Fox, ed., *Religion and Ritual*, Vol. 9, Indonesian Heritage Series, Singapore: Didier Millet, 1998, p. 21.

28 Lance Castles, "Notes on the Islamic School at Gontor," *Indonesia*, Vol. 1, April 1966, pp. 30–45.

Gontor soon gained a reputation for its excellence in Arabic instruction, as well as for its lively intellectual atmosphere. Its graduates were able to gain admission to prestigious universities in the Middle East. Its strategic emphasis on strengthening Islam seemed to align it with the religiously conservative side of the post-Masyumi Reformist movement led by Mohammed Natsir, and Indonesia's most publicized Islamic extremist, Abu Bakar Ba'asyir, attended Gontor. But Gontor became best known for producing religious liberals, including its most famous graduate, Nurcholish Madjid. It was partly in reaction to this situation that some disappointed pro-Islamic state activists, including Ba'asyr, founded Ngruki.[29]

Gontor had in common with the traditional *pesantren* that most of its students were from rural areas and small towns, not from big cities. Today Gontor is thriving; its emphasis on modernity has expanded to include educating girls (although not in a co-ed format) and offering vocational education, and it has branches all over Indonesia, as far away as Aceh. The original Gontor is located near another and equally famous *pesantren*, Tegalsari, which may be the oldest one in Indonesia, founded in the eighteenth century.

Pabelan and Vocational Education This *pesantren*, located north of Yogyakarta, was another offshoot of Gontor but with very different objectives. Pabelan originally taught its students only skills that would be useful in their villages and refused to grant diplomas in order to prevent graduates from getting jobs as civil servants, When the famous author V.S. Naipaul visited Pabelan on his "Islamic Journey," he was underwhelmed, observing that there was little point in teaching villagers how to be villagers.[30]

Development experts did not agree. Beginning in the 1970s Pabelan's vocational emphasis inspired non-governmental activists, both foreign and Indonesian, to begin various programs working through *pesantren* aimed at empowering the rural poor. The programs resulted in the gradual formation of a cadre of *pesantren* graduates specializing in rural development, while at the same time allowing the activists to circumvent a Suharto-era ban on political activity in rural areas.

---

29   Van Bruinessen, "'Traditionalist' and 'Islamist' pesantren."
30   V. S. Naipaul, *Among the Believers: an Islamic Journey*, New York: Vintage Books, 1982, p. 341.

Hidayatullah: A Bugis Variant The flourishing Hidayatullah network of 127 *pesantren*[31] serves primarily members of the Bugis ethnic group originally from southern Sulawesi, now widely scattered throughout Indonesia. Its "mother" *pesantren* is located in the East Kalimantan town of Balikpapan, and it operates schools or has offices in more than 200 districts around the country. Hidayatullah is headed by a former leader of the Darul Islam Rebellion, which was active in southern Sulawesi as well as in West Java and elsewhere. The ideology of Hidayatullah, expressed through its magazine, *The Voice of Hidayatullah*, is politically radical, replete with fierce jihadist rhetoric, but few if any of its graduates seem to have been caught doing anything violent, and in 2005 its leaders renounced any links with groups advocating violence.[32] Despite its fire-breathing pronouncements, Hidayatullah has consistently maintained good relations with the Indonesian government, marked by high-level visits, government awards, and even a valuable concession to exploit forest land in Kalimantan. Its politically influential Bugis constituency no doubt has much to with this apparent anomaly.[33]

Wealthy if Weird: The Strange Case of al-Zaytun Located in Indramayu, West Java, al-Zaytun has lavish facilities and a somewhat mysterious founder, Panji Gumilang. ("Panji" is a title suggesting heroic leadership.) A graduate of Gontor, Panji Gumilang was once a rebel Darul Islam commander operating in the same region, West Java, under the *nom de guerre* of Abu Toto. The al-Zaytun *pesantren* was supported by both the Suharto family (despite Suharto's famous antipathy to Darul Islam) and by his successor, Habibie, who presided over its official opening in 1999.

Al-Zaytun gained fame for its five-story dormitories housing 1500 students each, agricultural buildings and facilities and a mega-mosque with a capacity of 50,000. It drew criticism for allegedly heterodox views and practices, such as acquiring land without proper compensation. In response, the al-Zaytun community compared itself to the early followers of the Prophet in Mecca, before the first Islamic state was established in Medina, when many of the obligations of Islamic law were not yet established. At that time Muslims were a minority surrounded by heathens, and survival

---

31   The number is from ICG, *Jemaah Islamiyah in South East Asia: Damaged but Still Dangerous*, Asia Report No. 63, 26 Aug. 2003, p. 26.
32   Hefner, "Islamic Schools, Social Movements and Democracy," p. 83.
33   Van Bruinessen, "'Traditionalist' and 'Islamist' pesantren."

was their first priority. Van Bruinessen concludes that al-Zaytun, far from being a hotbed of radical Islamic politics, is an organization which has exploited an existing, formerly rebellious network to raise funds and recruit followers, while its leader, thanks to his high-level connections, has remained immune from serious criticism.[34]

Pesantren Daarut Tauhid: The Kiai as TV Personality Popular modern Sufism has become a global phenomenon, often mingling showmanship, profit motives and religion, occasionally at the expense of doctrinal precision. The most famous example from Indonesia is Pesantren Daarut Tauhid in Bandung, West Java, founded in 1987.[35] It is led by Abdullah Gymnastiar, better known as "Aa Gym," whose TV program emphasizing family values became popular nation-wide, especially with women. The *pesantren* complex, located in a once-poor neighborhood of Bandung, includes hostels, restaurants, schools, bookstores and lecture facilities. Aa Gym is not a trained cleric and supposedly acquired his expertise by miraculous means. His services do not follow old-fashioned *pesantren* practice, but do include induced ritual weeping as a sign of devotion. His wife and seven children, glowing with health, were prominently featured in his publicity. The *pesantren* attracted hordes of visitors and all went well until November 2006, when this exemplar of modern Islamic family values unexpectedly took a second wife. Within weeks his *pesantren* was deserted as his largely female clientele abandoned him in droves, and his financial backers worried that his enterprise would fail entirely.[36] It is not apparent at this writing whether Aa Gym will be able to regain his popularity.

The Sufi Brotherhoods (*Tarekat*) and Mysticism

A Sufi order or brotherhood is a group of devotees who worship together under the guidance of a master (*sheikh*), chanting holy texts repetitively according to a procedure which is the specialty of that particular order. Local orders are generally linked to international or national organizations (*tarekat*), often of ancient origin. The devotees keep track of their recitations

---

34 Van Bruinessen, *Ibid*; Azra *et al.*, "Pesantren and Madrasa," p. 197, n. 3.

35 Howell, "Sufism and the Indonesian Islamic Revival," p. 719; see also Patung, "Abdullah Aa Gymnastiar," *Indonesia Matters* website entry dated 26 Dec. 2006, accessed July 2008 at www.indonesiamatters.com/857/abdullah-aa-gymnastiar/ ; James B. Hoesterey, "Aa Gym: The Rise, Fall and Re-branding of a Celebrity Preacher," *Inside Indonesia* 90, Oct.-Dec. 2007, http://www.insideindonesia.org/content/view/1011/29/ .

36 Interview with Aa Gym, Bandung, 10 Feb. 2007.

1

1. Great bronze kettle drums such as this one in Jakarta's National Museum were the hallmark of a rich animist culture which predated all world religions in Indonesia and left a strong stylistic imprint on later art and architecture. | Pringle photo.

2. Early Islamic architecture often reflected Hindu-Buddhist prototypes, as in the case of this brick minaret studded with Chinese porcelain, part of the old mosque in Kudus, Central Java. | Leo Indrawan photo.

3. Some Javanese still pay due religious deference to the life-giving force of local volcanoes. Here a group ascends Mt. Merapi in Central Java. Indonesians do not agree about whether (or to what extent) such practices are indicative of imperfect Islam, but virtually all would agree that they are indisputably part of a many-layered national heritage. | John Stanmeyer/VII photo.

2

3

4. Diponegoro, Javanese aristocrat, scholar of Islam, and would-be "just king" or *ratu adil*, rebelled against the Dutch under the banner of Islam in 1825, and thereby earned a firm place in Indonesia's pantheon of national heroes. Ambassador to the United States Sudjadnan Parnohadiningrat is shown before an idealized portrait of the "*pesantren* prince" at the Indonesian Embassy in Washington. | Pringle photo.

5. During his decades as president, Suharto alternately repressed and nurtured political Islam. He welcomed contact with the Middle East, allowing a flood of Islamic educational support from Wahabist Saudi Arabia. He is shown here in 1995 with a Saudi visitor and Minister of Finance Mar'ie Muhammad (center), an Indonesian of Arab descent. | AFP/Getty Images.

6. In 1945 Indonesia's Muslim leaders declared a holy war against Allied troops who were reoccupying Indonesia on behalf of the Dutch, thereby arousing the youth of the nation to resist. When militants in the port city of Surabaya heard that the Dutch flag was once again flying over the town's major hotel, they raised the Indonesian flag in its place. A painting depicting this event hangs in the lobby of the hotel (formerly the Oranje, now the Majapahit). | Pringle photo used courtesy of Majapahit Hotel, Surabaya.

7

7. Suharto's greatest gift to Islam was economic growth, which stimulated further Islamization and heightened Islamic observance. But he also funded the construction of thousands of mosques built to a standard Javanese design, including this one in Depok, Central Java. The Suharto mosques were often adorned with a five-sided roof ornament representing the pluralistic state philosophy, Pancasila, surrounding the word "Allah" in Arabic script. | Yayasan Amalbakti Muslim Pancasila (the Presidential foundation which built many of the mosques).

8

8. Indonesia experienced a decade of turmoil resulting from the financial crisis of 1997, the fall of Suharto and the growing pains of a new, radically decentralized democracy. The results included sectarian conflict, Islamic terrorism, and vigilante intimidation such as this 2009 demonstration by members of the Islamic Defenders' Front (FPI) against the Ahmadiyah sect. Ahmadiyah claims to be Islamic but, contrary to mainstream Islamic belief, recognizes its own founder as a prophet or Mahdi. | Jewel Samad/Getty Images.

9. During Indonesia's decade of turmoil sectarian conflict between Muslims and non-Muslims killed about 11,000 people in several regions of the country, including Central Sulawesi, where government reinforcements are shown arriving in January 2007. | AFP/Getty Images.

9

10

11

10. The traditional Islamic boarding school or *pesantren* is a self-contained, rural institution with a mosque, teaching and boarding facilities, and farmlands on which the students grow food for their own consumption and for sale. Today there are numerous varieties of *pesantren*, many of them urban, and some operate *madrasah* (day schools) on the side. This one is in Aceh. | Pringle photo.

11. Indonesia has a large state-run Islamic university system, but there are many private Muslim universities as well. In this photo students at the private Paramadina University in Jakarta relax between classes. Paramadina reflects the pluralistic ideals of its late founder, Nurcholish Madjid, who was among the most famous Indonesian intellectuals of the Suharto era. | Pringle photo.

12

12. These young ladies are studying science at the Pabelan Pesantren in Central Java. Until recently most *pesantren* were devoted wholly to religious studies, but today most teach secular subjects as well, and the majority which accept government support are required to do so. Pabelan is famous for pioneering in the instruction of vocational subjects in rural areas during the Suharto era. | REUTERS/ Prasetyo Budi.

13. Indonesia's Traditionalist Islam, once thought to be a doomed anachronism, has boomed in recent years because of its new-look *pesantren*, television and radio ministries, and emphasis on appealing life-style themes. Abdullah Gymnastiar, better known as "AA Gym," was among the most popular of the new media clerics until he took a second wife in 2006 and many of his mostly female followers deserted him. He is shown here (wearing turban) with visiting British Prime Minister Tony Blair, Indonesian President Yudhoyono (far left) and Vice President Kalla. | Dimas Ardian/ Getty Images.

14. The Ngukri (or al-Mukmin) Pesantren near Yogyakarta was founded by radical clerics Abdullah Sungkar and Abu Bakar Ba'asyir because they felt that the majority of Indonesia's Islamic boarding schools were too moderate. Ngruki and some other *pesantren*, estimated at about 50 among a total of some 14,000, are suspected of providing both moral and organizational support for Indonesia's violent Islamic extremists. An Ngruki student is shown in 2004 tending to his laundry. | REUTERS/Andri Prasetyo.

13

14

15. Indonesia's repertory of mosque styles reflects community tastes and traditions. This old pagoda-style mosque is in the village of Lima Kaum, in the Minangkabau Highlands of West Sumatra. | Pringle photo.

16. Vendors selling roof tiles are a common sight along the roads of Java. They also offer pre-fabricated onion domes for those who may wish to "modernize" their pagoda-style mosques with a dash of "Arab" flavor. | Pringle photo.

15

17

18

19

20

17. A young couple with their new baby, obviously observant Muslims, pose proudly in front of a demonic guardian figure at Singosari, East Java, the site of a twelfth-century kingdom known for its bloodstained history and spectacular Hindu-Buddhist art. | Pringle photo.

18. The work of prominent Acehnese artist A.D. Pirous reflects a blend of contemporary and traditional styles, including both calligraphy and representational art, and reflecting what Pirous calls Islamic humanism. | Pringle photo.

19. Well-off teenage girls at a park in Bandung show off their style preferences, a casual mix of Islamic and secular chic. | Pringle photo.

20. A dried fish saleswoman in the central market of Yogyakarta, Central Java, wears a popular combination of headscarf, snug bodice and trousers. A recent study of female university students in the same city revealed that many of them wear headscarves to ward off unwanted advances by young men. | Pringle photo.

21. The National Monument in Jakarta enshrines Indonesian multiculturalism: a towering (male) *lingam* on a flaring (female) *yoni* are Hindu symbols even though only a small percentage of Indonesians, mainly on Bali, still adheres to that faith. The great Istiqlal Mosque (see Chapter 8) is in the background. | Pringle photo.

22. Young schoolgirls wearing Islamic uniforms prepare to tour the Minangkabau royal palace at Pagarruyung in West Sumatra, a magnificent example of pre-Islamic Minangkabau clan-house architecture. The palace was destroyed by an accidental fire in 2007, a few months after this photo was taken. | Pringle photo.

21

22

by counting them off with prayer beads, hence the deprecating reference by Clifford Geertz in his *Religion of Java* to old men counting beads.[37] (Geertz later acknowledged that he had underestimated the force and durability of Indonesian mysticism.[38]) The desired result of Sufi practices is increased closeness to God and understanding of His divinity, not unlike what Christians experience during holy communion, and sometimes referred to by the Greek-derived term "gnosis," meaning a special knowledge of spiritual mysteries.

Sufism facilitated Islam's arrival in Hindu-Buddhist Indonesia by contributing to a culture of tolerance for preexisting religious norms, as long as they were not blatantly at odds with the new faith (see Chapter 1). Since then the relationship between Sufism and Traditionalist religion has varied over time. The *kiai* who heads a *pesantren* may or may not also be the leader of a Sufi order meeting at his *pesantren*. Hasyim Asy'ari, Wahid's grandfather, banned *tarekat* activities in his own *pesantren*.[39] Two types of *kiai* are now generally recognized within the NU: scriptural specialists who study religious texts and those involved in *tarekat* work. The former have often enjoyed more prestige, while the latter have frequently had larger followings, including prominent public figures.[40]

Indonesian Traditionalists know full well that mystical practices involve a risk of heresy. Mysticism may cause individual insight (or passion) to overwhelm the hard requirements of scripture, for example by identifying one's self with divinity, or by suggesting that the formal requirements of Islam are merely a "starting point for beginners" embarking on a mystical journey.[41] The NU's formal position is that Muhammad al-Ghazzali, a famed twelfth-century Baghdad jurist and mystic, settled the issue by declaring that there was no conflict between Sufism and Islam as long as Sufi practitioners observed the major tenets of Islam, beginning with the Five Pillars of Islam.[42] But in fact that formula leaves some considerable

---

37 Clifford Geertz, *The Religion of Java*, paperback ed., New York: The Free Press of Glencoe, 1964, p. 183.
38 Clifford Geertz, "Religious Change and Social Order in Soeharto's Indonesia," *Asia*, No. 27, 1972 (lectures dedicated to the memory of Harry J. Benda), pp. 73, 80.
39 Martin Van Bruinessen, "Saints, Politicians and Sufi Bureaucrats: Mysticism and Politics in Indonesia's New Order" in Martin van Bruinessen and Julia Day Howell, eds., *Sufism and the 'Modern' in Islam*, London: I.B, Tauris, p. 100.
40 *Ibid.*, pp. 100–101.
41 Julia Day Howell, "Sufism and the Indonesian Islamic Revival," *Journal of Asian Studies*, Vol. 60, No. 3, Aug. 2001, p. 707.
42 On al-Ghazzali see Karen Armstrong, *Islam: A Short History*, New York: Random House, Modern Library Edition, 2000, pp. 88–90.

room for controversy. In general the NU's approach has been not to risk offending mystics by rushing to judge their practices as heretical or dangerously close to it, as Reformists have tended to do. This inclusive approach has continued to aid greatly in recruiting and holding converts to Islam. As one member of a *kiai* family explained, "... *tarekat* orders have brought Islam to the Javanese masses and the masses to Islam."[43]

The idea that repetitive activity (such as chanting scripture) increases religious awareness is of course common in many traditions. Sometimes such activity involves dancing, and the famous "whirling dervishes" of Turkey are Sufi Muslims. Similar practices are also well known in Christianity. The refrain of the famous nineteenth century American Shaker hymn comes to mind:

> When true simplicity is gained
> To bow and to bend we shan't be ashamed
> To turn, turn will be our delight
> 'Til by turning, turning, we come out right[44]

More spectacular forms of ecstatic worship seem to be absent from Indonesian Islam, although they were common enough in the preceding Hindu-Buddhist era, and trance-induced dancing still occurs in Javanese folk religion as well as, famously, on still-Hindu Bali. However it is well recognized in *pesantren* tradition that even the more restrained Sufi-style mystical observances are best left to the elderly, while the young should stick to learning holy writ.[45] Implicit in this cautious approach is awareness that mystical experience is a bit like playing with fire; it can get out of control unless it is carefully mentored, and adolescents are particularly prone to this risk.

Indonesian Reformists have also argued that the role of the Sufi "master" contravenes a central tenet of Islam – namely, that there should be no priest or intermediary between God and man. The Sufi reply to this criticism is that the master does not intervene; rather, he helps his followers to see God more clearly, much as eyeglasses can make reading possible. They argue that

---

43 Dhofier, *Pesantren Tradition*, pp. 139ff., quote from p. 145.
44 "Simple Gifts," composed by Joseph Bracken, from http://www2.gol.com/users/quakers/simple_gifts.htm.
45 Dhofier, *Pesantren Tradition*, p.138.

Sufi practice acts to *intensify*, not alter or replace, core Islamic practice.[46]

In recent years, with the growing popularity of Sufism and its spread into the middle classes, Sufi teachers have increasingly become vote-getters and political entrepreneurs. This is not wholly new; a political organization based on Sufism was founded in West Sumatra in the 1930s, and another was prominent in the Sukarno era.[47] Most of the brotherhoods represented in Indonesia, often with tongue-twisting Arab names and deep historic roots in the Middle East, are also found in other Muslim countries as far away as West Africa. They include the Shadhiliyya, Shattariyya, Sanusiyya, Naqshbandiyya, Qadiriyya and Tijanyya, plus an important Indonesian creation which combined Qadiriyya and Naqshbandiyya practices and is known, not illogically, as the Qadiriyya wa Naqshbandiyya.[48] (Pause for a deep breath.)

"Mainstream" *tarekat* such as these are among the 45 members of the NU-sponsored national organization, the Association of People of the Reputable Path (Jam'iyyah Ahlith Thoriqah al-Mu'tabaroh al-Nahdliyyah – JATMN), established in 1979.[49] Membership in this organization, which is only the latest in a series of such organizations, signifies that a *tarekat* has not strayed across the line between Islamic mysticism and heresy. There are many organizations in the booming world of modern Sufism which might have trouble obtaining this clerical seal of reputability.

Meanwhile non-Islamic mysticism, with ties to Javanese saints or *wali*, Hindu-Buddhist tradition, theosophy, freemasonry and more, is alive and well in Indonesia. Today it appeals primarily to the Javanese upper classes and is known by various terms including *kebatinan* (innerness) and *kejawen* (Java-ness). In the early days of the Suharto regime, Muslims objected to efforts to give official recognition to *kabatinan* groups. Later, Suharto's shift toward Islam and his personal sponsorship of Islamic mystics and healers boosted the popularity of mysticism generally, and this trend gained further strength under President Wahid, himself an aficionado of saint worship and other esoteric practices. Today anyone circulating widely

---

46 Howell, "Sufism and the Indonesian Islamic Revival," p. 702.
47 Van Bruinessen, "Saints, Politicians and Sufi Bureaucrats," p. 99.
48 M.C. Ricklefs, *Polarizing Javanese Society: Islamic and Other Visions (c.1830–1930)*, Honolulu: University of Hawaii Press, p. 75.
49 Van Bruinessen, "Saints, Politicians and Sufi Bureaucrats," pp. 101–03; the JATMN succeeded the earlier JATM; see also Michael Laffan, "National Crisis and the Representation of Traditional Sufism in Indonesia: The Periodicals *Salafy* and *Sufi*" in van Bruinessen and Howell, eds., *Sufism and the 'Modern' in Islam*, esp. p. 169.

among middle and upper class Indonesians will soon encounter Javanese who are fascinated by mysticism and like to reassure foreigners that it (not fundamentalist Islam) represents the core religious ethos of Indonesia.

Islamic Authority in Indonesia

Among the greatest sources of confusion about Islam, in Indonesia as elsewhere, is the question of how religious authority is derived and how it relates to state power. Apprehensive non-Muslims often believe that many devout Muslims favor an Islamic theocracy in which all law would be religious law. From this flows the erroneous idea that someone, somewhere, has defined a comprehensive Islamic law code or, at the very least, knows what it would be.

That there is in fact no agreed-upon central legal authority or code of law in Islam should come as no surprise, above all to Christians, who include in their ranks a dizzying array of believers from Roman Catholics to Quakers. The various churches of Christendom – if they exist as organizations at all – reflect radically differing approaches to issues of religious authority and what control it should exert, if any, over civil and criminal law.

There is nonetheless something called sharia law, much in the headlines in Indonesia and elsewhere. And there is also the term "*fatwa*" (plural *fatawa*) which, ever since Salman Rushdie, has become almost as alarming to non-Muslims as "jihad." What are these legal thunderbolts and who gives anyone the right to hurl them? Finally, what about the Islamic clergy? While there may be no priests in Islam, there certainly are clerics who, theory to the contrary notwithstanding, define for their followers what Islam requires of them, and seek, sometimes successfully, to influence or coerce their political behavior as well.

The position of the typical Traditionalist *kiai*, discussed earlier, helps to answer the central question of how Muslim leaders acquire and hold religious authority in Indonesia. Within the NU-centered system, the authority of the *kiai* is based on four factors: religious knowledge, an intellectual genealogy linking him to previous *kiai*, hereditary factors (his family tree), and managerial skills (e.g., operating a successful *pesantren*). One new factor has emerged more recently: affiliation with a recognized brotherhood (*tarekat*), a change reflecting the growing institutional strength of the Sufi orders.

No one of these factors is absolutely necessary, but some combination of them is needed to assure a level of recognition, first and foremost by fellow clerics, without which a *kiai* risks losing both peer and community support.[50]

Like their Traditionalist counterparts, Reformist clerics must have some degree of community support in order to survive and prosper. But Reformism lacks the *pesantren*-based philosophical consistency which is still important in the Traditionalist world. There was a time when Muhammadiyah provided an institutional base for the development of Reformist clerics, exercised especially through its educational system and prominent schools such as the Madrasah Mualimin Muhammadiyah in Yogyakarta, Central Java, which was started by Muhammadiyah's founder, Ahmad Dahlan. But since the advent of democracy the components of Reformism, especially those with radical tendencies such as the Justice and Prosperity Party (PKS), have grown in influence, and the sources of Reformist clerical authority have become relatively multi-polar and diverse compared to those of the NU.[51]

The question of what happens to a Muslim cleric who loses community support is illustrated by the story of Aa Gym, whose televised, family-oriented ministry suffered so dramatically when he took a second wife. His problem was that he offended his electronic community, not that he broke Islamic law, which allows polygamy with conditions. The importance of community support in legitimizing religious authority seems healthy and compatible with Indonesia's energetic democracy. But, needless to say, Indonesia's vast and varied array of Muslim communities don't always see eye to eye on religious issues.

Sharia and the Fatwa Phenomenon

Sharia (or sharia law) has been defined as "the whole corpus of Islamic jurisprudence," [52] from the beginning of Islam. Obviously, then, it is a body of knowledge and values, not some kind of legal code which can be pulled off a shelf and installed here or there. When news reports state, as they often do, that "sharia law" is being implemented in Saudi Arabia or Aceh, they are misleading. What is usually happening is that rulers are attempting to enact laws which *they believe* or hope are in accordance with

---

50 Based in part on interviews with Julia Day Howell in August 2007.

51 This paragraph is based in part on "Islamic Clerics among Modernist Muslims in Indonesia," an unpublished ms. by Ahmad Mutttaqin, a PhD student at Griffith University in Brisbane, Australia.

52 M.B. Hooker, "The State and Sharia in Indonesia, 1895–1995," in Timothy Lindsey, ed., *Indonesia, Law and Society*, Leichardt NSW: Federation Press, 1999, p. 97.

Vistors to Aceh are greeted at the airport by a large poster welcoming them to the land where sharia law is implemented. However, even in this most Islamic of Indonesia's provinces, the imposition of regulations dictating dress code and social behavior, and enforced by religious police, remains controversial. | Pringle photo

Islamic law, as enshrined in the jurisprudence interpreting the Koran, the Traditions of the Prophet (Hadith) and other sacred documents. But these rulers have no authority, beyond their own religious lawyers, for saying, for example, that it is contrary to Islam for women to drive automobiles. There is no unanimity of Muslim legal opinion on this issue or on many others relevant to modern life.

The underlying issue is whether or not early Islamic jurisprudence can be subject to reinterpretation in the light of changing values or advances in scientific knowledge, through the exercise of reason, a process known as *ijtihad*. Such reinterpretation was not uncommon in classical Islam, but in the Middle Ages Sunni Muslim scholars decided that "the gates of *ijtihad*" should henceforth be closed.[53] Reformers everywhere have generally argued, from a wide variety of political perspectives, that the gates should be reopened to allow Islam to deal with changing circumstances. But even if they were, profound questions would remain about what kind of reinterpretation is permissible or desirable. Fearing the social and moral consequences of such debate, fundamentalist (or scripturalist) clerics

---

53 Armstrong, *Islam: A Short History*. p. 200.

generally oppose reinterpretation and want to keep the gates closed. The argument is almost identical to debates in Christianity about the reinterpretation of Biblical texts that relate to homosexuality, evolution, abortion and other controversial contemporary issues.

The debate over the Jakarta Charter (see Chapter 2) is usually interpreted, including by Indonesians, as an argument about whether Indonesia should be an "Islamic state." Yet the seven words in question do not mention an Islamic state; they merely say that Muslims, not anyone else, would be bound by the tenets of sharia law. The authors of the Charter did not spell out how sharia law would be defined or enacted, hardly surprising given the stressful circumstances under which the Charter was written. No one is on record as having advocated a meaning broader than what the seven words actually say.

There are four schools of Islamic law in Sunni Islam, of which the Shafi'i school is dominant in Indonesia and elsewhere in Southeast Asia. These schools are important to legal scholars but in practice they "[do] not differ markedly from one another."[54] The NU follows the Shafi'i school but recognizes the other three, while Muhammadiyah, true to its Reformist philosophy, relies on a return to the Koran and the sayings of the Prophet as the primary basis for its legal opinions.[55]

Very few Indonesians seem to think that the Islamic state/Jakarta Charter debate has anything to do with establishing a formal theocracy. What they do perceive is a contest for power among politicians. A minority, mainly from Reformist Muslim backgrounds, would give constitutional political primacy to Islam, with as-yet undefined consequences. The opposing majority wants to remain within a pluralistic, multi-religious framework based on Pancasila, with its deliberately non-specific "Belief in One Supreme God." This majority suspects that the debate is really about abolishing the multi-religious status quo. Virtually no one in Indonesia is arguing for a purely secular state, even though many citizens are no doubt secular in their personal philosophies – hence the continuing and perhaps growing popularity of de facto secular political parties, mainly Golkar and the PDI-P (see Chapter 7).

Those Indonesians who want implementation of sharia have radically different views about what this should mean. Some argue for a restoration

---

54   *Ibid.*, p. 65.
55   Personal communication from Martin van Bruinessen.

of a transnational caliphate, modeled on an idealized concept of early Islam. Some want a literal interpretation of at least some elements of classical Islamic law, similar to the legal system of Saudi Arabia but not necessarily including its well-publicized harsh punishments for crimes like theft and adultery. Others believe that sharia should be implemented as a set of principles that would provide moral and ethical guidance to government, and would be fully compatible with internationally recognized human rights, including freedom of religion and social equality for women. [56] A global Gallup poll of Muslim opinion indicates that a similar debate is underway among Muslims elsewhere:

> Muslims who want to see *Sharia* as a source of law in constitutions... have very different visions of how that would manifest [sic].... Some expect full implementation of classical or medieval Islamic law; others want a more restricted approach, like prohibiting alcohol, requiring the head of state to be a Muslim, or creating *Sharia* courts to hear cases involving Muslim family law (marriage, divorce and inheritance). Still others simply want to ensure that no constitutional law violates the principles and values of Islam, as found in the Quran.[57]

It is unclear how many of the most vocal Indonesian advocates of sharia really want an Islamic state. They are aware that opinions differ on what it would mean in practice. They cannot be sure whose version of Islamic statehood would be chosen, or how the choice would be made. For Muslim politicians the Islamic state issue has been useful primarily as an enduring political symbol, one which tells the world that its proponents are serious about seeking greater respect for Islamic values and increased political influence for Islam generally.

Today's Indonesian legal system is a mosaic of seemingly disparate elements: modern Indonesian law, Dutch-Roman law, customary or *adat* law, and yes, sharia law. Indeed contrary to many alarmist interpretations, sharia is not just something that might or might not be imported from

---

56 See the discussion of a "substantive" application of sharia in Nadirsyah Hosen, *Shari'a and Constitutional Reform in Indonesia*, Singapore: ISEAS Series on Islam, 2007, esp. pp. 44, 50, 225–27.

57 John L. Espositio and Dalia Mogahed, *Who Speaks for Islam? What a Billion Muslims Really Think*, New York: Gallup Press, 2007, pp. 52–53.

Arabia in the future; important elements of it have been entrenched in the national legal system of Indonesia since Dutch rule, and indeed before that if the experience of pre-colonial Indonesian states is included. Moreover the borderline between custom and Islam is not precise. In many of the more fervently Muslim areas of Indonesia people believe, with some reason, that for them, custom and Islam are one and the same. Where there was conflict between sharia and customary law, the Dutch position was that custom prevailed, consonant with their effort to formalize and strengthen the division between activist Muslims and everyone else. It is a source of some annoyance to today's Islamic fundamentalists that this principle still has standing in Indonesian law.[58]

We have seen that Muslim desire for more control over the administration of Dutch-era Islamic law was an issue in the run-up to independence. A major change came with the creation of the Ministry of Religious Affairs in 1946, which expanded and formalized the position of sharia within the Indonesian legal mosaic. Today, for Muslims, elements of sharia apply in matters of marriage, divorce and inheritance as well as in the regulation and administration of the *haj*, Islamic religious foundations (*wakaf*) and more. In short, sharia already has a solid position in Indonesian jurisprudence which is generally accepted by everyone.

What about that most notorious aspect of sharia, the *fatwa*? A *fatwa* is a non-binding legal decree informed by sharia. In Indonesia such decrees are routinely issued by mainstream Muslim organizations, including both NU and Muhammadiyah, in order to provide informed religious guidance to the faithful.[59] Many of these are not controversial or alarming.

The *fatwa* problem is one of quality control, resulting from the fact that there is no system within Islam for deciding who can issue such a decree. To use a parallel from American frontier history, when "Judge" Roy Bean, a saloon keeper with no legal training and one law book, declared himself to be the Law West of the Pecos, a river in Texas, who was to say he was not? There were two possibilities: higher political authority could either tolerate or legitimize his decisions, or could deem them to be illegal. Or, absent higher authority, the local community could, Texas being Texas,

---

58   This was the so-called "reception theory", namely that Islamic law applies only to the extent that it is "received" into local *adat*: interview with Timothy Lindsey, Aug 6, 2007.
59   Nadirsyah Hosen, "Online fatwa in Indonesia: From fatwa shopping to Googling a Kiai," in Greg Fealy and Sally White, eds., *Expressing Islam: Religious Life and Politics in Indonesia*, Singapore: Institute of Southeast Asian Studies, 2008, p. 159.

have run him out of town. In Bean's case he was tolerated and eventually went into politics.

In Indonesia the *fatwa* question is similar to the question of how clerics derive their credibility. In both cases popular/community support is the key ingredient, as it was in the case of Roy Bean. Nevertheless, a *fatwa* issued by individuals without serious religious education or broad credibility can by no means be dismissed as harmless. If such a pronouncement incites violence, a mob obeys it, and the police do nothing, then the author of it is indeed the equivalent of Judge Roy Bean. Or the government can enforce the law against mob violence and arrest the perpetrators or otherwise stop it. The underlying issue in such cases is political will joined with sound statute law and administrative coherence.

Indonesia is hardly alone in struggling with the *fatwa* problem. In some countries there are so many conflicting *fatwa* available from various sources that anyone looking for some semblance of legal support can indulge in what has been termed "*fatwa* shopping." To quote from a recent news story about "*fatwa* chaos" in Egypt, "Muslims… seeking religious guidance may now turn to satellite television and the internet for opinions from as far afield as Indonesia – unless they follow the *fatwa* issued in 2004 by the Dar ul Ulum, India's largest Islamic seminary, that ruled Muslims shouldn't watch TV."[60]

In Indonesia the most famous or notorious *fatwa* in recent years amounted to a comprehensive attack on pluralism, announced in 2005 by the Council of Indonesian Ulama (Majelis Ulama Indonesia – MUI). The MUI was not always so illiberal; quite the contrary. It was created in 1975 as a means of mobilizing support for Suharto's development policies and some of its early decrees reflected not only subservience to the government, but also the views of a religiously progressive minority of clerics. The most important, issued in 1983 after much deliberation, gave Indonesia's family planning program a green light. Although the ruling did not endorse all methods of contraception, it is credited with overcoming much social resistance to the program and thereby helping to make it the success that it was.[61]

---

60 Daniel Williams Bloomberg, "Egyptian Scholars battle 'fatwa chaos' in Islam," *International Herald Tribune*, 7 Nov. 2007, p. 2.

61 Martin van Bruinessen, "Islamic state or state Islam? Fifty years of state-Islam relations in Indonesia," in Ingrid Wessel (Hrsg.), *Indonesien am Ende des 20. Jahrunderts*, Hamburg: Abera-Verlag, 1996, pp. 19–34, accessed July 2008 at http://www.let.uu.nl/~martin.vanbruinessen/personal/publications/State-Islam.htm.

After the fall of Suharto the MUI was anxious to survive and accommodate to the requirements of the new era, and it did so by backing the religiously conservative Muslims who seemed to be a rising force amid the chaos and sectarian strife of the transition to democracy. It is therefore regarded by many as a player in the ongoing debate, not as an impartial decision-making body. Its *fatwa* are no more legally binding than any others. But in the MUI's case its recent *fatawa*, discussed further in Chapter 7, have indeed provoked mob violence and other illegal behavior which the authorities have often been loathe to crack down on, for reasons of political expediency.

Muhammadiyah, NU and the Gender Struggle

During the presidency of Abdurrahman Wahid, at the height of the turmoil following the fall of Suharto, Indonesia's First Lady, Nuriyah, led a remarkable effort to reinterpret an early nineteenth-century Islamic legal text on the marital obligations of women in the light of modern norms and conditions. How could this have happened, and why was the supposedly *Traditionalist* NU in the lead? The story is told in an exceptional book by Pieternella van Doorn-Harder entitled *Women Shaping Islam: Reading the Qu'ran in Indonesia*.[62] It is important to clarify at the outset that not all Indonesian women are in favor of such reform, any more than all women elsewhere are feminists.

Muhammadiyah and the NU have two principal women's affiliates, 'Aisyiyah (established in 1917) and the Muslimat NU (established in 1946), plus organizations for younger women, male youth, and more. These organizations reflect the contrasting histories and philosophies of their parent organizations.

Muhammadiyah is more tightly organized and more heavily influenced by recent, often puritanical, trends from the Middle East. The largely home-grown NU, with older ties to the Middle East and conditioned by the *pesantren* world, has always been more willing to accommodate local cultural norms within its definition of Islam.

This fact, plus the diversity of the NU leadership, has enabled its women to press more effectively for reform than has been possible for

---

62 Pieternella van Doorn-Harder, *Women Shaping Islam: Reading the Qur'an in Indonesia*, Urbana and Chicago: University of Illinois Press, 2006. The balance of this section relies primarily on this book.

their counterparts in 'Aisyiyah, who have faced more serious theological constraints within Muhammadiyah.

As van Doorn-Harder relates, the crucial element in the story has been the willingness of the NU in recent decades to allow female *pesantren* students to study the sacred texts which are Traditionalist Islam's doctrinal backbone. Once women become truly expert, in a scholarly sense, they are deemed capable of criticizing and reinterpreting the texts through the exercise of reason (*ijtihad*). Such discussion and reinterpretation has continued within the Muslimat NU, which over time has exerted pressure on the male-dominated NU clerical establishment to allow steps toward a more modernized view of a woman's place in Muslim society. One of the early results of this process was the Council of Ulama (MUI) ruling in 1983 that put an Islamic stamp of approval on Suharto's family planning program. This decision was influenced by years of family planning advocacy by the women's organization, against initial male opposition.

The project to review the old text on female marital obligations took several years. The text [63] was steeped in the view that the primary role of women is to serve their husbands without question, including one extreme example stating that a wife is obligated to clean her husband's feet with her face. The reviewers found that over half the Traditions quoted in the text were false or weak. Their reinterpretation was based on the assumption that changing norms and conditions do matter, noting *inter alia* that the Koran, like the Bible, can be read as condoning slavery, which is nonetheless now abolished in both Muslim and Christian countries. Progressive NU clerics argue, no doubt somewhat optimistically, that the study of jurisprudence in the NU has shifted "from being a paradigm of 'orthodox truth' to being a paradigm of 'social relevance.'"[64] By 2006 the marital text had been revised and widely circulated. That, of course, has not ended the broader debate about Islam and the role of women.[65]

Women in Indonesia enjoy many advantages compared to those elsewhere in the Muslim world. Across the spectrum of traditional Indonesian societies, they often had relatively high status. Today, for the better off, there are few barriers to professional advancement. Indeed, the availability of childcare

---

63 The "*Kitab Syarh 'Uqud Al-Lujjain fi Bayan Huquq Al-Zaujain*," or "Notes on the mutual responsibility concerning the clarification of the rights of spouses," in Van Doorn-Harder, *Women Shaping Islam*, p. 167.
64 Van Doorn-Harder, *Women Shaping Islam*, p. 190.
65 A portion of the revision, together with a fierce rebuttal of it, is in Fealy and Hooker, eds., *Voices of Islam*, pp. 307–311.

through extended families or affordable household help arguably makes it easier for women to pursue careers in Indonesia than in some developed countries. Female parliamentarians and ministers have been unexceptional for decades, and one of Indonesia's six presidents to date was a woman. In the run-up to the 2009 parliamentary elections, a female coalition succeeded in getting a law through parliament requiring that one-third of all candidates for election be women.[66]

As this suggests, Indonesia's legal structure is ahead of that in many Muslim-majority countries. Under the marriage law of 1974, for example, a man can take a second wife only with the consent of the first. Divorce must be obtained by mutual consent and witnessed by an Islamic court judge, 14% of whom are women.[67] Indonesia is one of the few countries where women can become recognized experts on Islamic law, with a degree from an Islamic state university. It is true that women still cannot lead the ritual Friday sermon in a mosque, but they can lecture on religious subjects and have done so for many years.[68]

But the reality is not yet as benign as all this would suggest. Politically controversial laws in Indonesia can be ignored, and this is certainly the case with the marriage law of 1974. Polygamy is still practiced widely, often without genuine spousal consent, not least among the NU's clerical establishment, which, as noted earlier, consists of family networks based largely on multiple marriages. Moreover, under Indonesia's new democracy, hard-line religious conservatives are fighting back, glorifying polygamy and asserting men's rights as Muslims. They attack gender reform as a product of western (Christian) interference, pointing to the support given by the Ford Foundation and other foreign organizations to NGOs which have supported Indonesian women's groups like 'Aisyiyah and Muslimat NU.

In 2007, a prominent polygamist asked the Constitutional Court to review the restrictions on polygamy in the 1974 marriage law. He claimed that, however weakly enforced, they restricted his freedom of religion. The Court ruled against him on the grounds that polygamy falls under the rubric of social relations, not religion, and that the state is obligated to

---

66   Sally White and Maria Ulfah Anshor, "Islam and Gender in Contemporary Indonesia," in Fealy and White, *Expressing Islam: Religious Life and Politics in Indonesia*, Singapore: Institute of Southeast Asian Studies, 2008, p. 149.
67   Van Doorn-Harder, *Women Shaping Islam*, p. 42.
68   There is still debate among Indonesian Muslims over whether a woman can lead prayers of any kind if a male Muslim is present (information from Julia Day Howell and her Indonesian graduate students at Griffith University, Brisbane, March 2009).

regulate it. Female activists were pleased but not satisfied; they want to see polygamy outlawed.[69]

Female circumcision is still widely practiced in Indonesia and, like head scarf wearing, may have increased as part of the general trend toward increased Islamic observance. That this is so is partly due to the growing prevalence of symbolic, non-invasive procedures, such as a pin-prick in the genital area, which, arguably, are not really circumcision at all. Such procedures are becoming common in urban areas,[70] but there seems to be little information on female circumcision in rural areas. The practice is controversial but receives little public attention. Scholars debate the authenticity of the Tradition (Hadith) on which it is based, the Ministry of Health is trying to ban it in hospitals and clinics, and it is opposed by liberal Muslim organizations, including the female youth wing of the NU. In general, female circumcision is considered as a lower priority in Muslim law and tradition than male circumcision,[71] once seen as nearly synonymous with conversion to Islam.

Muslim women, divided themselves, especially along generational lines, are very conscious of the fact that they still cannot achieve progress on specific reforms without the approval of male clerics. But although the gender struggle continues, van Doorn-Harder concludes that "women themselves see dramatic improvement in their condition,"[72] due in no small part to the efforts of the mainstream women's organizations.

We can now return to the Indonesia of 1998, on the cusp of crisis, with regional violence already threatening the future of the country, and look at how the trouble started, what the role of Islam was, and why conflict has diminished since 2005.

---

69 White and Anshor, "Islam and Gender," pp. 147–49.
70 Sarah Corbett, "A Cutting Tradition," *New York Times Magazine*, 20 Jan. 2008.
71 White and Anshor, "Islam and Gender," pp. 143–45.
72 Van Doorn-Harder, *Women Shaping Islam*, p. 263.

6

Communal Conflict and Violent Islamic Extremism

On October 12, 2002 two bombs exploded in crowded nightclubs on the predominantly Hindu island of Bali, killing more than 200 people. It was a devastating experience at many levels. For the Hindu Balinese, it proved that they were not, as they had thought, immune from the disorder that was making headlines elsewhere in Indonesia. For other Indonesians it made clear that the gathering storm of violent extremism threatened the entire nation, because beautiful Bali was a national icon and its booming tourist business, apparently now on the brink of ruin, a national source of revenue. For nervous foreigners it confirmed that Indonesia was mortally threatened by fanatical Islam.

The situation was not as bad as it seemed at first. In the months that followed, the Indonesians made solid progress in tracking down the perpetrators, with help from the Australians and under the leadership of a capable Balinese police officer who subsequently went into politics and was elected Bali's governor. Tourism would indeed plunge, but then recover to record highs, despite a second although much less serious bombing in 2005. Perhaps most important, the Bali bombing had a kind of Pearl Harbor effect on Indonesian public opinion. At first there was denial and conspiracy theorizing – it must have been a CIA plot to besmirch Islam, etc. – but as the results of the investigations emerged, the truth was gradually accepted that this was indeed the work of Indonesian extremists bent on violent jihad. The perpetrators were caught and three of the most prominent executed in November 2008.[1]

The complex factors that caused the onset of systemic violence in

---

[1] "Anger Erupts After Executions in Bali Blasts," *Washington Post*, 10 November 2008. In fact the protests were localized and not of national significance.

Indonesia experienced widespread regional and sectarian violence beginning in the final years of the Suharto era. This map shows the areas most affected, but it is not comprehensive.

Indonesia at the end of the Suharto era are now reasonably clear, and it is equally evident what caused it to wind down, leading to over three years free of major violence, from 2006 to mid-2009. But as the July 2009 bombings demonstrated all too well, the problem was not definitively solved. Most of its underlying causes, whether local, national or international, have not been completely eliminated. Temporary recurrences of regional violence have taken place in Maluku and are not unlikely elsewhere. Despite recent progress, it remains to be seen whether Indonesia will succeed in developing a reliable, long-term capacity to resist illegal violence sufficient to withstand the inevitable political and economic vicissitudes of the future.

This chapter will first examine episodes of regional communal violence in post-Suharto Indonesia during the period 1997–2005. It will then look at the activities of Islamic extremists who intervened in two of the regional conflicts, Maluku and Central Sulawesi, and who also carried out acts of terrorism, defined as the killing of innocent victims to achieve political ends, elsewhere. The treatment of regional conflict is selective, focusing on the three most important cases. It looks at underlying causes common to all three and offers some conclusions about the downward trend in violence which began at about the time of the Bali bombing.

Three other major regional problems, Aceh, Papua and Timor, are briefly discussed in a separate section. None of them involved terrorism or extended communal violence, but each in its own way must be considered in order to understand Indonesia's struggle to achieve a more perfect union.

Violent Regional Conflict, 1996–2005

The cases are listed chronologically by the date that major violence began.

West and Central Kalimantan 1996–2001 Violence in this region between Muslim immigrants and native inhabitants killed almost three thousand people and displaced many more.[2] The two provinces affected have a total population of between five and six million people.

The island of Borneo, divided between Malaysia and Indonesia, and known as Kalimantan in Indonesia, is huge and thinly settled, the ecological opposite of Java. Given centuries to develop, magnificent forests thrive on its infertile soils. Today, however, tropical timber is highly prized and easily extracted. Logging has been the main cause of growing environmental havoc, best exemplified by catastrophic forest fires raging through cut-over areas and spreading smoke over large areas of Southeast Asia in recent years. At the time of the violence, three-quarters of West Kalimantan's forested area had been apportioned to loggers.[3]

Beginning in 1996, there were recurrent episodes of indigenous "Dayaks," a blanket term for the ethnically diverse, non-Muslim peoples of the interior, attacking Muslim immigrants from the island of Madura. The proximate cause was friction between the aggressive, entrepreneurial Madurese and a native population watching helplessly as their way of life vanished in a wave of development: logging, the replacement of forests with oil palm plantations, and the extraction of coal, oil and other minerals.

Under Suharto, a new law allowed Jakarta to hand out logging

---

2   Unless otherwise noted, figures on provincial casualties in this section are from the table in Christopher Wilson, *Overcoming Violent Conflict*, Vol. 5, *Peace and Development Analysis in Indonesia*, Jakarta: Crisis Prevention and Recovery Unit, United Nations Development Program, 2005, p. 5. See also Gerry van Klinken, *Communal Violence and Democratization in Indonesia: Small Town Wars*, London: Routledge, 2007.

3   Rohman Achwan *et al.*, *Overcoming Violent Conflict*, Vol. 1, *Peace and Development Analysis in West Kalimantan, Central Kalimantan and Madura*, Jakarta: Crisis Prevention and Recovery Unit, United Nations Development Program, 2005, p. 9.

concessions irrespective of customary rights to land, which were essential to the traditional Dayak way of life based on hunting, gathering and shifting cultivation.

The Madurese were the victims of pent-up frustration and hostility. In most cases the Dayaks, many of them recent converts to Christianity, initiated the violence. Their resistance took on aspects of what anthropologists call a "nativistic movement," a reactive, emotional effort by vulnerable societies to restore a destroyed way of life, often by appeal to the supernatural. In both West and Central Kalimantan, the Dayaks operated in part through new, pan-Dayak organizations which bridged old ethnic differences.[4] There were no reports of external agents becoming involved. Although Muslim-Christian friction did exist, it was not a major causal factor; in West Kalimantan indigenous Muslim Malays also attacked Muslim Madurese. But lurid reports of Christian (or animist) Dayak headhunters massacring Muslim Madurese did not go unnoticed elsewhere in Indonesia. The Borneo violence, horrific in its own right, was a factor in raising Muslim-Christian tension nationwide as well as a prelude to more widespread strife. As in most other cases of regional unrest, the underlying causes of the conflict have not been fully resolved.[5]

Interestingly, the violence did not spread to the neighboring Malaysian state of Sarawak. The Malaysian and Indonesian territories on Borneo have much in common, including some of the same Dayak groups and a recent history of wholesale logging at the expense of customary rights. This may have been because Madurese immigrants stayed on the Indonesian side of the border, or because the security apparatus of the Malaysian government was better organized, or because the greater prosperity of Malaysian Borneo compared to the Indonesian provinces reduced the pain of social change.

Maluku and North Maluku 1999–2004 Violence in Maluku was critically important because it was the first case of severe Muslim-Christian bloodshed during Indonesia's transition to democracy. It provoked the first use of Islamic and Christian militias, and it was the first conflict where Islamic fighters who were veterans of Afghanistan were key actors. The Maluku violence severely inflamed religious tension throughout

---

4   For details on the pan-Dayak organizations, see *Overcoming Violent Conflict*, Vol. 1, p. 15 and pp. 19–20.
5   "Ethnic-based conflict continues to haunt West Kalimantan," *Jakarta Post*, 8 Feb. 2008.

Indonesia. The death toll from 1999 through 2003 was at least 5,000, the highest in any of the conflicts discussed in this chapter.

In 1999 Maluku was separated into two provinces, Maluku and North Maluku, a division which contributed to political unrest. The two provinces cover a north-south swath of archipelago stretching over 1,000 kilometers, from just south of the Philippines to just north of Australia. There are coral reefs as gorgeous as any in the world and big, forested islands, including Halmahera and Buru, the site of the New Order's infamous political prison camp.

Maluku is known mainly for its fabled Spice Islands. Because of them there is an important Christian minority, originally Roman Catholic thanks to the sixteenth-century ministrations of St. Francis Xavier, but later converted to Protestantism courtesy of the Dutch. The current population of the two provinces, slightly under two million, is 85 percent Muslim, although Maluku, with almost two-thirds of the total population, is fairly evenly divided between Christian and Muslim.

The outbreak of violence in 1999 resulted from a perfect storm of past and present aggravations. The Dutch had favored Christians from Ambon, the island where the old provincial capital was located, as professional soldiers in the colonial army. During the Indonesian struggle for independence some of them fought on the Dutch side. Later, other Christian Ambonese attempted to form a breakaway Republic of South Maluku (Republik Maluku Selatan – RMS). They were defeated and, while some went to Holland, other pro-RMS elements remained behind, a disgruntled but influential Christian element associated with treason in the eyes of other Indonesians. Christians remained a favored elite in many areas of Maluku, but here as elsewhere there was a growing Muslim immigrant presence, which began to create a religiously defined underclass. Old ways were fading under the impact of social change. One consequence was the decay of traditional, village-level peacekeeping mechanisms, a factor which some have blamed for the rapid spread of violence once it got started.

Towards the end of his presidency, as part of his move toward Islam, Suharto encouraged Islamization of the Maluku bureaucracy under a Muslim governor. The decision to divide the province aggravated political rivalries, as did the shift toward a decentralized democracy, which began under President B. J. Habibie in 1999. Last but hardly least, it was alleged, but never proven, that the Indonesian Army tacitly encouraged growing disorder in Maluku to show President Abdurrahman Wahid, who succeeded Habibie in October 1999, that the new, democratic Indonesia could not survive without a strong military.

Violence seems to have commenced in January 1999 when a fight between an Ambonese Christian bus driver and an immigrant Muslim passenger set off two months of rioting which killed over 1,000 people.[6] Reciprocal bloodshed then took place in both Maluku and North Maluku. There were Christian as well as Muslim militias, and in 1999, following more violence occasioned by the division of the province, the Maluku Protestant Church called on Christians to join a holy war. Military efforts to control the situation on the ground were at first lamentably ineffective. At the national level, Islamic sentiment was rapidly inflamed, with senior Muslim politicians vying with each other to voice support for endangered Muslims in Maluku. In January 2000 the agitation peaked with a rally in Jakarta protesting the massacre of Muslims in Tobelo, North Maluku. Shortly thereafter the first Muslim militias left for Maluku, where they were not very effective.

On April 6 an Indonesian Muslim cleric, Ja'afar Umar Thalib, of Hadrami Arab descent, led a crowd of white-robed, spear-carrying followers to call on President Wahid. Thalib was a veteran of the anti-Soviet campaign in Afghanistan and the leader of Laskar Jihad, a new and formidable Islamic militia. He threatened to take Laskar Jihad to Maluku, and the president replied that he would be arrested if he did. In the event, Thalib had no trouble getting his men to Maluku because the Indonesian Army did nothing to stop him. Within a short time Laskar Jihad had fielded 7,000 suspiciously well-armed and equipped volunteers[7] and it was soon the dominant military force in Maluku, carrying out what amounted to ethnic cleansing in some areas.

It is usually harder to define how and when regional conflicts go into decline than to explain how they got started, and Maluku was no exception. The Indonesian military got along better with Wahid's successor as president, Megawati Sukarnoputri, who took office in July 2001, and was no longer motivated to cause trouble by tolerating or supporting

6   Graham Brown, *Overcoming Violent Conflict*, Vol. 4, *Peace and Development Analysis in Maluku and North Maluku*, Jakarta: Crisis Prevention and Recovery Unit, United Nations Development Program, 2005, p. 15.
7   Noorhaidi Hasan, *Laskar Jihad: Islam, Militancy, and the Quest for Identity in Post-New Order Indonesia*, Ithaca NY: Cornell Southeast Asia Program, 2006, p. 220.

Ja'afar Umar Thalib, Afghan war veteran and leader of Laskar Jihad, preaches at a mosque in Aceh in 2002. Laskar Jihad was a major participant in Indonesia's violent sectarian strife, especially in Maluku, until the violence became unpopular and it was disbanded. | Voja Miladinovic/Getty Images

the Islamic militias in Maluku. In time, new and more effective army and police forces were deployed to the region. Laskar Jihad was increasingly plagued by financial problems and factionalism. At the beginning of the conflict in mid-1999 Thalib had succeeded in eliciting religious opinions (*fatawa*), albeit cautiously phrased, from eminent Saudi religious scholars supporting his Maluku jihad. But late in 2002 Thalib's opponents obtained new rulings from the Saudis which effectively reversed the earlier ones.[8] Times had changed; the threat of Osama bin Laden, a deadly foe of the Saudi rulers, was growing, and the Saudi religious establishment was no doubt sensitive to its rulers' concerns.

Almost everyone in Indonesia, at both local and national levels, grew weary of the bloodshed. Negotiations began and a peace accord was signed in February 2002. After the unfavorable ruling from the Saudis, Laskar Jihad disbanded and the conflict ceased, except for a brief recurrence in 2004. Thalib himself stepped down in October 2002, withdrew to the relative obscurity of his *pesantren*, and was seen participating in Sufi

---

8   ICG, *Indonesia Backgrounder: Why Salafism and Terrorism mostly Don't Mix*, Asia Report No. 83, 13 Sept. 2004, pp. 12–18.

observances of a kind normally abhorrent to a radical, puritanical Muslim.[9] It was probably not coincidental that his retirement took place shortly after the Bali bombing, which shocked Indonesia and the world. Thalib tried briefly to revive Laskar Jihad after the temporary outbreak of violence in 2004, but got nowhere.[10]

Central Sulawesi: Poso 1998–2007 Sulawesi is the big island east of Borneo, once known as "The Celebes" because early European explorers weren't sure how many islands it was. It is mostly mountainous, with pockets of flat land, some of it quite fertile. It is also relatively close to the southern Philippines, the scene of a centuries-old Islamic insurgency, and it was one of the earliest of the post-New Order conflict zones. The town and district of Poso, the hub of the violence, are located on the eastward-facing bay that dominates northern Sulawesi. From 1999 through 2003, there were over 600 deaths in this conflict, according to UN figures.[11] In 2000 the province of Central Sulawesi had only slightly more than two million inhabitants.[12]

The Poso conflict resulted from a melding of traditional and religious grievances. The pre-colonial settlement of the region included Muslim Malays on the coast and warlike animists in the mountainous interior. The religion of the hill people, part of the broader Toraja group, centered around rituals associated with slavery and headhunting. Early in the twentieth century, the Dutch abolished the old headhunting rituals, partly as a security measure. They then encouraged Protestant missionaries to convert these people, who had effectively been deprived of their old religion.[13] In time this effort succeeded in creating a Christian population with access to missionary education. Those thus educated often moved out of their mountain homes and found government jobs as clerks and teachers, forming a new Christian elite living in close proximity to Muslims.

At the same time the Dutch were bringing in rice farmers from Java and Bali and settling them in fertile valleys, where the local people knew

---

9   Hasan, *Laskar Jihad*, pp. 211–13.
10 ICG, *Salafism and Terrorism*, p. 18.
11 *Overcoming Violent Conflict*, Vol. 5, table p. 5.
12 Graham Brown and Yukhi Tajima with Suprayoga Hadi, *Overcoming Violent Conflict*, Vol. 3, *Peace and Development Analysis in Central Sulawesi*, Jakarta: Crisis Prevention and Recovery Unit, United Nations Development Program, 2005, Table 1, p. 10.
13 Hildred Geertz, "Indonesian Cultures and Communities" in Ruth McVey, ed., *Indonesia*, New Haven: Yale Southeast Asia Studies, esp. "Swidden Farmers of the Interior: the Eastern Toradja," pp. 75–76.

nothing about irrigated rice cultivation. The government of independent Indonesia continued this practice. These official "transmigrants" were, as elsewhere, supplemented by spontaneous migrants, including Muslim traders and shopkeepers from entrepreneurially inclined peoples like the Bugis of neighboring South Sulawesi and the Minangkabau of West Sumatra, who augmented the original Muslim population.

An initial wave of Muslim-Christian violence occurred in the 1950s, when Darul Islam fighters from South Sulawesi pushed north into Christian territory, but the most recent fighting is usually dated from a Muslim-Christian scuffle around the Poso bus station in December 1998. Then came a chain reaction of violence, followed eventually by an abortive peace settlement in August 2000. But fighting resumed after a lull, and by late 2001 there were at least seven Islamic militias from outside the area operating in Central Sulawesi.[14] They did not always get along; indeed they sometimes fought with one another. They included Laskar Jihad, although it was never as important in Poso as it was in Maluku, and Jemaah Islamiyah (JI), al-Qaeda's principal ally and sometime agent in Indonesia, Malaysia and the Philippines. According to press reports based on interrogation of captured trainees in Manila, JI set up an allegedly al-Qaeda training camp in Poso for Muslim rebels from the southern Philippines as well as for Indonesians.[15] These reports seemed to confirm fears that Indonesia was becoming a regional hub for terrorism.

In December 2001 Jusuf Kalla (then Coordinating Minister for Peoples' Welfare, later to be Indonesia's Vice President), himself a Muslim native of South Sulawesi, brokered a peace accord for Poso. Implementation was painfully slow and ineffective at first. But although conflict continued, its nature changed, from widespread communal violence to targeted assassinations of officials and others, directed by Muslim extremists. This shift apparently reflected the thinking of JI, which had decided that remote Poso would be an ideal base for insurgency, in line with its belief that the achievement of an Islamic state would require the establishment of devoutly Islamic base areas first. JI needed enough violence in Poso to keep the warrior spirit of its local followers alive without making it

---

14 ICG, *Indonesia Backgrounder: Jihad in Central Sulawesi*, Asia Report No. 60, 3 Feb. 2004, p. 11. See also John T. Sidel, *Riots, Pogroms, Jihad: Religious Violence in Indonesia*, Ithaca NY: Cornell University Press, 2006, pp. 153–68.
15 ICG, *Jihad in Central Sulawesi*, p. 12.

impossible to pursue its teaching and recruiting activities.[16]

The government continued to implement reconciliation programs and to arrest those responsible for violence. These efforts led to a large-scale police raid on Poso in January 2007, which killed fourteen well-armed insurgents. Muslim politicians in Jakarta as well as some foreign observers felt that the police had used excessive force, but the raid got positive results. Tough police work was followed by a shower of carrots, including a pair of new, high-profile Muslim and Christian schools, as well as a vocational training program for ex-trouble makers which morphed into a mechanism for getting hotheads from both sides together. The police pursued behind-the-scenes efforts to make sure that those captured in 2007 did not receive unduly harsh jail sentences. Special favors, such as pilgrimages to Mecca, were doled out to relatives of leading radicals.

Vice President Kalla was the driving force behind the conflict resolution effort in Poso, as he was during the peace negotiations that ended the war in Aceh. His personal involvement assured abundant funding, to the point that critics began focusing on corruption, and there were rumors that the security authorities were encouraging sufficient conflict to keep the money rolling in. But the International Crisis Group concluded in January 2008 that after almost a decade of conflict, and despite problems ranging from massive corruption to residual distrust of the police, Poso "is in much better shape."[17]

Common Causes of Local Conflict

The same causes in various combinations were behind all three of these conflicts. Muslim vs. non-Muslim hostility was a major factor in Maluku and in Poso, but not as important in Kalimantan and never in isolation from other causes. At the local level, grievances which had accumulated over long periods, but were suppressed during the Suharto years, broke out anew. Some of these were traditional feuds clothed in modern, sectarian dress.

In Poso, for example, there was an uneasy relationship between headhunting mountain tribes and coast dwellers long before the Dutch converted the mountain people to Christianity. Almost everywhere, accelerating population movement and attendant social change, some of

---

16 *Ibid.*, pp. 14–16.
17 ICG, *Indonesia: Tackling Radicalism in Poso*, Asia Briefing No. 75, 22 Jan. 2008, p. 11.

it attributable to economic development, made people feel insecure. Once violence erupted, country-wide publicity made it contagious, as when Muslims on Java who read about riots in Maluku rushed to support the formation of armed militias and joined them. Potent background factors included never-ending reports of violence in the Middle East, often oversimplified as persecution of Muslims, and vigorous missionary efforts by Christian evangelicals in Muslim areas such as West Sumatra.

Aggressive entrepreneurship by Muslim migrants was an irritant in every case mentioned above. The ubiquity of the Minangkabau with their trademark Padang restaurants has long been a national joke among Indonesians, who are fond of saying that the first astronaut to land on the moon was greeted by a Padang restaurant with its chili-saturated food on display. But the phenomenon was not always so funny to pre-existing populations, especially if they were Christians or animists, or just not quite as go-getting.

The onset of Indonesia's new, radically decentralized democracy, legislated in 1999, was another common irritant. Suddenly, hoary disagreements about district boundaries and local leaderships came back to life. The splitting of provinces, as in Maluku, and the creation of gerrymandered districts, as in Central Sulawesi, may in some cases have been part of a well-intentioned plan to share representation among ethnic groups, but initially such moves were always controversial. The first candidates in local elections were often aligned along ethnic or religious fault lines, and the notion that this could be a prelude to healthy democratic competition, rather than violence, was not always realistic. Hierarchical clan chiefs sometimes became demagogues. Control of natural resources, including mines and forests, was an issue in a number of places.

Confusion at Indonesia's center was arguably the most important indirect cause of regional violence. Interim President B.J. Habibie (May 1998–October 1999) initiated a flood of political reforms and was then voted out of office. The hard job of managing the consequences was left to Abdurrahman Wahid (October 1999–July 2001) and Megawati Sukarnoputri (July 2001–October 2004), neither of whom seemed able to control events.

The resulting sense of uncertainty and weakness emanating from Jakarta was compounded by an army that was often part of the problem, as demonstrated by its ill-concealed toleration (or worse) of violence in Maluku in order to discredit a sitting president.

Finally it is worth noting that these three major areas of communal violence, which killed roughly 9,000 people up to 2003[18] and displaced many more, have a total population of about nine million, roughly three percent of Indonesia's current population.

Aceh, East Timor and Papua: Three that Don't Fit the Pattern

Unrest in three areas other than those discussed above encouraged the impression that Indonesia might be falling apart, but none of them involved either major sectarian conflict or significant incidents of terrorism, as opposed to thuggery or guerilla warfare. It is nonetheless worthwhile to review briefly how these three contributed to Indonesia's broader problems of national security and coherence.

Aceh It will be recalled that it took the Dutch more than 30 years of warfare to subjugate Aceh. Moreover peace did not survive independence from Dutch rule for long. Having supported the Indonesian Revolution, the Acehnese joined the Darul Islam Rebellion which lasted, for them, from 1953 to roughly 1959.[19] Then there was relative calm until, under the Suharto regime, the Acehnese declared independence in 1976, followed by more fighting until 1982. By 1989 a new and potent separatist organization, the Free Aceh Movement (Gerakan Aceh Merdeka – GAM) was on the scene, and it carried on the struggle until a settlement was reached in 2005.

If you were to conclude that the Acehnese are a stubborn lot, you would certainly be correct. They are also devout Muslims, as proud of their Islam as anyone anywhere. But the historical record also makes it quite clear that their fight has always been about regaining control of their own affairs, not about turning Indonesia into an Islamic state. The GAM rebellion was very serious indeed, the biggest challenge to Jakarta of any of the three cases discussed here. The Indonesian army repeatedly did its best to re-establish control of Aceh both before and after the fall of Suharto, but never came close to succeeding. Enormous damage was done in the process.[20]

---

18 Extrapolated from *Overcoming Violent Conflict*, Vol. 5, p. 5, which gives a figure of 11,160 fatalities for the entire country from 1990 to 2003, including violence in regions other than the three covered here.

19 See Chapter 3 above and M. C. Ricklefs, *A History of Modern Indonesia since c. 1200*, 4th ed., Stanford CA: Stanford University Press, 2008, pp. 303, 364.

20 For background see Damien Kingsbury, *Peace in Aceh: A Personal Account of the Helsinki Peace Process*, Jakarta: Equinox, 2006, pp. 5–14.

One might have thought that the Acehnese would fall easy prey to international Islamic extremism. But during all the years of the most recent insurgency, punctuated only by sullen cease-fires, mainstream GAM never made common cause with al-Qaeda or others bent on international Islamic statehood. (Splinter elements of GAM, apparently in the pay of Indonesian intelligence, did participate in some of the violence outside Aceh, according to an International Crisis Group Report.[21]) Equally surprisingly, GAM did not demand Islamic statehood for Aceh itself. Despite this, President Habibie began the process of bestowing the right to enact sharia law on Aceh in 1999, as part of what eventually became the final peace agreement. Jakarta assumed that the Acehnese would be pleased, and apparently did not consult with them in depth. [22]

In fact the question of sharia law and the religious bureaucracy which it has empowered remains controversial even in fervently Islamic Aceh. GAM has always opposed it. The first freely elected governor of autonomous Aceh, former GAM leader Irwandi Yusuf, has made it clear that he regards Habibie's gift as a distraction from the more urgent business of development and reconstruction after decades of war and the 2004 tsunami.[23] Experts agree that the tsunami itself was not, as is often stated, the key event that catalyzed the achievement of peace, although it helped the process along. The settlement resulted primarily from war fatigue combined with a determined effort led by President Susilo Bambang Yudhoyono, elected in 2004, and Vice President Kalla, who was already a seasoned peace-maker after his experience with Maluku and Poso. However, it is not wholly clear whether, or for how long, the widely praised peace agreement defining an autonomous Aceh will survive the implementation stage.[24]

---

21 ICG, *How the Jemaah Islamiyah Terrorist Network Operates*, ICG Asia Report No. 43, 11 Dec. 2002, pp. 6–9.

22 The granting of autonomy to Aceh was a complex process that included legislation passed in 1999, 2001 and 2006. See Arskal Salim, "Epilogue: Shari'a in Indonesia's Current Transition: an Update" in Azra Azyumardi and Arskal Salim, eds., *Shari'a and Politics in Modern Indonesia*, Singapore: Institute of Southeast Asian Studies, 2003, p. 222; Donald K. Emmerson, "What is Indonesia?" in John Bresnan. ed., *Indonesia:The Great Transition*, Lanham MD: Rowman and Littlefield, 2005, pp. 36–40.

23 Irwandi Yusuf, "My Vision of Aceh: Our Hopes and Concerns," remarks at the United States-Indonesia Society, 13 Sept. 2007, Washington DC: USINDO Brief.

24 For a summary of problems facing Aceh see ICG, *Aceh: Post-conflict Complications*, Asia Report No. 139, 4 October 2007. Re-emerging threats to the peace process are discussed in Sydney Jones, "Aceh on a Knife Edge: There Are Big Dangers in Declaring Success Too Soon," *Inside Indonesia* 95, Jan.–March 2009, http://insideindonesia.org/content/view/1179/47/.

East Timor The Indonesian Army invaded the Portuguese colony of East Timor in 1975, leading to almost a quarter century of brutal occupation and resistance. The resulting international condemnation did great damage to Indonesia's reputation and the legitimacy of the Suharto regime. In 1999 President Habibie acted courageously to end this national nightmare by approving a referendum on independence, held on August 30, 1999. But when pro-independence forces won the referendum, the Indonesian Army unleashed its anti-independence militias in an orgy of violence. Less than a year later the military would play a similarly disruptive role in Maluku by tolerating, if not supporting, Laskar Jihad. Not surprisingly, East Timor remained chronically unstable and vexed by disorder well after the Indonesian departure.

The long Indonesian occupation of East Timor provided an interesting example of New Order religious policy and its sometimes unexpected consequences. It began in the heyday of anti-communism, when everyone was required to "have a religion" (*beragama*) in accordance with Pancasila's dictum of Belief in God Almighty. Islam was virtually non-existent in East Timor. The majority of East Timor's roughly 800,000 inhabitants were animists, believing in More than One God. The Catholic Church was of course present, but weakly represented, especially among the rural population. But Indonesian policy now provoked a flight from animism to Catholicism, comparable to the short-lived flight from communism to Hindu-Buddhism and Christianity in Java after 1966. The Catholic Church not only tripled its communicants, from approximately 30% to approximately 90% of the population;[25] it also became a bastion of East Timor's decades-long struggle for independence.

Papua In the late 1990s Papua was often cited with Aceh as evidence that Indonesia might be falling apart. Vast in size, with a population of only 2.7 million,[26] the western half of the island of New Guinea has been a source of controversy ever since the Dutch refused to relinquish it to newly independent Indonesia. Sukarno fought back with his usual

---

25 Don Greenless and Robert Garran, *The Inside Story of East Timor's Fight for Freedom*, Sydney: Allen and Unwin, 2002, p. 17; Robert Archer, "The Catholic Church in East Timor" in Peter Carey, ed., *East Timor at the Crossroads: The Forging of a Nation*, Honolulu: University of Hawai'i Press, 1995, p. 127.

26 Population figure is rounded from Thomas Brinkhoff, "City Population: Indonesia," constructed 20 Jan. 2008, using *Badan Pusat Statistik* figures accssed March 2008 at http://www.citypopulation.de/Indonesia.html.

flamboyant zeal, and in 1962 the US pressured the Dutch into giving it up. After that, Irian Jaya, as the Indonesians called it, was largely left to Christian missionaries until the mid-1970s, when its wealth of minerals and timber began to be exploited. A Papuan nationalist movement seeking independence from Indonesia has existed for over 40 years.

Making sense of Papua is difficult partly due to its incredibly fragmented, mainly Melanesian ethnicity. One might expect the Papuans to yearn for union with their next-door neighbor, independent, almost-wholly-Melanesian Papua New Guinea (PNG). However, the Papuans have never seriously pursued such a goal, perhaps due to reports of rampant crime and corruption in PNG, plus lack of interest on the part of the Papua New Guineans. Papua's unrest is further stimulated by competition for natural resources among both Papuans and non-Papuans. Partly because the economic stakes are higher in Papua than was the case in Aceh, the issues are taking longer to sort out.

The political and administrative maneuvers involved in Jakarta's relationship with Papua are too complex to relate here. The territory was granted autonomy in 2001 and is currently and somewhat tenuously divided into two provinces, Papua and West Papua. There has been some progress in integrating Papua (both provinces) into the Indonesian state – more Papuans are attending Indonesian universities than ever before, for example. Although there has been some sectarian violence it has not been on the scale of Kalimantan, Maluku or Poso.

That could change. Muslim immigration has caused irritation in Papua as in other areas mentioned earlier. Between 1964 and 1994 the proportion of Muslims in the Papuan population rose from 6.5 to 23.1 percent. Only one-tenth of them are indigenous Papuans, concentrated in two of the region's 19 districts.[27] Most Papuans are former animists who have been converted to Christianity for many years, and many are beginning to feel threatened by the Islamic influx.

The Yudhoyono regime was sufficiently concerned to take the unusual step of banning a Papuan-authored book entitled *The Landlord that Becomes a Guest (Tuan Rumah yang Menjadi Tamu)* in 2007, making it an instant best-seller. The fervently Christian District of Manokwari has issued local regulations banning mosque construction in certain areas.[28] The Muslims

---

27 Number of districts is from 2005 and may have changed.
28 "Right on cue, Bible-based ordinances appear," *Jakarta Post*, 3 June 2007.

are equally aggrieved. They remember what happened in Maluku, which is not far away, and a number of militant or activist groups such as Hizbut Tahrir and the Prosperous Justice Party (PKS) are represented in Papua among the immigrant Muslim community.[29]

Violent Extremism: Laskar Jihad and Jemaah Islamiyah

All three cases of regional sectarian unrest described earlier – in Kalimantan. Maluku and Poso – were essentially home-grown, but two of them, Maluku and Poso, were aggravated by the intervention of Islamic militias from elsewhere in Indonesia. The militias felt that they were coming to the aid of Muslims under threat, and some of their leaders were in pursuit of more elaborate political goals (e.g., Jemaah Islamiyah's hope of creating an Islamic enclave in Poso as a prelude to an Islamic State).

However, some extremists, in this case mainly JI, also carried out bombings across Indonesia that had nothing to do with communal conflict. These incidents were undeniable examples of terrorism. The strikes were aimed initially at Indonesian Christians, later at foreigners seen as associated with the US-led global war on terror, which in Indonesia was widely viewed as a war on Islam. The perpetrators intended them as revenge pure and simple, but also as a way to undermine and discredit an Indonesian government which they judged to be insufficiently Islamic.

As we have seen, violent extremism has roots in Indonesian history. JI in particular was built around portions of the old Darul Islam movement, which, although militarily defeated in the Sukarno era, still had scattered groups of followers. Darul Islam's smoldering embers flamed anew as a result of New Order policies in the 1980s, combined with international conflicts which aroused Muslim resentment. Suharto's refusal to allow Reformist Masyumi to re-enter national politics marginalized Masyumi's aging moderates and encouraged its radical religious conservatives. They in turn built new connections with the Middle East. As explained in Chapter 4, these ties resulted in a flood of both financial and intellectual support for the kind of puritanical Islam supported primarily by Saudi Arabia and often known as *Salafi*.

Pure Salafism condemns efforts to overthrow a Muslim government,

---

29 Unless otherwise indicated, information in this paragraph is based on ICG, *Indonesia: Communal Tensions in Papua*, Asia Report No. 154, 16 June 2008, and on personal experience in Papua New Guinea.

or for that matter any involvement in organized politics, in favor of non-violent religious study and reform. But some Indonesians, chafing under Suharto's repression, were impatient with this other-worldly approach.

Among them were Abdullah Sungkar and Abu Bakar Ba'asyir, the two Indonesians of Arab descent who had co-founded the radical Ngruki *pesantren* in 1976. Both were jailed in Indonesia in 1978. They were released and fled to Malaysia in 1985. Between 1985 and 1995 Sungkar, who was senior to Ba'asyir and the first leader or "*amir*" of JI, recruited between two and three hundred Indonesians for service in Afghanistan, sometimes ordering his own followers to go there. Although Sungkar visited Afghanistan, it seems that neither he nor Ba'asyir served in the battle zone for any length of time.

In Afghanistan the Indonesians, including Ja'afar Umar Thalib, future founder of Laskar Jihad, fought with the Afghan *mujahidin* against the Russians. They were trained and inspired by Osama bin Laden and his lieutenants and met like-minded Malaysians and Filipinos. In summer they roasted in desert tents and in winter they wondered at the snow. They participated in heroic battles against the Soviets, including one, the Battle of Jaji, that was a turning point of the Afghanistan war. It is well known, but worth mentioning anyway, that they were all, directly or indirectly, beneficiaries of CIA support for the *mujahidin*. In 1993 Sungkar and Ba'asyir founded Jemaah Islamiyah, dedicated to the creation of an Islamic State in Southeast Asia, as an organization distinct from Darul Islam.[30]

Of all the ties that united the violent extremists, the Afghanistan experience was the most important in both psychological and technological terms. In 1985 a group of Komando Jihad adherents had tried to smuggle a bomb to Bali, but it blew up on their bus and killed one of them. In 2002 when JI adherents tried the same thing, this time with individuals led, trained and motivated by veterans of Afghanistan, they succeeded all too well.[31] As the Afghan experience faded into the past, the extremist leaders hoped that fighting in Maluku, Poso or the southern Philippines would provide an equally powerful experience for young recruits.

---

30 Previous two paragraphs are based on ICG, *Jemaah Islamiyah in Southeast Asia: Damaged but Still Dangerous*, Asia Report No. 63, 26 Aug. 2003, esp. pp. 2–10. Date of Jemaah Islamiyah founding is from Greg Fealy, Virginia Hooker and Sally White, "Indonesia," in Greg Fealy and Virginia Hooker, eds., *Voices of Islam in Southeast Asia: A Contemporary Sourcebook*, Singapore: Institute of Southeast Asian Studies, 2006, p. 49.

31 Robert Pringle, *A Short History of Bali: Indonesia's Hindu Realm*, Sydney: Allen and Unwin, 2005, pp. 205–206.

There were and still are additional unifying factors at work among the leaders of JI, including an "old boy" loyalty to the Ngruki *pesantren* and a scattering of other radical schools. The leaders send their children to a group of *pesantren* which one researcher has labeled the "JI Ivy league."[32] JI members have established marriage ties with each other and with their Malaysian colleagues in a manner reminiscent of the Traditionalist clerical establishment in the *pesantren* world of East Java.

It is now generally accepted that JI or its offshoots was responsible for the setting of 300 bombs in eleven cities across Indonesia on Christmas Eve 2000 (which killed 19 and wounded almost 200 people) as well as for both Bali bombings, in 2002 and 2005 (which together killed over 200). JI and its splinters also carried out bombings in Jakarta at the Marriott Hotel, the Australian Embassy, the Atrium shopping mall and other targets. These were typically tightly controlled operations in which each cell operated without knowing the identity of colleagues in other cells. The extremist leaders recruited foot soldiers, including suicide bombers, often from Islamic schools. They also sponsored out-and-out criminality, utilizing "*preman*" (thugs or hoodlums) to raise money by robbing busses, stealing cars and holding up banks.[33] JI operated dozens of training camps, not just the most publicized one in Poso.

The 2002 Bali bombing, far and away the more serious of the two, marked a shift in JI's focus, away from intervening in regional conflicts such as Poso and towards targeting westerners and resisting the US-led war on terror. By 2002, however, JI was confronting much more effective police work in Indonesia, and by the end of 2003 it had lost several of its top operatives, most notably Ridwan Isanuddin (alias Hambali), a major strategist and fund-raiser.[34] Hambali was arrested in Thailand and turned over to the US. This became an issue between the US and Indonesia because the Americans refused to allow the Indonesians to interrogate him. The problem diminished after the US agreed to share transcripts of its interrogations of Hambali with the Indonesian government.

After the Bali bombing, divisions developed in JI's always-informal hierarchy. Ba'asyir favored cutting back on violence and taking more advantage of Indonesia's newly emerging democracy to work for an Islamic state, a stance which caused some of his colleagues to conclude

---

32 ICG, *Damaged but Still Dangerous*, pp. 26ff.
33 ICG, *How the Jemaah Islamiyah Terrorist Network Operates*, pp. 24ff.
34 *Ibid.*, p.1.

that he was not radical enough. The most lethally active JI splinter was led by Noordin Mohammed Top, better known simply as Noordin Top, a Malaysian national who left JI in about 2004.[35] Top repeatedly evaded the security forces and was almost certainly behind the Jakarta bombings of July 2009, discussed below. Meanwhile the mainstream of Jemaah Islamiyah established a thriving publishing business partly devoted to terrorist memoirs, with the proceeds allegedly devoted to caring for the families of those incarcerated.[36]

What about JI's links to al-Qaeda? The International Crisis Group (ICG) concluded in 2003 that JI has probably received some funding from al-Qaeda, but that al-Qaeda does not exert operational control over JI.[37] The relationship is more perhaps a matter of shared ideals (or fanaticisms) than of systematic bureaucratic links, which of course does not make it less dangerous.

In trying to sort out JI's operation in Poso, an ICG researcher ended on a note of perplexity:

> If JI leaders are involved in Mujahidin KOMPAK [a militia generally considered to be a JI affiliate], does that make Mujahidin KOMPAK a proxy of JI? Not necessarily. If local Mujahidin leaders are trained by JI, does that make what they do thereafter JI's responsibility? Probably not. What is the relationship between JI-trained locals and the religious outreach activities carried on by JI members in the same area? Not clear. If there are lessons to be learned, they are that nothing is black and white, and it is impossible to predict JI's behavior accurately based on an assumption that it is a monolithic organization with a single set of goals.[38]

Why Terrorism Waned

From 2006 through mid-2009 Indonesia enjoyed more than three years free from major regional conflict or terrorism. But on July 17, 2009, near-simultaneous bombings at two American-brand hotels in Jakarta killed at least nine people and dashed hopes that violent extremism had been defeated for good. The bombings were assumed to have been the work

---

35 ICG, *Noordin Top's Support Base*, Asia Briefing No, 95, 27 Aug 2009, p. 1.
36 ICG, *Jemaah Islamiyah's Publishing Industry*, Asia Report No. 147, 28 Feb. 2008, esp p. 12.
37 ICG, *Damaged but Still Dangerous*, pp. 29–30.
38 ICG, *Jihad in Central Sulawesi*, p. 24.

of Noordin Top's JI splinter group, and Top was killed resisting police in Solo, Central Java, two months later.[39] The renewal of terrorism came hard on the heels of the 2009 parliamentary and presidential elections, in which parties favoring an Islamic state made a poor showing and President Yudhoyono was handily re-elected, suggesting that some extremists might have concluded that good behavior was getting them nowhere.

Even during the 2006–2009 hiatus Indonesia was never wholly free from political violence. Some of Noordin Top's followers came close to bombing a hotel in Palembang in 2008 before they were arrested. Scattered episodes of vigilantism and thuggery aimed primarily at Christian churches[40] and at the Ahmadiyah sect continued. Nevertheless, impressive progress against widespread disorder was made from 2002 onwards, and it is clear what the ingredients of continuing progress are likely to be.

The most important reason for the waning of extremist violence was the restoration of coherent central government. Just as the chaos of the late Suharto years fuelled the fires of sectarian strife, so the successful growth of Indonesia's democracy began to restore confidence and reduce paranoia. Almost equally important was the fact that violence became increasingly unpopular. The unrest of 1998–2005 brought far more pain than gain for most Indonesians including, of course, most Muslims. Figures for the fourteen provinces most affected by sectarian strife show a total of slightly more than 11,000 killed from 1990 to 2003, including some episodes dating to the Suharto era and others occurring in a few regions not discussed above. The year 1999 was the most violent year, and Maluku was the deadliest conflict.[41]

It mattered that Indonesians did not take kindly to being stigmatized as citizens of an incipient failed state. The Bali bombings were a particular affront to national pride. Muslims who were initially preoccupied with the plight of their co-religionists began to realize that what had been touted as a holy war killed mainly other Muslims. The rise and fall of Laskar Jihad from 2000 to 2002, and the path of its leader from national hero to obscurity, reflected this sea change in public opinion.

---

39 "Top Terror Suspect Killed, Indonesian Officials Say," *New York Times*, September 18, 2009, p. A11.
40 On continuing episodes of anti-Christian violence, see Robin Bush, "One Step Forward..." in *Inside Indonesia* 89, April–June 2007; Douglas E. Ramage, "Indonesia in 2006: Democracy First, Good Governance Later" in Daljit Singh and Lorraine Carlos Salazar, eds., *Southeast Asian Affairs 2007*, Singapore: Institute of Southeast Asian Studies, p. 149.
41 *Overcoming Violent Conflict*, Vol. 5, table p. 5.

At the same time the Indonesian security forces evolved from being part of the problem, epitomized by the army's role in Maluku, to playing an increasingly productive investigative and peace-keeping role. By 2007, in the words of one commentator, Indonesia had "perhaps the best record of any state in Asia of combating terrorism."[42] A Habibie-era reform transferred anti-terrorism responsibility from the army to the police. It was counterproductive at first because the army did not give the police its files, all-important in a situation where terrorist networks were based on historical entities such as the Darul Islam networks. However, after that, the police greatly improved both their effectiveness and their public image.

The investigation of the first Bali bombing marked a turning point. As an International Crisis Group report noted at the time, "...the professional pride of the police is at an all-time high with the Bali successes. This may be the first time that the police are taking pride across the country as a force getting results through dogged pursuit of leads, rather than money or coercion."[43]

While no police force anywhere is perfect, the improvement that became evident in the case of Bali continued in Poso and elsewhere. The Indonesian police seem to have been well ahead of their counterparts in some fully developed countries in recognizing that honey catches flies, treating terrorist suspects almost as privileged guests rather than torturing them, and making sure their families were also well treated, in order to induce cooperation.[44]

The renewed bombing in 2009 caused some critics to charge that government had gone too far in the direction of coddling arrested terrorists. The International Crisis Group was reluctant to agree, noting soon after the event that no one implicated in previous crimes seemed to have been among the 2009 bombers. It did, however, call for more monitoring of the minority of radical *pesantren*, estimated at about 50 in number, although it recommended against attempting to close them down.[45] The 2009 bombings made painfully clear that individuals bent on lawless, violent jihad could still evade arrest and find refuge in Indonesian communities, not just in radical *pesantren*. This remained true despite the general unpopularity of extremist violence and the improved quality of Indonesia's police work.

---

42 Ramage, "Indonesia in 2006," p.136.
43 ICG, *How the Islamiyah Jemaah Terrorist Network Operates*, p. 25.
44 Seth Mydans, "A Jailhouse Conversion Splits Relatives and In-Laws," *New York Times*, 15 March 2008; on broader police effectiveness, see Douglas E. Ramage, "A Reformed Indonesia," *The Australian Financial Review*, 12 Oct. 2007, p. 1.
45 ICG, *The Hotel Bombings*, Asia Briefing No. 94, 24 July 2009, p. 7.

What has enabled terrorists to operate in Indonesian communities despite their unpopularity? It relates in part to the fact that Indonesian Islam has lost none of its diversity. In addition to the moderate majority there remains a minority of radicals who condone or engage in illegal violence. The extremist networks (JI and others) are harassed but alive. The bitterness aroused by the communal violence of the recent past will undoubtedly linger for a long time.

There are other reasons. The foreign backdrop of conflict in the Middle East and Afghanistan continues to feed extremist opinion, and there is plenty of it on display in the free and fecund Indonesian press. Financial support from foreign sources may be a factor, although it is probably less important than support from Indonesian sympathizers and low-level criminal activity of the type traditionally employed by JI to raise money. Hostility to Christian missionary work can nurture local radicalization, so much so that the Indonesian government is being urged to attempt the difficult task of developing policies to counter this Muslim backlash without compromising freedom of religion.[46]

The only antidote to renewed violence in conflict-damaged regions like Poso and Aceh is to reconcile the former antagonists by intensive local efforts, including but not restricted to resettling those displaced by the conflict and creating employment for former fighters. There are other less obvious post-conflict goals, such as making sure that Indonesia's prison system does not become a nurturing ground for future violence by mingling hard-core extremists with ordinary criminals.[47] No one would argue that this post-conflict agenda is proceeding as fast as it should, much less that the threat of terrorism has been vanquished for good, despite the generally encouraging record of recent years.

As noted above, there has been a rift in Indonesia's violent extremist ranks since about 2005 between those who advocate violence and others who feel that it is time to take advantage of Indonesian democracy and pursue a radical religious agenda by peaceful means, including intimidation as needed. Many observers, both foreign and Indonesian, feel that intimidation is indeed the more dangerous long-term risk to pluralism and democracy. The next chapter will examine this proposition.

---

46 ICG, Indonesia: *Radicalization of the "Palembang Group*," Asia Briefing No. 92, 20 May 2009, p. 15.
47 ICG, "*Deradicalization" and Indonesia's Prisons*, Asia Report No. 142, 19 Nov. 2007.

7

Islamic Extremism
and Democracy

I believe in Pancasila [the five basic principles of the Republic].
I'm a pluralist. In my extended family we have Muslims,
Catholics, Protestants and Buddhists – we're always having festivals!

– Inul Daratista, celebrated *dangdut* dancer,
protesting against the 2006 anti-pornography bill.[1]

A monstrous statue looms over the courtyard of the National Museum in Jakarta, where it has frightened generations of visiting schoolchildren. It has none of the serene beauty of much early Indonesian art, exemplified by the ninth-century Borobudur in Central Java. The statue depicts a large male figure standing on a corpse, which lies on a pedestal garlanded with human skulls. The statue is thought to be a portrait of King Adityavarman, the founder and ruler of a fourteenth-century state in what is now the devoutly Islamic province of West Sumatra, the home, then as now, of the Minangkabau people. It represents the monarch as an adherent of the Bhairava Cult of Tantric Buddhism (Bhairava being a demonic aspect of Shiva), which for macabre qualities surely has never been surpassed.

An inscription found by the Dutch archeologists who unearthed the statue relates how "the king was consecrated on a burial ground where he sat alone on a pile of corpses, laughing demonically and drinking blood, while the flames of a great human sacrifice spread an unbearable stench which, to the initiate, was like the fragrance of ten thousand million flowers."[2]

By now you may be confused – what is a Hindu God doing as part of a

---

1   Duncan Graham, "Inul Daratista: Getting to the bottom of the pornography bill," *Jakarta Post*, 3 June 2006.
2   Claire Holt, *Art in Indonesia: Continuities and Change*, Ithaca NY: Cornell University Press, p. 80.

Adityavarman was among the last rulers of a Hindu-Buddhist state in West Sumatra, homeland of the now devoutly Islamic Minangkabau people. Here he is portrayed as a demonic incarnation of Shiva-Buddha, standing on a garland of human skulls. | National Museum in Jakarta, photo by Tara Sosrowardoyo

Buddhist cult? You may be tempted to think "How very Indonesian!" In fact, Shiva-Buddha cults were not uncommon in Mahayana Buddhist tradition elsewhere in Asia, and this one was presumably related to the state religion of the Java-based Majapahit Empire, of which the Minangkabau state had previously been part.

Granted, Tantric Buddhism was sometimes way, way out. Granted also that this image represents a period when Hindu-Buddhism in Indonesia was in decay, beset by a recrudescence of traditional animism on one side and the first encroachments of Islam on the other. But consider the ongoing complexity of West Sumatran history. By the early nineteenth century the province had long been converted to Islam. In the 1820s it experienced a vigorous jihad, the Padri War, a struggle described in Chapter 2 between fundamentalist reformers returning from Mecca and traditional rulers. The old rulers won, with the help of the Dutch, but the contest between Reformist and Traditionalist Islam continued in Minangkabau country, as elsewhere. Then, in the 1920s, this agricultural province was the scene of a genuine communist uprising, of all things, basically because a new cash economy was causing social upheaval.

West Sumatra was also among the very first provinces in Indonesia to take advantage of new opportunities for education under the Dutch. It produced leaders of all political persuasions in the developing nationalist movement, including Mohammad Hatta, Indonesia's first Vice President (moderate Islamic); Sutan Sjahrir, first prime minister (western-style secular-socialist-intellectual), Mohammed Natsir, another early prime minister (advocate of an Islamic state), and Tan Malaka (communist and rebel leader). The province is proud of all its famous figures. As of early 2007 more than a dozen biographies of them (three of Tan Malaka alone) were on sale at the provincial airport bookstore.

Aside from their restaurants serving red-hot food, found in every corner of Indonesia, the Minangkabau ("Minang" for short) are perhaps most famous for being one of the few matrilineal Muslim societies on earth. This means that descent and inheritance pass through the female line, and although women do not become rulers (their brothers and nephews do) matrilineality nevertheless gives Minangkabau women real authority, as anyone who has met a sampling of them can attest.

Matrilineality is a robust carryover from early history, before Islam and before Hinduism, when there was a strong animist, bronze-iron age Minangkabau society. Its most famous manifestation is the traditional dwelling style, featuring sweeping, uplifted roofs, designed to house an entire extended family. Today this style is represented everywhere in the province: the Padang airport terminal, the new regional assembly building, even hotels and filling stations.

So how have the Minang people managed to digest this amazing cultural stew, with all its various lumps? Certainly it has not been without a lot of stress and turmoil over the years, usually about the difficulty of reconciling custom (*adat*) and Islam. But the Minang finally declared victory (according to regional folklore the name Minang is first cousin to the Indonesian word *menang* meaning "to win") with a saying to the effect that both Islam and custom are part of one social structure, end of discussion.[3]

---

3 The proverb is "*Adat bersendi syarak* [sharia], *syarak bersendi Kitabullah* [the Holy Koran]." It means "Custom is joined to (or depends on) sharia, sharia is joined to (or depends on) the Holy Koran." It is widely regarded as a Malay as well as a Minangkabau proverb, which is not contradictory given that the geographic term *Melayu* was once applied to the Minangkabau domains, and that Minangkabau is in many ways a subset of the broader Malay culture.

The provincial museum in Padang is a good place to sample the thinking of the Minangkabau people about their own diversity. The museum is intended for Indonesians, not foreigners, and it is devoted to local culture. There are photos and models of the famous customary houses, and others devoted to the superb old Minangkabau mosques built in a pagoda style derived from Hindu-Buddhist practice. There is a sign, in Indonesian only, which says (paraphrasing): "Know your own culture, it is the best way to resist [unwelcome] foreign influence."

Democracy isn't making it any easier to fit so many disparate cultural elements together. The Padang municipal government has been among those which have enacted elements of sharia law. One proposed ordinance would have ruled that women could not be outside during hours of darkness. Since Minangkabau women dominate market commerce, and since that requires pre-dawn activity, the ordinance, after nation-wide publicity, was rejected. Not long afterwards, the mayor was winding up a three-day celebration of Chinese New Year, during which he exhorted the Chinese business community to take good care of their picturesque old shop houses, saturated with pork fumes, because they are a tourist attraction.

Of course West Sumatra is not typical of Indonesia as a whole, nor is any other province. Of this fact Indonesians are quite aware, as they are also aware of the political challenge that such diversity entails. In a world of growing conformity, Indonesian diversity often seems appealing, but hardly practical as the basis for a democratic state, especially when the state has 240 million people living on thousands of islands spread across 3,000 miles of ocean. Some observers doubt that such a state can possibly stand against a hard, directed ideology such as violent, extremist Islam as embodied by al-Qaeda and its copycat franchises and affiliates.

We will look at the logic behind this pessimism and then at a different hypothesis invoking the reality of Indonesian diversity as a barrier to monochrome extremism. This is not an exercise in setting up a straw man and then knocking it down; there is some merit in both points of view, substantial bias on all sides, and plenty of room for debate. Everyone would agree that trying to predict the future in Indonesia is at least as unwise as anywhere else.

Intimidation and Vigilante Violence

The chaos that followed the fall of Suharto resulted not only in terrorism and regional conflict, as described in the previous chapter; it also created an atmosphere where Islamic extremists were emboldened to intimidate their opponents. The first extra-legal Islamic militias were formed to help endangered fellow Muslims in Maluku and elsewhere, but they soon had counterparts on the streets of Jakarta. Continuing warfare in Afghanistan, the Gulf and Iraq gave new credence to old conspiracy theories involving Jews and the United States abroad and their supposed allies in Indonesia, including ethnic Chinese, Roman Catholics (many of them Chinese), and various prominent NGOs, both foreign and domestic. Radical fundamentalists felt that the time was right to assert their ideological goals and to strike at liberal Muslims who had emerged as a significant intellectual force, thanks partly to the proliferation of middle-class Islamic styles in the Suharto years.

Several factors fueled concern and reciprocal paranoia on the part of foreign observers and Indonesians alike. For foreigners, the increasing visibility of Islam in Indonesia, epitomized by the growing use of head-scarves, suggested that a dangerous retreat from pluralism was indeed under way. The increase in observant Muslim representation in the armed forces initiated by Suharto (see Chapter 4) was also worrisome, notwithstanding that Christians had previously been overrepresented in the army because of their better education, and that some redress of this disparity was overdue.

The use or threat of violence to intimidate opponents was and remains a more serious concern. Among the most famous targets of such violence has been the Liberal Islam Network (Jaringan Islam Liberal – JIL), a coalition of intellectuals which challenges religious conservatism by asserting that independent judgement can be applied to reinterpret doctrine in the light of modern values and scientific knowledge. Many of JIL's activities (publications, radio broadcasts, discussion groups, etc.) take place at the Utan Kayu Theater complex in Jakarta, owned by veteran journalist, poet and gadfly Goenawan Mohamad. The Utan Kayu location is almost as famous as Goenawan himself. It became so after the weekly news magazine *Tempo* was banned in 1994. Goenawan, then *Tempo*'s chief editor, turned it into a center for anti-Suharto activities.[4]

JIL has been the target of fundamentalist wrath since its establishment in 2001. The next year an obscure radical group issued a *fatwa* "authorizing"

---

4   Utan Kayu's pro-democracy work was initially supported by the US Agency for International Development. See Janet Steele, *Wars Within: The Story of Tempo, an Independent Magazine in Suharto's Indonesia*, Singapore: Institute of Southeast Asian Studies, 2006, pp. 260–63.

*Journalist and poet Goenawan Mohamad at his Utan Kayu
complex in Jakarta. Utan Kayu was the target of extremist
intimidation, eventually unsuccessful, in 2005. | Pringle photo*

the death of its founder and head, Ulil Abshar-Abdalla.[5] In mid-2005 the
Islamic Defenders Front (Front Pembela Islam – FPI) tried to enlist the
support of the local mosque near Utan Kayu to drive the liberals from
the neighborhood. A tense standoff ensued over a period of months, but
after Goenawan made repeated calls for police assistance, utilizing high-
level connections from his days as a prominent editor, the police finally
intervened and the FPI backed off. It was nonetheless, by Goenawan's own
account, a close call.[6] The danger seems to have passed as far Goenawan and
his group are concerned, but as of this writing the FPI is still intimidating
other targets, sometimes violently.

The assault on the Liberal Islam Network was one result of 11 famous
religious opinions *(fatawa)* issued in 2005 by the quasi-official Indonesian
Council of Ulama (Majelis Ulama Indonesia – MUI), which ruled that
liberal and pluralistic ideologies, presumably including Pancasila itself,
should be forbidden to Muslims. The MUI coined an acronym, "SIPILIS,"
implying that secularism, pluralism and liberalism were comparable to
venereal disease.[7] As noted in the previous chapter, the MUI is, as its

5   Greg Barton, *Indonesia's Struggle: Jemaah Islamiyah and the Soul of Islam*, Sydney: University of
    New South Wales Press, 2004, p.85.
6   Interview with Goenawan Mohamad, Utan Kayu, 1 March 2007
7   Jeremy Menchik, "Illiberal but not Intolerant: Understanding the Indonesian Council of
    Ulamas," *Inside Indonesia*, 90, Oct.–Dec. 2007, http://www.insideindonesia.org.

language implies, a partisan player. Although it was government-created, its opinions are not government-approved, and it has no more authority to issue *fatawa* than anyone else with a claim to religious expertise. But not everyone understands that the MUI is not fully official, and those who agreed with its pronouncements naturally welcomed them. At the same time, prominent Muslim intellectuals, including mainstream figures, challenged the MUI edicts in a well-publicized debate.[8]

Another of the MUI's 11 *fatawa* condemned the Ahmadiyah sect as heretical, and shortly afterwards a mob attacked Ahmadiyah's headquarters in Bogor. Founded in late nineteenth-century India (now Pakistan), Ahmadiyah has had a branch in Indonesia causing controversy since the 1920s and now has about 200,000 followers there.[9] It claims to be Islamic and follows many of the tenets of Islam. But it also asserts that although Muhammad was the perfect Prophet, he was not necessarily the final one, and that Ahmadiyah's founder was a genuine (if subordinate) prophet and/or the promised Mahdi and Messiah.[10] To most Indonesian Muslims this viewpoint is unacceptably contrary to the core teachings of Islam, and Ahmadiyah's resulting unpopularity, further stimulated by its pursuit of new followers, has made it a soft target for opportunistic violence.

Ahmadiyah's relationship to Islam resembles that of Mormonism to Christianity. Mormonism, a Christian offshoot which also had its own founding prophet, was violently persecuted in the United States for many years despite the guarantee of religious freedom in the US constitution. The Mormons were forced to flee into what was then known as the Great American Desert, where they founded Salt Lake City and prospered. They eventually adopted changes in doctrine, such as disavowing polygamy, that made Mormonism acceptable to most mainstream American Christians. Ahmadiyah has thus far been unwilling to compromise in this manner.

When a group of religious rights supporters, including prominent Muslims, demonstrated in favor of Ahmadiyah at the National Monument in Jakarta on June 1, 2008, Muslim vigilantes attacked them and a dozen

---

8   Robin Bush, "Pluralism, Tolerance and Religious Freedom in Indonesia: Setbacks and Pushback in 2005," remarks at the United States-Indonesia Society, 1 Feb. 2006, Washington DC: USINDO Brief.

9   Harry J. Benda, *The Crescent and The Rising Sun: Indonesian Islam under the Japanese Occupation, 1942-45*, The Hague: Van Hoeve, 1958, pp. 50, 52, 54.

10 A good short description of Ahmadiyah can be found in Gordon D. Newby, *A Concise Encyclopedia of Islam*, Oxford: One World Publications, 2004, p. 22. Ahmadiyah's doctrine on the position of its founder – whether prophet or *mahdi* – has varied among its adherents.

were hospitalized, causing widespread public outrage. This time President Yudhoyono ordered the arrest of the attackers, including their leader. Then on June 9 the government issued a decree ordering Ahmadiyah to freeze its activities, meaning, apparently, that its followers could continue to worship but should not try to convert others. No one was pleased with this ambiguous result and at this writing it is uncertain whether the organization will be able to survive in Indonesia.[11]

When I spoke with Goenawan Mohamad about Liberal Islam's close encounter, I asked if he felt that Indonesia needs stronger legal safeguards against infringement of religious and other freedoms. He answered no, the government just needs to enforce the law, as the police finally did in his own case. Most Indonesians I spoke with felt the same way: there are enough laws, they said; what we need is timely and consistent enforcement. They were referring primarily to Article 29(2) of the Constitution, which reads, "The state guarantees the freedom of every person to worship according to his or her religion or belief."

Despite this constitutional guarantee, however, religious freedom in Indonesia is constrained and confused by a number of laws and by unwillingness to implement those that do (or should) protect it. The state recognizes only six "religions": Buddhism, Confucianism, Roman Catholicism, Protestantism, Hinduism and Islam, while other "beliefs" such as non-Islamic mysticism have separate and lower, if any, official status. Confucianism was dropped from the list in 1979, then restored to it in 2006, as part of an effort to eliminate anti-Chinese discrimination. Moreover, Pancasila, which is part of the preamble to the Constitution, enumerates belief in a singular supreme God (*Ketuhanan yang Maha Esa*) as a principle of the state, leaving animists, atheists, agnostics, non-Islamic mystics, various messianic groups and others potentially out in the cold.

According to census statistics only 0.2 percent of all Indonesians do not profess one of the fully recognized faiths, a figure which is absurdly low. It results partly from widespread cheating in order to obtain an official identity card, required for everyone, which identifies the holder's religion and is necessary to obtain such major government services as health care. Islam is the only faith for which one does not have to present proof of religion to obtain a card, resulting in a sizeable cohort of "Identity Card Muslims"

---

11 For a detailed account of the Ahmadiyah controversy see ICG, *Indonesia: Implications of the Ahmadiyah Affair*, Asia Briefing No.78, 7 July 2008.

(for obvious reasons no one knows how many there are). This anomaly is probably due less to religious bias than to bureaucratic inertia; it originated as part of the Suharto-era drive to stamp out the embers of communism by requiring everyone to "have a religion (*beragama*)." Another law dating to the Sukarno era, but recently revised and strengthened, prohibits slander against, or the false interpretation of, the core principles of any of the six recognized faiths. Like the recognition regime itself, this law is open to abuse. The officials and police who are charged with enforcing it are hardly experts on theology.[12]

Among the most widely publicized efforts to restrict individual freedom (or licentiousness, depending on your point of view) is the anti-pornography law introduced in 2006. The original legislation prohibited practically anything that might arouse lust, including kissing in public and immodest female dress. It appealed to genuine fear among many Indonesian Muslims that they are losing the battle, not to another religion, but to rampant secularism – the same fear that plagues many devoutly religious people elsewhere, including Christians. The legislation was nonetheless seen by others, including some mainstream Muslim leaders, as going too far and being un-Indonesian in its disregard for diversity.

Papuans and Balinese charged that such a law might stigmatize their traditional dress, or absence thereof, and some Balinese threatened secession. Women, artists and poets were outraged. Women wanted to know why it was always female, never male, behavior that was seen as a threat to morality. Dangdut dancer Inul Daratista, the possessor of the most famous posterior in Indonesia, if not in the world, got into the act, protesting that she was a good Muslim and warning that her neighbors would protect her against violence (one of her karaoke lounges had been attacked by a mob). The protests worked up to a point and the legislation was withdrawn, but parliament passed a toned-down version in 2008. At last word a group of Balinese lawyers were challenging the law's constitutionality before the Constitutional Court.

The underlying problem, the weakness and inconsistency of Indonesian law on freedom of religion and expression, remains unsolved. My own opinion is that Indonesia will continue to attract justified international criticism until it enacts and enforces, if not a bill of rights, then something

---

12   For material in previous two paragraphs see Robin Bush, "One Step Forward…" in *Inside Indonesia* 89, Jan.–March 2007.

else that will clarify and enforce basic, internationally recognized freedoms. The state also needs to act consistently to curb religious vigilantism. Until it does so the country will not fully realize the moral benefit that its democracy and diversity warrant.

Intimidation is not a problem restricted to urban areas or to the harassment of controversial sects. Historian Merle Ricklefs has documented recent episodes in rural areas of Java where militant Reformists have bullied and browbeaten co-religionists who do not adhere to fundamentalist beliefs. He suggests that what appears to be ongoing growth in conversion to Christianity in urban areas of Java such as Solo (Surakarta) may result at least in part from reaction to well-publicized fundamentalist excesses.[13]

Extremism by a Thousand Cuts?
Local Sharia Law and Stealth Tactics

Another phenomenon frequently cited as a harbinger of creeping Islamic extremism is the widespread issuance of sharia or sharia look-alike regulations at the district and city level, known as *peraturan daerah*, or just "*perda*" in common parlance. These edicts have included restrictions on the activities of women, like the proposed female curfew in West Sumatra; anti-prostitution and other anti-sin ordinances; requirements for Muslims to prove knowledge of the Koran as a condition for government employment, marriage or admission to university; and restrictions on church construction in Muslim areas and on mosques in Christian areas (e.g. in Papua). Many of them have been issued in regions where the Darul Islam movement was strongest, which have historically favored Islamic statedom. Interestingly, such regulations have often been introduced not by hard-line Muslims, but by non-Muslim politicians seeking to appease Muslim constituents.

The sharia regulations are one aspect of Indonesia's new and sometimes frenetic decentralized democracy, where everyone gets to vote for six different officials: president, members of parliament (both houses), provincial governor, district head or city mayor, member of district or city assembly, and village head. The greatest shift in democratic power has been from Jakarta to the district/city level, covering about 460 entities (the number constantly changes). It is there that fledgling politicians, including non-

---

13 M.C. Ricklefs, "Religion, Politics and Social Dynamics in Java: Historical and Contemporary Rhymes" in Greg Fealey and Sally White, eds., *Expressing Islam: Religious Life and Politics in Indonesia*, Singapore: Institute of Southeast Asian Studies, 2008, esp. pp. 122–33.

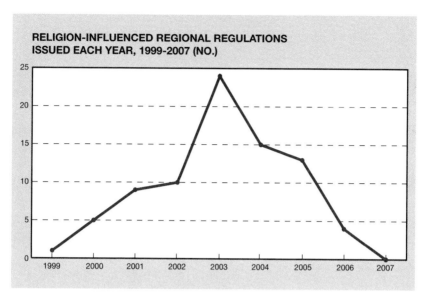

RELIGION-INFLUENCED REGIONAL REGULATIONS ISSUED EACH YEAR, 1999-2007 (NO.)

Approximately eighty local regulations supposedly based on sharia law, or in some cases on Biblical strictures, have been issued since 1999. However, as indicated by this chart, the number of these religious and morality decrees issued each year declined sharply after 2005 and stopped in 2006, apparently because they proved to be unpopular. | "Figure 10.3: Religion-influenced Regional Regulations Issued Each Year, 1999-2007 (no.)" first appeared in Expressing Islam: Religious Life and Politics in Indonesia *edited Greg Fealy and Sally White (2008), p. 179. Reproduced with the kind permission of the publisher, Institute of Southeast Asian Studies, Singapore.*

Muslims, have tried to please everyone, including the most conservative (or politically extreme) Muslims.

What seems most disturbing about the local religious regulations is that they are apparently illegal. Indonesia is not a federal system, meaning that it was not formed by independent states coming together, granting certain powers to the center, and retaining for themselves whatever powers were left. Rather it is a centralized state which has delegated certain enumerated powers to the local level and retained those that were not delegated. Purposely, the powers given to the districts in 1999 did not include religion, because the framers of the decentralization law felt that having different religious regimes by district would be unsettling. (Aceh is an exception; as noted earlier, Jakarta gave it authority to enact sharia law at the provincial level as part of the peace process.)

There are several ways that the central government could annul such local regulations, including a decision from the Ministry of Interior or a Constitutional Court ruling. As of 2008, the most informed explanation of why the regulations had not been challenged was that President Bambang Susilo Yudhoyono, not seen as a pious Muslim himself, was dependent on Muslim party members to get his most important legislation through a narrowly divided parliament. He did not wish to offend potential supporters on issues deemed to be of lesser importance. In other major democracies this kind of political behavior is known as "pandering." It is seen as mildly reprehensible, but hardly abnormal, much less undemocratic.

Only recently has it become evident that *perda* issuance peaked in 2003 and may have been a temporary phenomenon. As of early 2009, none had been issued since 2006, when there were five.[14] What happened? The decline in *perda* issuance coincided with the beginning of direct elections for local officials who were previously indirectly elected by local legislatures. This coincidence suggests that politicians facing the test of direct elections discovered that the religious regulations offended more citizens than they pleased. If so, this is a case where Indonesia's democracy has been working after all, however slowly.

The government's reluctance to implement the law against illegal local ordinances suggested that Indonesia might well be vulnerable to another kind of creeping Islamic extremism: not intimidation per se, but the exploitation of political democracy and freedom of expression to pursue anti-democratic ends, and the use of "stealth" tactics to conceal power grabs. It will be recalled that the radical Jemaah Islamiyah split on exactly this point after the first Bali bombing: whether or not it might be more effective to bore from within Indonesia's democracy rather than risk death by indulging in highly unpopular episodes of terrorism in public places.

In recent years the most publicized alleged practitioner of extremism-by-stealth has been the Prosperous Justice Party or PKS (Partai Keadilan Sejahtera – formerly PK, Partai Keadilan). Here is the way a leading believer in the power of creeping Islamization in Indonesia looks at the PKS:

> Of the two [violent-extremist Jemaah Islamiyah and the PKS], the Justice Party [PKS] is by far the larger threat to Indonesia. With its suicide bombings Jemaah Islamiya has set itself up for a confrontation with the government that it cannot hope to win.

---

14 The decline of *perda* popularity and its cause is explained in Robin Bush, "Regional Regulations in Indonesia: Anomaly or Symptom?" in Fealy and White, eds., *Expressing Islam*, esp. p. 179.

In contrast, the Justice Party uses its position in parliament and its metastasizing network of cadres to advance the same goals incrementally, one vote at a time. At the same time, by throwing its weight behind Jemaah Islamiya's Bashir, the party complicates the government's efforts to crack down on terrorists. Indeed, peaceful methods aside, the Justice Party's success can only help terrorists: the more people believe that the problem with society is too much modernity, and that a purified Islam is an answer to twenty-first-century problems, the more likely it is that hotheads among them will use terrorism to achieve their goals.[15]

Founded in 1998, the PKS is a spin-off of the fragmented Reformist movement. Many observers agree that it does have fervently Islamic, if not radical, goals despite its position as a member of President Yudhoyono's parliamentary coalition. But since these goals are still not popular among mainstream Muslims, the PKS has downplayed or disguised them and emphasized clean government and the battle against corruption: like the Fascists in Italy it would make the trains run on time. The PKS slogan for the 2009 elections was "clean, caring and professional."[16] This approach has appealed to many voters who are not particularly interested in the party's religious agenda.

The PKS has also profited from its disciplined, cell-type organization, inherited from its roots in the Suharto-era, campus-based *tarbiyah* (education) movement, its effective use of the internet, and its brainy, well-educated following.[17] The party pioneered in the development of "integrated" Islamic education, which seeks to infuse Islamic values into the entire curriculum rather than teaching them as a separate subject, an effort which has earned the respect of many Muslim intellectuals and has

15 Sadanand Dhume, "Indonesian Democracy's Enemy Within: Radical Islamic party Threatens Indonesia with Ballots more than Bullets," *Yale Global*, 1 Dec. 2005, accessed Feb. 2008 at www.http://www.yaleglobal.yale.edu/article.print?id=6579. See also his more recent book, *My Friend the Fanatic: Travels with an Indonesian Islamist*, Camberwell, VIC: Penguin Group (Australia), 2008. Dhume's views on Indonesia's intimidation problem have moderated following the poor showing of the pro-sharia parties, including the PKS, in the 2009 elections, discussed below.

16 R. William Liddle and Saiful Mujani, "From Transition to Democratization," ms. from forthcoming book on democratization, courtesy of the authors.

17 Robert W. Hefner, *Islam in Indonesia's Political Future*, Alexandria VA: CNA Corporation Center for Strategic Studies, 2002, p. 34; Saiful Mujani and R. William Liddle. "Muslim Indonesia's Secular Democracy," *Asian Survey*, July–Aug 2009, pp. 581–82.

parallels among Christian fundamentalists in the West.[18]

The PKS has disavowed support for the Jakarta Charter[19] (symbolizing Islamic statedom) in favor of a Medina-style charter (or constitution), referring to the brief period in early Islamic history when Jews, Christians and Muslims lived together in Medina under a pluralistic system established by the Prophet. The concept of the Medina Charter suggests tolerance and was earlier proposed as a possible guide for contemporary Indonesia by renowned Muslim intellectual Nurcholish Madjid, a champion of pluralism. The PKS has even gone so far as to nominate Christian candidates for certain elections in Papua, in line with its support of the Medina Charter.

However, critics of the PKS note that espousing the Medina Charter can also be read as an advocacy of an Islamic state model under which "people of the book" (Jews and Christians) are indeed tolerated, but only as *dhimmi*, people subject to Islamic political supremacy. The critics maintain that disavowal of the Jakarta Charter is just a smokescreen; the true objective of the PKS is indicated by its alleged efforts to gain control of mainstream Muhammadiyah by boring from within the organization.

The obfuscation-cum-stealth strategy of the PKS, if that is what it is, worked well at first, to the point of increasing its share of the vote from less than two to about eight percent between 1999 and 2004.[20] But in 2009 its share of the vote increased by less than one percent, far short of its 15 percent goal, although it still fared better than any other Muslim party. The PKS record in recent local elections has been mixed, including significant victories in gubernatorial races in West Java and North Sumatra in 2008, proving that it can still attract voters looking for change when it has appealing candidates. But as the party begins to look more and more like just another opportunistic political party it has started to lose its idealistic following among students, who were its original constituency,[21] and it has arguably become far too well known to be truly stealthy.

If stealth isn't working, what about intimidation? In short, the verdict is still out. Thus far, not too many Indonesians seem to have been intimidated. But many are concerned about the possibility, much as many Christians in the West are concerned about the political inroads of fervent, fundamentalist

---

18 Robert W. Hefner, "Islamic Schools, Reform Movements, and Democracy in Indonesia," in Hefner, ed., *Making Modern Muslims: The Politics of Islamic Education in Indonesia*, Honolulu: University of Hawaii Press, 2009, pp. 73–74.
19 Lilian Budianto, "PKS rejects idea of Islamic state," *Jakarta Post*, 28 April 2008.
20 Mujani and Liddle, "Muslim Indonesia's Secular Democracy," p. 581.
21 Interview with Saiful Mujani and Anies Baswedan, March 2, 2007.

Christianity. If so, why do moderate Muslims not speak out more strongly against obvious abuse of political freedom when it occurs? Why are they so quick to criticize the use of armed force against real, armed terrorists, as they did in the case of the police raid in Poso in January 2007, which seems to have been effective against undoubted criminals? Why are they so prone to paranoid conspiracy theorizing in which Muslims, whether in the Middle East or at home, are always the victims?

Partly it's because Muslims in Indonesia have not yet gotten over the persecution of the early Suharto years, or the heritage of their own historical marginalization. The violence and sectarian conflict that followed Suharto's fall increased Indonesian sensitivity to reports of violence against Muslims worldwide. Christian missionary activity in Indonesia, often well funded, has remained an irritant capable in some cases of stimulating violent extremism, as noted in Chapter 6. The uncharted waters of competitive democracy have resulted in heightened ethnic and religious sensitivity and assertiveness across the board.

In addition, many mainstream Muslims have genuinely conservative religious views. Such people often share with their conservative counterparts in the Christian West a fear that profane secular norms and habits are getting completely out of hand. They don't like much of what they see on the internet and they fear its popularity with youth. They are not sympathetic to the Muslim liberals, who tend to flaunt their liberalism a little too much, and certainly not to apostates like Ahmadiyah. All this does not, however, add up to a satisfactory explanation.

There have been encouraging signs. The same shift in public opinion that gradually eroded support for violent extremism also made flamboyant verbal militancy less appealing. In early 2006 the Majelis Mujahidin Indonesia (MMI) issued a statement reversing its earlier definition of "jihad" as including the use of violence.[22] In tandem with its successful anti-terror efforts, the government began to reassert the importance of pluralism, most notably when President Yudhoyono gave a major speech endorsing tolerance, pluralism and Pancasila and implicitly rejecting the notion that people of one religious persuasion could dictate morality for all Indonesians.[23] Yudhoyono's subsequent failure to act decisively against the persecution of Ahmadiyah was a clear step backwards, no doubt driven

---

22   Robin Bush, "Pluralism, Tolerance and Religious Freedom," p. 3.
23   Rendi Akhmad Witular, "SBY Urges end to debate on Pancasila's Merits," *Jakarta Post*, June 2, 2006.

by pre-election year politics and his dependence on Muslim votes. But the record of election results, indicating long-term Islamic moderation at the political center, is still a valid indicator of long-term trends, despite the real flaws in Indonesia's protection of religious freedom.

Ballot Boxes and Pollsters

Indonesia has had four free and fair national elections since independence: in 1955, 1999, 2004 and 2009. In 1955, 42 percent of voters favored parties advocating an Islamic state (the Jakarta Charter, or a state based on sharia law). Since then that minority has declined to less than half its strength in 1955: 14 percent in 1999, over 15 percent in 2004, and about 13 percent in 2009. [24]

These numbers are not exact and must be treated with caution. The figure of 42 percent for the pro-Islamic state vote in 1955 was probably an exaggeration and should be substantially discounted, although just how much is impossible to know. As explained in Chapter 3, Islamic statehood was not a well-defined issue in the 1955 election, and inclusion of the NU as supporting it is particularly questionable. It also needs to be kept in mind that for a variety of reasons not all supporters of Islamic statehood necessarily vote for a party that endorses that goal.

It is nonetheless clear that over more than half a century only about one-fifth of the electorate, representing about one-quarter of the Muslim population, has supported the idea of a state in which Islam, the majority religion, would at minimum be the basic principle of government, as opposed to the Pancasila principle under which all religions which recognize one supreme god have equal status. If anything, the pro-Islamic state vote has declined; it has certainly not increased. The consistency of this voting pattern is all the more remarkable given the "piety boom" – the spread of Islam among previously non-observant Muslims, which accompanied the growing prosperity of the Suharto era. Using the old Geertzian terminology, it seems that many of those nominally Muslim *abangan* who became observant Muslim *santri*, after brief flirtations with Hinduism and Christianity, have now become more pious as well as more affluent, but have not changed their voting habits.

---

24 See discussion in Chapter 3 for 1955 figures; 1999, 2004 and 2009 figures are based on National Election Commission statistics cited in Mujani and Liddle, "Muslim Indonesia's Secular Democracy," p. 581.

The results of local elections in decentralized Indonesia – about 500 of them between 2005 and 2009 – offer additional evidence that even muted fundamentalism is having a hard time at the polls. Having concealed or downplayed its religious objectives, the PKS has been able to win only in coalition with other parties. To be sure, most elections in Indonesia are won by coalitions. Still it is striking that "less than five percent of [local] contests are won outright by Islamist [pro-sharia] party candidates *and no party or candidate has been successful by running on an Islamic law platform* [emphasis added]. "[25] Indeed religion and ideology seem to be ignored in local contests, which remain focused on issues affecting voter welfare and in which incumbents have been ousted about 40 percent of the time.[26]

Indonesia now has sophisticated public opinion polling which offers additional insights on voter preferences. In general, voters asked to comment on Islamic issues respond in a manner which emphasizes their support for Muslim values. No surprise, then, that a typical poll in 2002 showed 71 percent of respondents favoring sharia.[27] Such numbers set off alarm bells for non-Muslim westerners, but it must be remembered that "sharia" means the whole corpus of Islamic doctrine, beginning with the fundamentals: belief in one God and the other pillars of the faith.

It is thus not surprising that Indonesian Muslims respond to questions about whether they favor sharia in much the same way that many Christians do when asked if they believe in Christian values. A positive response does not reveal how the respondent may feel about abortion, gay clergy, stem cell research or evolution; a positive response in Indonesia does not reveal how the respondent may feel about cutting off thieves' hands, polygamy, or theocratic rule.[28] Most people everywhere want to be faithful to the tenets of their respective faiths as long as they are not required to do things that are difficult or abhorrent for them.

To get at specific issues, pollsters have learned, more specific questions must be asked. In the 2002 poll cited above, fewer than half as many respondents favored harsh measures (such as government-enforced fasting, or the severe penal code of the Wahabi) as those who favored sharia in

---

25 Douglas E. Ramage, "A Reformed Indonesia," *Australian Financial Review*, 12 Oct 2007, p. 2.
26 *Ibid*, p. 2.
27 Saiful Mujani and R. William Liddle, "Politics, Islam and Public Opinion." *Journal of Democracy*, Vol. 15, No. 1, Jan 2004, p. 113.
28 Interview with Anes Baswedan, Feb. 13, 2007.

principle.[29] And of course, as explained in Chapter 5, there is no such thing as universally agreed upon or codified sharia law.

Additional polling conducted from 2004 to 2008 indicated a decline in support for extreme measures (opposition to a female president declined from 41% to 22% during this period) and a noticeable increase in support for the major secular/nationalist political parties, Golkar and PDI-P, as compared to Muslim parties of all kinds. That trend seems to have been born out by the decline in pro-Islamic state electoral support between 2004 and 2009, and a more general decline in support for all five major Muslim parties, three of which support Islamic statehood, from 36% to 26% in the same period.[30]

Nonetheless, although many fewer Indonesians favor harsh sharia-based measures than support sharia in the abstract, the level of extremist sentiment expressed in some polling is still disturbing.[31] A 2007 poll in the series cited above also showed that one-fifth of respondents still favored executing apostates and approved of the attacks on the World Trade Center. In other recent polling substantial support, ranging up to one-half of respondents, has been shown for jailing those who misinterpret the Koran, stoning adulterers, not allowing the Ahmadiyah sect to exist, favoring government regulation of female dress (57%), restricting women's mobility at night, and even approving of the generally unpopular Bali bombings. It should be noted that some of the inconsistency in the polling probably results from variations in sample selection.[32]

Taken together, the evidence from both the ballot box and public

---

29 Mujani and Liddle, "Politics, Islam and Public Opinion," pp. 113ff. See also 2004–2006 polling conducted by Robert Hefner cited in Hefner, "Islamic Schools, Social Movements and Democracy," pp. 92-3, which gives a slightly lower but comparable proportion favoring sharia in the abstract versus harsh, allegedly sharia-based punishment.

30 The five are PAN, PBB, PKB, PKS and PPP, of which PBB, PKS and PPP support Islamic statehood. See list of political parties at the end of this book.

31 From polls conducted by Lembaga Survei Indonesia described in Mujani and Liddle, "Muslim Indonesia's Secular Democracy."

32 See, for example, polls conducted by the Center for the Study of Islam and Society (PPIM – Pusat Pengkajian Islam dan Masyarakat) of the National Islamic University (UIN) Syarif Hidayatullah in Jakarta, cited in Greg Barton, "Indonesia's Year of Living Normally: Taking the Long View on Indonesia's Progress," in Daljit Singh and Tin Maung Maung Than, eds., *Southeast Asian Affairs 2008*, Singapore: Institute of Southeast Asian Studies, pp. 134–37. Positive results for regulation of female dress and mobility are from a 2008 USAID poll, "Indonesia Democracy and Democratic Governance Issues – 2008" http://www.usindo.org/publications/briefs/index.html accessed March 2009. The results of Indonesian public opinion polling vary considerably depending on sample selection. For example the PPIM polling was restricted to Muslims as opposed to the Lembaga Survei Indonesia's nationally representative sample.

opinion polling leads to substantially the same conclusion: that there is a historically stable mass of Indonesian Muslims constituting a majority of the entire population who are averse to religious extremism, although often supportive of religious conservatism. They are represented *inter alia* by the two umbrella organizations, Nahdlatul Ulama and Muhammadyah, unique to Indonesia, both justifiably described as "mainstream." These organizations, Traditionalist and Reformist respectively, are "big tents" with substantial internal differences, and they can and do work with each other despite broad philosophical and doctrinal differences. Their moderation stands in contrast to a persistent minority with both domestic and foreign antecedents whose members embrace either peaceful fundamentalism or, a minority within a minority, violent extremism.

The political consistency of Islam in modern Indonesia can, I believe, be partly explained by the nature of Indonesian diversity, a phenomenon which is expressed, celebrated and strengthened by a many-facetted national mythology, a subject explored in the next chapter.

8

The Resilience of Diversity: A Summing Up

In 2000 Thomas Friedman wrote a column describing a category of states that are "too big to fail; too messy to work."[1] Friedman's examples included both Russia and Indonesia, and had he written five years later he might have added his own country, the United States, by then rancorously deadlocked over crucial issues including the war in Iraq, immigration and health care. "Messiness" can have many components, but in developing countries, ethnic and religious divisions, exacerbated by historical and regional complications, often head the list, with the Balkans as the classic example.

Americans have a double standard about diversity. They see American diversity as an asset for many reasons – the genius of our Founding Parents, who (we think) invented federalism, and our skill as compromisers and political managers. Our diversity is OK because we know how to put everyone in a big pot and melt them down, except maybe when there are just too many immigrants. It gives our system energy, creativity and aesthetic appeal. But we often regard other people's diversity as dangerous. Developing countries have not yet learned how to handle it. They have "tribes" rather than benign linguistic categories like "Hispanic." Their pots aren't melting nearly fast enough. They don't yet understand the difference between non-lethal political competition and mortal combat.

In other words the United States, like most countries, has a national mythology, which its citizens use as a basis for comparison in judging other countries. Like most, the American mythology is a blend of selected, positive

---

1   Thomas Friedman, "Wahid's New-Look Indonesia is Frankly a Mess," *International Herald Tribune*, October 4, 2000, p 8., cited by Donald K. Emmerson, "What is Indonesia?" in John Bresnan, ed., *Indonesia: The Great Transition*, Lanham MD: Rowman and Littlefield, 2005, p. 72, n. 73.

historical facts and outright fiction (e.g., the fable of George Washington confessing to his father that he had indeed cut down the cherry tree, a myth which enshrines honesty and courage as national values). National mythology leaves out or downplays corrosive unpleasantness (genocide against Native Americans for example). Or it converts national disasters like the American Civil War into sources of inspiration (with a little help from Abraham Lincoln). But for all its fictional or fiddled aspects, the American national mythology is essentially true, which is why it helps us to maintain faith in the future – "the audacity of hope," as Barack Hussein Obama has phrased it.

Indonesia's National Mythology

As we have seen, Indonesia's founders were acutely aware of the need for a national mythology, and they did a much better job of creating one than most people – including some Indonesians – seem to realize. Their founders had been told by the Dutch *ad nauseum* that all those islands could never be one country, and they needed to prove otherwise. They aimed for "Indonesia" (singular) in place of the East Indies (plural). As we have seen, they happily accepted the gift of a national language, the already ubiquitous "Malay" which the Dutch had helped to establish as an Indies-wide official lingua franca, and renamed it "Indonesian."

The Dutch tried to play on differences in every way possible. In 1946 they dangled a poison-pill federation, to be under Dutch control of course, hoping to woo away regions wary of Javanese control. The tactic didn't work, but it took half a century for Indonesians to forget it sufficiently to realize that empowerment of local governments, however risky and problem-ridden, makes sense. The Dutch made customary local law (*adat*) into a component of national law, along with legal distinctions for "foreign orientals" (mostly Chinese) and of course for Europeans. The Indonesian nationalists fought back by reference to pre-colonial empires, especially Majapahit, which Dutch scholars had researched for them. They piled on the necessary symbols: national flag, national anthem, national hat (the famous *peci* that Sukarno always wore). Eventually the Dutch did them the ultimate favor of provoking a national revolution, costly to be sure, but extraordinarily effective as a nation-building force. (Where would the United States have been without George III?)

The Indonesians recognized that while diversity might be a long-term asset it was a huge short-term problem, for all the reasons the Dutch cited.

Both communist and radical Islamic insurgencies within the national, anti-Dutch struggle drove home the point. Fortunately the Indonesians had Sukarno, who insisted with unflagging energy and eloquence that every single Dutch East Indian could, regardless of ethnic or religious attributes, be an Indonesian. "Look at me," he cried, "I, Sukarno, am everything!" The more that fervent Muslims faulted him for ignoring the fine print of their faith, the more he persevered, eventually ruling by decree and proclaiming a national ideology that mixed the unmixable: nationalism, religion and communism. He crossed the line into logical absurdity and Indonesia melted down into Muslim-Communist fratricide in 1965–66, leading to three decades of military rule. Based on that, many foreigners judged Sukarno to have been an irresponsible demagogue and a failure. But he is looking better in retrospect, essential in his time both as architect and component of Indonesia's identity. This is certainly the way he is regarded by most Indonesians today.

As explained in Chapter 2, Sukarno and his colleagues originated Indonesia's pluralistic national philosophy, Pancasila, with its fundamental element of belief in an undefined almighty god-ness, a formula that seems to accord with Indonesia's diversity, notwithstanding decades of subsequent dissent by a minority of Muslims. Less appreciated is the sophistication of the national motto, Bhinneka Tunggal Ika, usually translated "Unity in Diversity," which suggests that although diversity is desirable, maybe inevitable, it can also be stressful, even risky. I have been unable to find out who originated the slogan in 1950. It was probably Muhammad Yamin, a passionate nationalist writer and politician from West Sumatra, and he may have been partially inspired by the US equivalent, E Pluribus Unum, although neither of these points is certain. In any case it is hard to imagine a guiding dictum more appropriate for a large, multicultural state.

Diversity is not an abstract concept in Indonesia; it is visible in the streets, in music, dress, architecture and the arts, in folklore and humor, and as a source of national pride. It can be smelled and tasted in street food, arguably the best eating in the country. Much Indonesian cuisine is presented as the specialty of region x or y: *Sate Madura* (Madura kebab), *Soto Banjar* (Banjar Soup), *Ayam Goreng Yogya* (Yogyakarta fried chicken), proclaimed on banners above simmering pushcarts. At the airport when a domestic flight arrives you can often identify its place of origin by the edible souvenirs that disembarking passengers are carrying.

Regional stereotypes abound. Indonesians are proud of beautiful

Hindu Bali, but irritated when foreigners go there without visiting other attractions in Indonesia – sometimes without even realizing that Hindu Bali is part of Indonesia. However, although the Balinese are great for tourism, their art and culture is a bit too noisy, colorful and direct, especially for the Javanese. As for the Javanese, they – at least the upper classes – are exquisitely refined; but the most powerful Javanese are the grotesque, farting clowns of the *wayang* world, who are in fact gods, controlling the super-cool aristocrats and death-dealing warriors. Everyone knows that the Acehnese grow high-grade marijuana and use it as a condiment in their cooking: no wonder they are a bit crazy. The Protestant Batak Christians of North Sumatra are direct and garrulous; some of them have been known to brag to Americans that their forebears were cannibals who ate the first American missionaries to enter the Batak homeland. As stereotype would have it, the Protestant Bataks are exceeded in their pushiness only by the fervently Islamic Madurese.

Humor is the lubricant of Indonesia's diversity. The Javanese infatuation with mysticism (both Islamic and pre-Islamic) is a national joke. President Abdurrahman Wahid's midnight séances at the tombs of saints, not to mention his assignations with the Queen of the Southern Ocean, a potent, pre-Islamic deity, drew criticism from more conventional clerics but also amused the citizenry. Sukarno's (mis)behavior, which often reflected his eclectic world view, was also a source of endless gossip, resentment and amusement. In the mid-1950s he hired a Christian Batak architect-friend to design the great Istiqlal Mosque in Jakarta's central square, the biggest Muslim house of worship in Southeast Asia. When it was finished, news immediately flew around town that there were 12 columns supporting its central dome, which is true. The story continued that the architect had inserted them in the design to represent the 12 apostles of Christianity, which was probably *not* true, but too funny not to be gleefully repeated.[2]

The Istiqlal mosque is adjacent to another of Sukarno's creations, the National Monument ("Monas"), a towering column standing on a flaring base, a massively unsubtle version of the Hindu linga-yoni symbols representing male and female sexual organs. Inevitably, it was soon referred to as "Sukarno's Last Erection." It must be offensive to some Muslims, but as far as I know no one has proposed that it be de-erected. As elsewhere, religious humor in

---

2   On the Istiqlal Mosque see Hugh O'Neil, "Islamic Architecture under the New Order" in V.M. Hooker, ed., *Culture and Society in New Order Indonesia*, Kuala Lumpur: Oxford University Press, 1993, pp. 156–58.

The Istliqlal Mosque in Jakarta, Indonesia's largest, was designed by an architect friend of Sukarno's who happened to be a Christian Batak from North Sumatra. This inevitably set off tongue-in-cheek speculation that the 12 central pillars supporting the massive dome, several of them visible here, must have been intended to represent the Twelve Apostles of Christianity. | Leo Indrawan photo

Indonesia can sometimes get a bit tasteless. In January 2008, at the time of former President Suharto's death, the weekly *Tempo* did a lead story on his career with a cover depicting the general as Christ at the Last Supper, surrounded by his most famous/notorious henchmen. Catholics protested, and *Tempo* apologized and replaced the cover on its web site.

When I visited Indonesia in early 2007 speculation about rampant intimidation was at its height, so I tried to find evidence of it. Goenawan Mohamad and his liberals had been targeted by mobs, but certainly not silenced. There is a great deal of Islamic literature in bookstores representing all points on the political spectrum, but alongside it are books on Christianity and mysticism, in numbers roughly proportional to each belief's share of the Indonesian population.[3]

True, women at all levels of society are wearing headscarves more than they used to, but the reasons are complex. Partly it's a matter of global style. Headscarves are in fashion throughout the Muslim world, notwithstanding controversy almost everywhere. They need not appear

---

3   Based on visits to the Gramedia bookstore chain, operated by a Roman Catholic-owned
     publishing house.

dowdy or demeaning: "Islamic chic" modes are widespread, not least in Indonesia. Among younger Indonesians, headscarves combined with tight jeans and form-fitting bodices are common. But when anthropologist Nancy Smith-Hefner did research on headscarves in Central Java she found that young ladies, often from families that have never sent their daughters to school in big cities before, utilize the headscarf to send a signal to young men not to attempt unwanted advances.[4]

Headscarves are also one example of a broader trend towards the conscious advertisement of ethnic and religious identity. It comes to a peak at wedding time, when the parents of mixed couples negotiate the details of how each family's regional dress will be featured in the ceremony. Indonesia's ethnic Chinese used to be cautious about wearing Chinese dress for fear of arousing nationalist prejudice. But today they habitually do so, especially around Chinese New Year which has become a high-profile national holiday.

The arts remain as pluralistic as ever. I spoke with artists, teachers and educators, and found no one cowed by the menace of Islamic intimidation. One of my interviewees was the Minangkabau filmmaker Nia Dinata whose films are often about potentially sensitive subjects, such as polygamy (*Shared Husband* – a critical account, based partly on personal experience) and homosexuality (*The Gathering* – a sympathetic account). She looked at me in mild disbelief when I asked her if she was worried about hard-line Muslim pressure, although she admitted to getting occasional nasty e-mails As a matter of common sense, she avoids prurient or otherwise tasteless content that would be cut anyway by the multi-religious government censors who review all films. But none of this seems to have crimped her style; what bothers her much more than puritanical pressure is the difficulty of competing with unrestrained foreign imports, which are favored by Indonesia's quasi-monopolistic theater owners.[5]

Specifically Islamic art remains relatively rare in Indonesia. A.D. Pirous, an Acehnese painter resident in Bandung, has probably done more than anyone else to promote art which reflects the spirit of Islam. In 2002 he pioneered a series of Islamic art festivals held at the Istiqlal Mosque in Jakarta, the same one designed by Sukarno's Batak friend. In his own

---

4   Nancy J. Smith-Hefner, "Javanese Women and the Veil in Post-Soeharto Indonesia," *Journal of Asian Studies*, Vol. 66, No. 2, May 2007, pp. 389–420.
5   Interview with Nia Dinata, 26 Feb. 2007; see also Jane Perlez, "Indonesian Filmmaker's Personal Take on Polygamy," *New York Times*, 26 Aug. 2006, p. A3.

work he uses a mixture of styles, abstract and representational, as well as calligraphy. He says there is no Islamic injunction against representational art. Pirous is most interested in using art to campaign against war and human suffering, and he did so effectively to publicize the impact of the 2004 tsunami on his home province.[6]

Pirous' house-studio in Bandung is not far from a studio-gallery-restaurant complex belonging to a wealthy Balinese sculptor who is making a 146 meter tall statue of the Hindu God Shiva on his mount, the mythical bird Garuda. It is being shipped to Bali in sections, to be reassembled not far from the airport. Some may think it tasteless, a monumental display of Balinese kitsch, but there have been no complaints from Muslims, who know that Bali has the right to be Bali.

I had also heard that mosque architecture was being influenced by increasing Islamic piety, and that new mosques, funded with money from Saudi Arabia and elsewhere, were now uniformly being built in "Arabic," onion-dome style. Onion domes are not really "Arab" at all, but descended from Byzantine models. That aside, Indonesian mosques are still being built in a wide variety of styles, the choice of which seems primarily to reflect local taste. Sukarno's Istliqlal Mosque with its huge dome would be at home in any Middle Eastern city. In contrast, Suharto's mosque-building program of the 1980s used a standardized version of the Javanese pagoda style, modeled on an ancient prototype in Demak, Central Java, but topped by a five-sided Pancasila emblem surrounding the word "Allah" in Arabic script, a touch which no doubt irritated the minority of Muslims who see the state philosophy as anti-Islamic.[7]

While the pagoda form is still dominant on Java, syncretically inclined congregations who want to demonstrate up-to-dateness can buy shiny, prefabricated metal onion domes from roadside vendors to top off their pagoda-style mosques. These come in all sizes, some with Buddhist-style finials just to hype the diversity a bit more. Truly magnificent examples of pagoda-style mosques, some of them centuries old, can be found on Java and also in the Minangkabau province of West Sumatra; the trip there is worth it for them alone.

---

6   Interview with A.D. Pirous, 2 Feb. 2007; see also his collected articles in *Melukis Itu Menulis*, Bandung: Penerbit ITB, 2003.
7   O'Neil, "Islamic Architecture under the New Order," pp. 159–61; also (no author) *Masjid YAMP*, Jakarta: Yayasan Amalbakti Muslim Pancasila, 2004, esp p. 11. This book was published by the Suharto foundation which built his standardized mosques.

Javanese Not-Quite-Hegemony

Many multi-cultural states have problems with a dominant ethnic group resented by all the others. What, then, about the role of Java and the Javanese? Ethnic Java, not counting West Java, which is not Javanese but Sundanese, has roughly one-third of Indonesia's population on a little over one-tenth of its land area. The island of Java is geographically "Inner" Indonesia; the rest is "Outer." It was the crown jewel of the Dutch Empire. It has the national capital (Jakarta), the biggest seaport (Surabaya), and most of the industry – although not most of the natural resources. Five of Indonesia's six presidents since independence have been Javanese. Java has arguably the most intense culture, due to its long, heavily Indianized past, leading its upper classes to put on airs. Because they provided clerks and officials for the colonial regime, the Javanese got a head start in formal education and administrative experience. However, they have never controlled the national economy, thanks in part to the powerful role of the ethnic Chinese and the commercial energy of certain other groups, including the Muslim Minangkabau and Buginese.

To the extent that it does exist, Javanese political domination has certainly stirred some resentment. It was a factor in the 1958 Outer Islands Rebellion and aggravated Acehnese separatism. Javanese pervasiveness in the military and the bureaucracy has never been popular beyond Java, to cite just two of many problems. But one may nonetheless wonder why the Javanese role in Indonesia has not been far more divisive than it has.

Part of the answer is that the Javanese language, highly stratified (unlike Malay-Indonesian), with different vocabularies for speaking to people of different social status, is not the national language. Had it been, there might well have been more trouble. But the Javanese never pressed for such a thing, and there has never been a serious Javanese nationalist movement in modern times. The Javanese ability to minimize the onus of hegemony is usually attributed to Javanese tolerance, derived from the Hindu assumption that all religions are part of one great spiritual stream. "We Javanese can get along with Christians and Buddhists. We see truth in all religions and are not exclusive in our beliefs."[8] The publication from which this quotation is drawn appeared in 1965, a year when massive Muslim killings of "communists" would demonstrate the limits to Javanese

---

8   Benedict R. O'G. Anderson, *Mythology and the Tolerance of the Javanese*, Ithaca NY: Cornell University, Modern Indonesia Project, Monograph Series, 1965, p. 2.

tolerance. But as a general rule, and despite this catastrophic exception, the tolerant outlook of the Javanese has been a major national asset.[9]

Summing Up

Why should it matter that Indonesian diversity is alive and well? Of course it is aesthetically attractive. It is good for tourism. It is a major reason why foreigners, especially those who have a chance to live there, find the country appealing, despite its traffic jams, floods, mud volcanoes and Years of Living Dangerously.

But Indonesian diversity is not merely a feel-good phenomenon, swathed in *wayang* theatre and mosque styles; it has hard, fundamentally important political content. It pushes Indonesian leaders, who cannot avoid coping with it, toward the political center. This was true even under Suharto, who was no democrat but also no fool; it is all the more true under a democratic system where politicians must compete for votes. In other words diversity acts as a brake, however imperfect, on ideological, religious or political extremism.

The strength of Indonesian diversity derives from a combination of deep roots and pervasive national mythology. Awareness of it is imbibed with mothers' milk, although better history instruction in the schools certainly wouldn't hurt. The most important political consequence of diversity is that any effort to force people out of cultural and religious patterns which are basic to their identity risks doing fatal damage to the painfully woven fabric of the country. The bloody, tragic destruction of communism on Java in 1965–66 happened primarily because the communist party pushed its radical reforms too hard, mortally threatening the economic base of a powerful Islamic culture. Suharto's failed, end-of-regime effort to make Pancasila into a coercive ideology is another case in point, as is the fact that Pancasila rapidly regained its original meaning as an expression of pluralism.

The great majority of Indonesian Muslims are aware of all this. They know that, despite its theoretical unity, Islam as practiced is diverse. They respect each others' religious styles without losing their own convictions. There is thus far no agreement among Muslims as to what sharia is or how it should be modified to accommodate modern norms. That is why the

9 For another discussion of Javanese hegemony, or the lack thereof, see Emmerson, "What is Indonesia?" pp. 44–48.

concept of a state based on sharia law, valuable as an ideal, loses traction when proposed as a specific objective.

Powerful as Indonesia's diversity may be, it is not a political panacea nor can it compensate for a breakdown of national leadership. The degeneration of the New Order led directly to the waves of regional conflict and sectarian violence from which Indonesia is just recovering. Visions of incipient state failure stirred paranoia and panic across the archipelago. In the short term, decentralized democracy exacerbated the resulting malaise, and only recently have democracy's longer-term curative powers begun to be evident.

Recovery since 2004 has been due in large part to firm, patient, democratically elected leadership at the center. President Yudhoyono and Vice President Kalla were a good team, reflecting elements of activism linked with prudence and Reformist Islam paired with a more Javanese religious style. President Yudhoyono was widely criticized for being slow to move, but patience is a fundamental requirement for governing a country blessed with mega-diversity. We cannot be too critical when Indonesia's leaders behave like elected politicians in more seasoned democracies and are swayed by short-term political expediency.

Diversity has conditioned the culture and politics of Islam in Indonesia. The two mainstream groups, Traditionalist NU and Reformist Muhammadiyah, tolerate and work with each other while each strives to manage its own internal complexities. Both have some doctrinal radicals in their far-flung ranks, but they do not embrace those who would resort to criminal violence. They are well aware that Indonesia still has its share of corrupt politicians, jihadists and potential messianic rebels. Everyone accepts that the state must deal with those who break the law; everyone hopes that extremism – fundamentalism if you will – can be kept within peaceful bounds. No one thinks it will vanish any time soon.

More basic and most difficult for foreigners to grasp, Islam in Indonesia remains a majority religion but a minority political philosophy. As we have seen, this distinction began to develop centuries ago because of pre-existing regional diversity. Where Hindu-Buddhist tradition was strong, especially on Java, Islam often accommodated to the norms of local society. As a modern economy grew under the Dutch, Islam expanded its natural constituency among traders and the urban middle classes both on Java and in Outer Indonesia, only a small portion of whom had been deeply "Hinduized." Intellectual links with the Middle East expanded rapidly after the opening of the Suez Canal, bringing new emphasis on Islamic modernization and reform, both to renew and invigorate Islam itself, and to enable it to compete more effectively with colonialism.

This centuries-long process gave rise to the overarching dualism in Indonesian Islam which still exists. It is notoriously difficult to label. I have used "Traditionalist" and "Reformist," but the terms *"abangan"* and *"santri"* popularized by Clifford Geertz are still used, if no longer quite correctly, to describe the same thing. This dualism remains the most important single fact about Indonesian Islam, and about Indonesian politics as well. It has often been distorted and misunderstood, especially by foreigners (including Geertz himself), who accepted too easily Reformist allegations that Traditionalism was an "unorthodox" blend of Islam, animism and Hinduism. After downplaying Traditionalism for decades, scholars have now clarified beyond any doubt that Traditionalist Islam is indeed real Islam, just as Roman Catholicism is real Christianity, despite what the early Protestants said about it.

We have seen how Islamic diversity was further affected by the events of the anti-Dutch Revolution and early Independence. Most Indonesians and hence most Muslims supported the Revolution. However many, primarily from the Traditionalist side of the dichotomy, ended up identifying themselves politically as nationalists. The growth of essentially secular nationalism left political Islam as a minority category, feeling increasingly marginalized. Marginalization was aggravated by the extremist Darul Islam insurgency during the Revolution and by the Outer Islands Rebellion, both of which left political Islam tainted with treason.

Suharto's three decades in office, and especially the high economic growth over which he presided, stoked a surge of Islamic piety. It is often referred to as an Islamic "renaissance," but it was really a "naissance," a new phenomenon. It did not destroy the existing dualism, but it did result in a new wave of diversification affecting both Traditionalists and Reformists. Critical to this process was the growth of a new, predominantly urban middle class. Islam was further affected by Suharto's repression of the Reformists, who became partially radicalized as a result, and the by the expansion of ties with the Middle East. This is a source of anxiety and concern to many liberal observers, both foreign and Indonesian.

The internet age, globalization on steroids, has of course extended the reach of international Islamic norms, but it has also and more profoundly stimulated the spread of secular norms, especially among youth. This in turn has thrown religious conservatives everywhere on the defensive and given a fillip to fundamentalism from Kansas to Bandung. Like their Christian counterparts elsewhere, Muslim conservatives in Indonesia sense that they are standing against a secular tide which is undermining religious values. The result has fuelled religious radicalism and aggravated the pre-existing paranoia resulting from Indonesian Islam's paradoxical status as a political minority.

However, it may well be that the most important religious trend of recent decades has been the largely unexpected resurgence of Traditionalist, Sufi-influenced Islam. The reason for this resurgence is that Traditionalism makes ample room for inner devotion and spirituality, as opposed to the external, formal requirements of Reformist Islam. Sufism is enjoying a global revival because it appeals to rising middle classes and to women. It has rapidly morphed into new forms, from shop-front operations to television ministries. It is in most cases a politically moderate phenomenon, an effort to reconcile Islam with modern social norms and requirements. No one can say where the growth and diversification of Traditionalism will end, but it seems likely to have an enduring impact on the social and political character of Indonesian Islam.

The diversity of Indonesian Islam exists alongside the fundamental doctrinal unity that is basic to all Islam. This coexistence is not without the tension suggested by the epic poem from which the Bhinneka Tunggal Ika motto is drawn. However, despite the continued existence of some extremism, Islamic diversity is overwhelmingly healthy, not fratricidal. It is compatible with the broader pattern of Indonesian diversity. Awareness of diversity inhibits the great majority of mainstream Muslims from trying to force their religious styles on others. It encourages Indonesians to seek new ways to bring religious and social goals into harmony. The best example remains the overwhelmingly positive role of Islamic education discussed in Chapter 5. Foreigners who see Islamic education in Indonesia as a nurturing ground for terrorism are seriously misinformed. The fact that the only American buried in the Kremlin wall went to Harvard does not mean that Harvard was a nest of communists.

However, diversity should not be confused with democracy. While Indonesians have known about diversity for a long time, they are still learning about democracy, especially in its new, decentralized format. All things considered, democracy is working well at the moment under capable national leadership, but we do not yet know whether it would survive a bout of bad leadership or a serious crisis of some kind, both of which are inevitable sooner or later. Many Indonesians are still uncomfortable with the expense and messiness of local democracy. The head of the NU, Hasyim Muzadi, has called for the abolition of direct elections at the local level, because they are too expensive – and there are just too many of them.[10]

Muzadi is not alone. Many Indonesians still find the ideal of benevolent authoritarianism appealing: the messianic vision of a just king (*ratu adil*) who will single-handedly bring good government is also embedded in Indonesia's national mythology. After all, even the most experienced democracies frequently yearn for strong, impartial leadership, often invoking imagined models from the past.

But even if Indonesia did abandon democracy, it could not escape its diversity. The *ratu adil*, if he did appear, would have to be a pluralist to succeed. If history means anything, he could not represent the views of extremist Islam or any other ideological or religious extreme and still be seen as "just." He would have to come to terms with modern, secular norms as well. Anyone aspiring to be such a benevolent, diversity-conscious ruler would most likely emerge from the ranks of the military, even though at this writing the military has withdrawn from politics to an extent which no one would have dared to predict only a few years ago.

The idea that Islamic zealots might impose their brand of extremism by stealth is not credible. The voting record and the polling data are credible. If ideologues cannot win elections by being honest, they can try to disguise their real intentions by claiming to be something they are not. But politicians who attempt this are on a slippery slope. Before long, as they strive to remain popular, they will start to become what they are claiming to be – a happy ending perhaps. Alternatively, they can try to infiltrate mainstream organizations, as the PKS has been accused of doing with Muhammadiyah. But Reformism's major organization has hosted competing exponents of different views, including fundamentalism and advocacy of an Islamic state, ever since its founding in 1912, without being taken over by any one of them.

The only other option open to Islamic (or any other) extremism is to abandon democratic pretense altogether and resort to force. However an extremist Islamic coup would face fierce resistance both from the diverse majority of the population and from an unsympathetic security apparatus, and everyone knows it.

---

10 "Direct Elections Consolidate Democracy in RI," *Jakarta Post*, 29 Jan. 2008.

As with any democracy, there are many aspects of Indonesia's decentralized model that are problematic. As noted in Chapter 7, the much-discussed problem of local-level efforts to impose elements of sharia law seems to have been cured by the same decentralization it initially exploited. Moreover, it is now becoming apparent that muscular local government is resulting in increased regional economic growth, reducing the historic pattern of over-concentration in Jakarta.[11] But no one would suggest that Indonesia has solved myriad other problems involving conflicts between national and local goals, on matters ranging from natural resource management to family planning.

Many problems of Indonesian democracy may turn out to be growing pains. Whatever solutions are eventually worked out will probably be imperfect from an outsider's perspective. Indonesians may conclude, for example, that some degree of local latitude in enacting regulations based on sharia makes political sense. In that case a national standard will still be needed to make sure that serious abuse of religious freedom is avoided.

Indonesian Islam is the product of both imported elements and local conditions, interacting over time. But of these two, and despite Islam's status as a universal faith, national context has always been the dominant force in the long run. Doctrines imported from the Middle East to Indonesia have consistently been reshaped, sometimes dramatically.[12] This is no doubt true to some extent in other largely Muslim states like Iran, Nigeria and Pakistan which are also culturally diverse. My guess would be that in each of these places, as in Indonesia, Islam cannot be understood without intensive study of its national setting.

The western democracies remain understandably focused on the threat of violent Islamic extremism, in Indonesia as elsewhere, seeing it as a pervasive, global menace much as they once saw communism. The result, unfortunately, is that the positive aspects of Islam, such as its constructive role in civil society, are too often ignored. The moderate majority of Muslims is overshadowed by the existence of a small, unpopular, criminal minority, which has neither the organizational strength nor the doctrinal coherence of Soviet-style communism.

---

11 See James Castle, "Indonesia, Global Crisis, Domestic Economy and the 2009 Elections," remarks before the Southeast Asia Studies Program of the School for Advanced International Studies (SAIS), Johns Hopkins University, Washington DC, 8 Oct. 2008.
12 Giora Eliraz cites as an example Mohammad Abduh's thinking; see his *Islam in Indonesia: Modernism, Radicalism, and the Middle East Dimension*, Brighton: Sussex Academic Press, 2004, pp. 21–22.

To overemphasize extremism in this way is a serious impediment to good policy. It inhibits cooperation with the moderate majority, whose strength shows no sign of waning. It leads foreigners to become preoccupied with their own security and diplomats to ghettoize themselves. It has made exchange programs increasingly difficult. Inevitably it is seen as demonization of Islam in general. Correcting this error will enhance, not detract from, effective prosecution of the "war" on terrorism, which, as Indonesia's case has demonstrated, is not a "war" at all, but a matter of improved police work in a context of good governance generally.

What can we expect the future of Islam in Indonesia to be? Despite the recurrence of terrorism in 2009, there is little reason to doubt that lawless killing in the name of Islam remains unpopular with the majority of Muslims, or that the application of improved police work in a democratic setting will in the long run be able to bring it under better control. Unfortunately it may never be possible to predict with certainty that terrorism has been vanquished for good, in Indonesia or anywhere else.

Several trends and social realities visible in recent decades and discussed in this book will almost certainly remain important. Indonesia's diversity will continue to buffer secular and ethnic extremism unless there is another failure at the center, as there was in 1998. At the same time, a small minority of Islamic radicals will continue to exploit sentiment stirred by international conflicts which can, rightly or wrongly, be interpreted as anti-Muslim aggression. The influence of global secular culture will continue to wax strong, especially among urban youth.

Devout Muslims, predominantly moderate in their politics, will continue to be unnerved by the pace of secularization and to react by emphasizing the importance of religious values. Some of them will remain attracted by fundamentalist doctrines, and this in turn will provoke disagreement with those Muslims who believe that there is no conflict between Islam and internationally accepted rights, such as freedom of religious expression and equality for women.

Those who espouse compatibility between modernity and Islam will continue the age-old argument with those who disagree over whether holy scripture can be reinterpreted by scholars in the light of modern norms and values. In the heat of such debate, Indonesian Muslims will from time to time accuse other Muslims of being bad Muslims, or worse. Outsiders should be wary of taking sides by concluding that one or the other side is right, or that there is only one true, "orthodox" style of Islam. There will be no agreed-upon definition of sharia among Indonesians, which would be tantamount to agreement on all the components of Islamic culture. Indeed the diversity of Indonesian Islam will surely continue to increase, although the broad distinction between Traditionalist and Reformist will remain significant.

Despite the behavior of a small minority of violent extremists, political Islam has played a robust role in the development of Indonesian democracy. In the process, as we have seen, politicians of all religions have sometimes appealed to Muslim voters by supporting measures which threaten or violate the rights of others, thereby calling into question Indonesia's constitutional commitment to freedom of religion. This has been one of the most visible imperfections of Indonesia's democracy and it will remain the subject of public anxiety for the foreseeable future. The four-fifths of Indonesians who favor pluralism, symbolized by Pancasila, have pushed back against anti-pluralist excesses with varying degrees of success and will continue to do so.

The 2009 bombings drew renewed attention to the problem of radical *pesantren* and their apparent role as indoctrination centers and communication nodes for violent extremism. Any attempt to shut down these schools, fewer than one percent of all *pesantren*, could easily backfire by arousing paranoia among Muslims generally and might further complicate Indonesia's freedom of religion dilemma. Adroit policy measures and sophisticated police work will be required if increased monitoring of the radical schools confirms that they truly are a threat to public safety.

Should a larger proportion of Indonesians shift towards favoring a more clearly Islamic state, it will be reflected in election results, and not necessarily irreversible. What such a shift would mean in practice, other than more prominent display of Islamic symbols, is more difficult to discern. But it seems likely that Indonesian voters will continue to be more interested in improved living conditions than in religion, a preference increasingly evident in virtually all recent elections, whether local or national.

It is to be hoped that the non-Muslim world will recover fully from the trauma of the World Trade Center attacks and their aftermath and realize that Islam in general should not be viewed through a distorting prism of fear. In Indonesia, Islam is and will remain a healthy component of a multifaceted national culture. Outsiders should focus primarily on this success, without denying the threat of violent extremism, or the ongoing tension between fundamentalism and pluralism.

Further Reading on Islam in Indonesia

This book is designed for generalist readers and students, some of whom will want to know more about complex topics only briefly discussed in the text. The following are writings that I have found useful in my own research, and in many cases they are also entertaining to read. The selection only scratches the surface of what has been written on Islam in Indonesia, much less on Islam generally. More complete bibliographies are contained in several of the works listed.

Print Publications (Books and Articles)

Armstrong, Karen. *Islam: A Short History*. New York: Random House, Modern Library Edition, 2000.
Anyone interested in Indonesian Islam who is not already versed in the basics of global Islam will find this book useful, sensible in its approach to contentious topics, and a pleasure to read. See also John Esposito's *What Everyone Needs to Know about Islam*, cited below.

Aspinall, Edward. *Islam and Nation: Separatist Rebellion in Aceh, Indonesia*. Stanford, CA: Stanford University Press, 2009.
Aceh is hard to deal with in any work on Indonesia as a whole, because many of the general assumptions about the country do not apply to its northernmost province, not least with regard to Islam. For those who want to know more about Aceh, especially about the complex interplay between Acehnese nationalism and Islam, this is a good place to begin.

Azra, Azyumardi. *The Origins of Islamic Reformism in Southeast Asia: Networks of Malay-Indonesian and Middle Eastern 'Ulama' in the Seventeenth and Eighteenth Centuries*. Sydney and Honolulu: Allen and Unwin and University of Hawaii Press, 2004.
Azyumardi Azra is a prime example of a distinctively Indonesian phenomenon, the modern, Traditionalist scholar of Islam who is also an active commentator on public affairs and a strong supporter of political moderation and democracy. In this intensely researched book, based on his Columbia University PhD thesis, Azra explores a subject of great importance in Traditionalist Islam, the history of the scholarly networks which have maintained and transmitted Islamic knowledge. Azra is professor of history at Jakarta's State Islamic University (UIN) and recently served as its rector.

Barton, Greg. "Indonesia's Year of Living Normally: Taking the Long View on Indonesia's Progress" in Daljit Singh and Tin Maung Maung Than, eds., *Southeast Asian Affairs 2008*. Singapore: Institute of Southeast Asian Studies, 2008, pp. 123–45.
Barton is one of Australia's leading commentators on Indonesian Islam. This article reflects a growing consensus among both policy makers and academics that Indonesia has been making solid progress on all fronts away from the chaos of the post-Suharto years. *Southeast Asian Affairs* is an annual review of the region published by the Institute of Southeast Asian Affairs (ISEAS) in Singapore. Its country-specific articles, written by scholars of differing viewpoints, are an excellent starting place for anyone doing research on Indonesia or other countries in the region.

Bruinessen, Martin van, and **Julia Day Howell,** eds. *Sufism and the 'Modern' in Islam*. London: I.B. Tauris, 2007.
This collection of essays covers one of the most important recent developments in Indonesian Islam: the emergence of new and revitalized forms of Islamic mysticism (Sufism), which have great appeal for Indonesia's growing middle class. The collection includes three excellent essays on Indonesia, with the balance of the book on other parts of the world, for Sufism in modern dress is a global phenomenon, as much or more so than violent extremism.

Bush, Robin. *Nahdlatul Ulama and the Struggle for Power within Islam and Politics in Indonesia.* Singapore: Institute for Southeast Asian Studies, 2009.
Robin Bush devotes most of this book to an analysis of pro- vs. anti-Islamic state politics during the presidency of Abdurrahman Wahid. But in the process she goes much further, helping to explain how the tension between Modernists (or Reformists) and Traditionalists originated and why it has persisted to the present. Her work is strongly recommended reading for anyone seeking to understand the great dichotomy in Indonesian Islam.

Cribb, Robert and **Audrey Kahin.** *Historical Dictionary of Indonesia,* Asian Historical Dictionaries No. 9. Lanham MD: The Scarecrow Press, 2004.
A revised edition of a constantly useful reference work.

Dhofier, Zamakhsyari. *The Pesantren Tradition: The Role of the Kyai in the Maintenance of Traditional Islam in Java.* Tempe AZ: Arizona State University, Program for Southeast Asian Studies, Monograph Series Press, 1999.
This book is a highly authentic, readable description of the *pesantren* world by an Indonesian who was born into it as a member of a *kiai* family. Originally published in Indonesian in 1982, it is informative on everything from the role of the *kiai* to the place of Sufism in Traditionalist Islam. The author was prescient in concluding that the flexibility of Indonesia's Traditionalist Islam would insure its continuing strength.

Dhume, Sadanand. *My Friend the Fanatic: Travels with an Indonesian Islamist.* Camberwell VIC: Penguin Group (Australia), 2008.
Dhume, who is quoted in Chapter 7, is an Indian journalist formerly assigned to Jakarta. In this Naipaulesque memoir he argues, as he has elsewhere, that the hot knife of fanatical Islam is slicing inexorably through the butter of Indonesian soft-statehood. If you want a point of view quite different from the one expressed in this book, Dhume's is a good place to start. Dhume has moderated his pessimism since this book was written, thanks to the poor showing of pro-sharia parties in the 2009 elections.

Eliraz, Giora. *Islam in Indonesia: Modernism, Radicalism and the Middle East Dimension.* Brighton: Sussex Academic Press, 2004.
Eliraz explains how Indonesian Islam relates to Middle Eastern Islamic reform movements, and to my knowledge it is the only book that does so in such a concise yet comprehensive manner.

Esposito, John L. *What Everyone Needs to Know about Islam.* Oxford: Oxford University Press, 2002.
This book for the general public by a leading interpreter of Islam focuses on widely held questions and anxieties about Islamic politics and attitudes toward modernity. It makes a good reference companion to Karen Armstrong's *Short History*, cited above.

Fealy, Greg and **Virginia Hooker,** eds. *Voices of Islam in Southeast Asia: A Contemporary Sourcebook.* Singapore: Institute of Southeast Asian Studies, 2006.
An indispensable collection of documents and writings by prominent Southeast Asian Muslims, arranged by topic, representing the entire spectrum of Islamic political and doctrinal variation, with short biographic sketches of each author. The book includes articles on Islam in each country covered (Brunei, Burma, Cambodia and Vietnam – the two are treated together – Indonesia, Malaysia, The Philippines, Singapore and Thailand), an extensive bibliography, and a good glossary, drawn on for the glossary in this book.

Fealy, Greg and **Sally White,** eds. *Expressing Islam: Religious Life and Politics in Indonesia.* Singapore, Institute of Southeast Asian Studies, 2008.
This volume is a lively collection of articles on economic and social topics, from gender issues to the commercial spin-offs from growing Islamic piety. It provides in-depth treatment of important subjects (such as Islamic banking) which are touched on only briefly in this book.

Fox, James J., ed. *Religion and Ritual*, Indonesian Heritage Series, Vol. 9. Singapore: Editions Didier Millet, 1998.
A beautifully illustrated volume on Indonesia's religious history, culture and institutions, fun to read (or browse) and a first-rate source on all of Indonesia's major faiths, from animism to Islam.

Geertz, Clifford. *The Religion of Java*. New York: The Free Press of Glencoe, 1960.
Even though mainly about Java, this classic work, by the most famous social scientist ever to work on Indonesia (with the possible exception of Margaret Mead), taught a generation of foreigners (and many Indonesians) how to think about Indonesian Islam in general, and especially about the socio-religious distinction between observant (*santri*) and nominally or non-observant (*abangan*) Muslims. While there aren't as many non-observant Muslims today as there were when Geertz did his field work in East Java, the distinction he described has not gone away.

Hefner, Robert W. *Civil Islam: Muslims and Democratization in Indonesia*. Princeton: Princeton University Press, 2000.
Suharto ruled Indonesia for more than half its life span to date as an independent country. He tried to suppress Islam, but unwittingly stimulated it, much as the Dutch had, through his successful economic policies. Hefner does a fine job of telling this story in a short space. He argues persuasively that Islam is compatible with democracy, as demonstrated by the Indonesian case. This book is usefully read in conjunction with R.E. Elson's *Suharto: A Poltical Biography*, Cambridge: Cambridge University Press, 2001.

Hefner, Robert W. "Islam in Indonesia, Post Suharto: The Struggle for the Sunni Center," *Indonesia*, No. 86, October 2008, pp. 139–60.
In this review of several scholarly publications, the author of *Civil Islam* (see above) summarizes his more recent thinking on the subject.

Hefner, Robert W. "Islamic Schools, Social Movements and Democracy in Indonesia," in Robert W. Hefner, ed., *Making Modern Muslims: The Politics of Islamic Education in Southeast Asia*. Honolulu: University of Hawaii Press, 2009, pp. 55–105.
Anyone wanting to learn about Indonesia's Muslim school system and its place in the broader society would be well advised to start here.

Mujani, Saiful and **R. William Liddle.** "Leadership, Party and Religion: Explaining Voter Behavior in Indonesia," *Comparative Political Studies*, Vol. 40, No.7, July 2004.
This article is one result of an ongoing, productive collaboration. Saiful Mujani is the Executive Director of the Lembaga Survei Indonesia, among the premier public opinion institutes in Indonesia; Liddle is a professor of political science at Ohio State University and the author of many writings on Indonesian politics. Their current work is yielding valuable insights into trends in political Islam: for example, an apparent movement since 2004 away from Muslim parties of all stripes and toward quasi-secular Golkar and PDI-P, despite the headline-grabbing exploits of the extremist minority.

Pires, Tome. *The Suma Oriental of Tome Pires: an Account of the East, from the Red Sea to China, Written in Malacca and India in 1512–1515*, 2 vols., Armando Cortesao, ed., reprint ed. New Delhi: Asia Educational Services, 2005.
Tome Pires was an astute apothecary in the service of the Portuguese conqueror of Malacca. He traveled widely and wrote the best surviving first-hand account of sixteenth-century Indonesia, still in the formative phase of Islamization. Lost for centuries, then rediscovered in 1937, his *Suma Oriental* is a unique resource for modern historians. This handsomely bound reprint edition produced in India is a bargain for bibliophiles and history buffs.

Ramage, Douglas E. "Indonesia: Democracy First, Good Governance Later," in Daljit Singh and Lorraine Carlos Salazar, eds., *Southeast Asian Affairs 2007*, Singapore: Institute of Southeast Asian Studies, Singapore, 2007, pp. 135–157.

Ramage was until recently the Country Representative for the Asia Foundation in Jakarta, and writes frequently on Indonesian affairs. He is optimistic about the country, including its democracy and the role of Islam therein, but, as this title suggests, he is also realistic about Indonesia's many problems. His major book is *Politics in Indonesia: Democracy, Islam and the Ideology of Tolerance*, London: Routledge, 1995.

Ricklefs, M.C. *A History of Modern Indonesia since C. 1200*, 4th ed. Stanford CA: Stanford University Press, 2008.
Ricklefs' history of Indonesia begins with the advent of Islam and marches resolutely up to the present. No bells, no whistles, just solid, well-researched, analytical history from a consensus perspective – but those who may be into bells and whistles will find they can't live without this book.

Ricklefs, M.C. *Polarizing Java: Islamic and other Visions (c. 1830–1930)*. Honolulu: University of Hawaii Press, 2007.
This book is a sequel to the author's *Mystic Synthesis in Java: A History of Islamization from the Fourteenth to the Early Nineteenth Centuries*, Norwalk CT: Eastbridge, 2006. The two volumes build on the author's decades of research and publication on Javanese history to portray the origins and evolution of Indonesia's two Islamic styles, Traditionalist and Reformist. The result is a major step forward in the study of Indonesian social history.

Taylor, Jean Gelman. *Indonesia: Peoples and Histories*. New Haven: Yale University Press, 2003.
Taylor's history, designed for teaching, is organized around themes rather than chronological narrative, and is especially pertinent to social issues; lighter reading than Ricklefs' *History of Modern Indonesia*, but less useful as a reference.

Van Doorn-Harder, Pieternella. *Women Shaping Islam: Reading the Qur'an in Indonesia.* Urbana and Chicago: University of Illinois Press, 2006.
Women Shaping Islam is a highly readable study of the women's branches of Muhammadiyah and Nahdlatul Ulama. The author focuses on the role of these organizations in working to reinterpret classical Islamic texts to gain greater equality for women on issues such as marriage rights and responsibilities, with adherents of the Traditionalist NU in the lead.

Online and on Television

Indonesia has gone electronic in a big way, wallowing in blogs and web sites. Nearly all major newspapers have web sites, most of them in Indonesian, and so do all the major political parties. The much discussed, allegedly radical, Justice and Welfare Party (PKS) even has a web site for its North American members. Beyond that, the web offerings are almost endless, and although they are mostly in Indonesian, many are bilingual, especially those catering mainly to youth. I have found that Wikipedia offerings regarding Indonesia (some in Indonesian, some in English) are often useful, although, as always, the open editing feature of Wikipedia makes it risky to rely on as a sole source.

Indonesia Matters
A mixed Indonesian-English language web site at http://www.indonesiamatters. com specializing in social issues, politically liberal in outlook, and known for critical commentary on fundamentalist Islam and its vigilante footsoldiers.

Inside Indonesia
A free, Australia-based, quarterly magazine at http://www.insideindonesia.org featuring short articles by young academics and others who know the country well, representing a wide variety of opinions. *Inside Indonesia* was established to bridge the gap between superficial press accounts and dense, hard-to-access academic studies. Since March, 2007, it has been published online only, and all back issues are available at its web site.

International Crisis Group (ICG)

The group provides analysis of Indonesia in both print and online versions, the latter at http://www.crisisgroup.org. Under the capable leadership of Sydney Jones, the Jakarta office of the ICG has set the gold standard for political analysis of conflict and crisis in Indonesia, from Aceh to Papua. ICG's focus is, of course, on trouble spots, both actual and potential, but its reports also say a lot about the broader political health of the country.

Jakarta Post

There is no better way to keep up with what is going on in Indonesia than to check in at the website of Indonesia's premier English language daily at http://www.thejakartapost.com. The *Post*'s news reports tend to reflect what ran in *Kompas* and other major Indonesian-language newspapers the day before, which is a plus for non-Indonesian readers. The op-ed commentary is lively and multi-opinioned.

Martin van Bruinessen's personal web site

Van Bruinessen, the foremost authority on Indonesia's Traditionalist Islam and Sufism, has put his scholarly articles on his personal website at http://www.let.uu.nl/~martin. vanbruinessen/personal/publications. It's a treasure trove of valuable essays on Traditionalist Islam and Sufism. Although he is Dutch, an anthropologist at Utrecht University, van Bruinessen writes better English than most native speakers, and he is an expert on Kurdish as well as Indonesian Islam.

Struggle for the Soul of Islam: Inside Indonesia

This U.S. public television documentary first aired on April 19, 2007 as part of the America at a Crossroads Series, Public Broadcasting Service (PBS). It outlines the conflict between politically extreme Islamic groups and more moderate voices in Indonesia. Perhaps inevitably, it hypes conflict and downplays moderation (the opening clip portrays the Bali bombing of 2002) but it is nonetheless an essentially balanced account and would be an excellent resource to accompany classroom discussion of the issues raised in the last three chapters of this book.

Tempo magazine

When it was founded in the early 1970s Indonesia's most famous weekly magazine imitated its namesake, *Time* magazine USA, by using the jazziest possible language, making it difficult for Indonesian-as-a-second-language readers. Today, *Tempo* is alive and well, having survived banning under Suharto, and there is now an English-language edition which is also published on the web at http://www.tempointeractive.com. *Tempo* is another great way to stay current on Indonesia.

Glossary

This glossary includes a selection of institutions and foreign language terms, primarily those which appear in the text. When an entry is discussed at length in the text, the relevant chapter is indicated. Political parties are listed separately. Spellings and italicization are based where possible on the glossary in Greg Fealy and Virgina Hooker, eds., *Voices of Islam: A Contemporary Sourcebook*, Singapore: Institute of Southeast Asian Studies, 2006, and on the *New Shorter Oxford English Dictionary*.

abangan Nominal or less than fully observant Muslim Javanese peasant; one of three terms used by anthropologist Clifford Geertz to describe cultural-religious lifestyles on Java. *Abangan* religion as described by Geertz in 1960 centered around village-level communal feasts, but it has largely been displaced in recent years by more observant styles of Islam. See also *aliran*, *santri*, *priyayi* and Note on Terms.

Aceh War 1873–1912 The Dutch campaign, never wholly successful, to subjugate Aceh, at the northern tip of Sumatra. See Chapter 2.

adat An Indonesian word of Arabic origin, meaning the customary law of local ethnic groups, usually but not always distinct from Islamic law. The Dutch made *adat* law part of Dutch East Indies law, in part as a strategy to isolate and control Islam, and it still has legal standing in Indonesia today.

Ahmadiyah A religious group founded in India in the late nineteenth century. It is controversial because its followers claim to be Muslims, but many of them also maintain that its founder was a prophet, an idea contrary to one of the basic tenets of Islam. See Chapter 7.

'Aisyiyah The women's branch of Muhammadiyah. See Chapter 5.

aliran Literally "stream," often used to refer to the cultural-religious categories popularized by Clifford Geertz. See also *abangan*, *santri*, *priyayi* and Note on Terms.

amir Commander, leader (as of Jemaah Islamiyah).

Ansor The male youth organization of the Nahdlatul Ulama, involved (with army support) in the post-coup killings of communists in 1965–66. See Chapter 3.

Arab In Indonesia often used to describe Indonesian descendants of immigrants from the Hadramaut region of Yemen, who today comprise a multi-faceted elite. See Chapter 3.

babad A traditional, usually pre-colonial, Javanese history or chronicle.

Barisan Hizbullah A military wing of the Masyumi, formed in December 1944.

Bhinneka Tunggal Ika Indonesia's national motto, often translated "Unity in Diversity." It is drawn from an Old Javanese epic still read in Bali, and implies a degree of tension between unity and diversity. See Chapters 1 and 8.

Budi Utomo (Noble Endeavor) An early, quasi-nationalist association established in 1908 to encourage awareness of Javanese culture, soon overshadowed by less genteel nationalist organizations.

dakwah, also *da'wah* An Arabic term meaning dissemination of Islamic doctrine and Islamic outreach; also proselytization activity among non- or nominal Muslims.

Darul Islam (1948–62) An Islamic insurgency centered in West Java, with chapters in Sulawesi, Aceh and elsewhere. Darul Islam left political Islam tainted with treason. It left behind networks of extremists who later contributed to the formation of Jemaah Islamiyah and other violent extremist groups. See Chapter 3.

DDII, Dewan Dakwah Islamiyah Indonesia (Indonesian Islamic Mission Council) Founded by former Masyumi leaders, after Suharto shut them out of politics, to disseminate Islamic teachings and proselytize among non-observant Muslims. See Chapter 4.

dhimmi Subject peoples; see discussion under **Medina Charter**.

DPD, Dewan Perwakilan Daerah (Regional Representative Council) See **MPR**.

DPR, Dewan Perwakilan Rakyat (Peoples' Representative Council) The Indonesian Parliament. See **MPR**.

dzikir Arabic for "remembrance," used to describe the repetitive chanting of holy texts common in Traditionalist Sufism.

Fatayat NU The young women's affiliate of the NU. See also **Muslimat NU**.

fatwa (plural ***fatawa***) A non-binding religious opinion, sometimes misleadingly translated as "decree," given by someone who claims, rightly or wrongly, to have authority and know-ledge of Islamic law. See Chapter 5.

fikh Islamic jurisprudence.

FPI, Front Pembela Islam (Islamic Defenders' Front) A vigilante group formed in 1998 in Jakarta to fight immoral activities, often by violent means such as raids on nightclubs and agitation against targets deemed to be un-Islamic, such as the Ahmadiyah sect. See Chapter 7.

FUI, Forum Ummat Islam (Indonesian Islamic Community Forum) An umbrella group of Islamic extremists set up in 2005 to support the anti-pluralistic edicts issued by the quasi-governmental Indonesian Council of Ulamas (MUI).

fundamentalist Someone advocating the letter of holy scripture as the principal source of religious and sometimes political authority. The term is confusing because in Indonesia, as elsewhere, Islamic fundamentalism has been invoked for a wide variety of political and doctrinal objectives.

GAM, Gerakan Aceh Merdeka (Aceh Independence Movement) An organization which led the Acehnese

independence struggle from the 1970s until a settlement was reached in 2005; it has continued as a political movement in Aceh.

Gerakan Tarbiyah Literally Education Movement. A sometimes clandestine, campus-based movement of the 1980s and 1990s to propagate Islamic revival, created partly to circumvent Suharto-era repression. See Chapter 4.

Hadith Traditions concerning the deeds and sayings of the Prophet.

Hadramaut The region in the southern Arabian peninsula from which most Indonesians of Arab descent emigrated. A *Hadrami* is someone from the Hadramaut.

haj The pilgrimage to Mecca.

Hizbullah See **Barisan Hizbullah**.

Hizbut Tahrir (Party of Liberation) An international organization founded in Jerusalem in 1953, with a branch in Indonesia since 1983 (Hizbut Tahrir Indonesia, or HTI), advocating a pan-Islamic agenda and restoration of the Caliphate; endorses resort to violence by others but is non-violent itself.

HMI, Himpunan Mahasiswa Indonesia (Islamic Students' Association) Reformist Muslim Students' Association formed in 1947 in association with Masyumi but unlike the latter survived and was prominent under the Suharto regime.

HTI See **Hizbut Tahrir**.

hudud Criminal offenses and punishments set out in the Koran and Hadith, often used in reference to controversial corporal punishments such as stoning to death for adultery and cutting off thieves' hands.

IAIN, Institut Agama Islam Negeri (State Islamic Institute) IAINs are part of the state Islamic university system; see also **UIN**.

ICMI, Ikatan Cendekiawan Muslim Indonesia (Indonesian Muslim Intellectuals' Association) Organization sponsored by Suharto in

1990 as part of his effort to reach out to Muslims; complex in its composition and motivation. See Chapter 4.

ijtihad Independent judgement based on Islamic scripture, used to reinterpret Islamic law in the light of contemporary circumstances, as opposed to *taqlid*, unchallenging acceptance of tradition or convention. See Chapter 5.

imam Muslim religious leader, especially a preacher or prayer leader; see also the Javanese term *kiai*.

al-Irsyad A social and religious reform organization founded by Arab immigrants in Indonesia in the early twentieth century, more recently known for its establishment of some religiously radical *pesantren* during the Suharto era; also an associated university in Solo.

Islamist A person for whom Islam is the fundamental guiding principle of life; also a person or organization espousing some kind of Islamic state (not necessarily defined) or a state founded on Islamic values. In western usage "Islamist" usually implies Islamic extremism.

Jakarta Charter (*Piagam Jakarta*). Seven words removed from the draft preamble of the Indonesian Constitution in 1945 that would have obligated Muslims (but not others) to obey sharia law (not defined). Widely regarded as symbolizing advocacy of an Islamic state (also not defined). See Chapters 3 and 5.

Jaringan Islam Liberal, JIL (Liberal Islam Network) Founded in 2001 by Ulil Abshar-Abdalla, JIL is an organization which advocates Islamic practice fully compatible with freedom of expression, democracy and modern social values.

JATMN, Jam'iyyah Ahlith Thoriqah al-Mu'tabaroh al-Nahdliyyah (Association of People of the Reputable Path) Established in 1979, JATMN is a professional association of Sufi orders affiliated to the Nahdlatul Ulama, a product of the continuing

spread and increasing political importance of Sufism. See Chapter 5.

Jemaah Islamiyah, JI Literally, "Islamic Community," a clandestine, cell-based regional organization founded in Malaysia in 1993 and later headquartered in Indonesia. A violent extremist organization with links to, but not necessarily controlled by, al-Qaeda. See Chapter 6.

jihad Struggle or effort, either non-violent or violent, but in popular western usage usually connoting war in the service of Islam.

JI See **Jemaah Islamiyah**.

JIL See **Jaringan Islam Liberal**.

kebatinan Mysticism, not necessarily Islamic. From the Arabic-origin Indonesian word "*batin*" meaning "inner."

kejawen Literally "Java-ness," non-Islamic Javanese mysticism.

khaul Commemorative prayers on the grave of the deceased, a distinguishing characteristic of Traditionalist Islam in Indonesia.

kiai or *kyai* A Javanese-language term for a cleric or scholar, including the head of a *pesantren*.

KISDI, Komite Indonesia untuk Solidaritas Dunia Islam (Indonesian Committee for the Solidarity of the Muslim World) Founded in the early New Order by frustrated Reformists; became an important link to Middle Eastern support for Islam in Indonesia, including Salafi variants. See Chapter 5.

kitab kuning Literally "yellow books," a defined corpus of scripture and commentary chanted and studied in Traditionalist *pesantren*. The name derives from the fact that the old books were often printed on yellow-tinted paper.

Komando Jihad (Jihad Commando) A possibly apocryphal violent extremist group (or groups) of the 1970s and 1980s, built on Darul Islam adherents but also covertly manipulated by Suharto's chief intelligence strategist, General Ali Murtopo, to prove that there was a new Muslim threat to replace the old, no longer credible communist threat to the state. See Chapter 4.

kyai See *kiai*.

Laskar Jihad (Holy War Fighters) Established in 2000 by Ja'afar Umar Thalib primarily to support Muslims in Maluku, disbanded in 2002. See Chapter 6.

LIPIA, Lembaga Ilmu Pengetahuan Islam dan Arab (Institute for Islamic and Arabic Studies) Branch of a major Saudi Arabian university which opened in Jakarta in 1980 and became an important distributor of Saudi educational assistance and publications.

Madiun Affair (1948) A communist uprising within the Indonesian Revolution which was, *inter alia*, an early indicator of political tension between nominally observant and devout Muslim communities in Java. See Chapter 3.

madrasah An Islamic day school.

Mahdi In Islam, the rightly guided one, a messianic figure who will appear to restore correct religion.

Majapahit The last great Hindu-Buddhist state in Indonesia, thirteenth to sixteenth centuries, based in East Java but with vague territorial claims extending elsewhere in the archipelago, including to areas now part of Malaysia.

Masyumi, Majelis Syuro Muslimin Indonesia (Indonesian Muslim Consultative Council) Japanese-sponsored Islamic umbrella organization created in 1943. It became a political party after independence and was banned by Sukarno in 1960.

mazhab A legal school in Sunni Islam. There are four: Shafi'i (predominant in Indonesia), Maliki, Hanafi and Hanbali.

"Medina charter," or Medina constitution A reference to the system of government said to have been established by the Prophet Muhammad after his flight to Medina, when he cooperated with Jews and other monotheistic non-believers, or "people of the book." The "charter" has been cited as proving that Islam is compatible with pluralism. Others claim that it refers to something resembling the practices of later Islamic regimes under which non-believers were tolerated but only as *dhimmi* or subject peoples, protected by the state but inferior in status and subordinate to Islamic rule. See Chapter 7.

MMI, Majelis Mujahidin Indonesia (Indonesian Mujahidin Council) An umbrella organization of Islamic militias headed by Abu Bakar Ba'asyir, established in Yogyakarta in 2000 at the time of the Christian-Muslim strife in Maluku.

Modernist See **Reformist**.

MPR, Majelis Permusyawaratan Rakyat (People's Consultative Assembly) According to constitutional amendment enacted in 2004 it is now bicameral, including members of parliament (DPR – Dewan Perwakilan Rakyat) and of a new Council of Regional Representatives (DPD – Dewan Perwakilan Daerah). The MPR amends the constitution and inaugurates/impeaches the President.

MUI, Majelis Ulama Indonesia (Indonesian Council of Ulama) A quasi-official body established in 1975, which in its early years issued opinions supporting Suharto's developmental objectives (e.g., family planning), but more recently has been stridently critical of religious pluralism. See Chapters 6 and 7.

Muhammadiyah The Reformist umbrella organization. Its Traditionalist counterpart is the Nahdlatul Ulama. Both are unique to Indonesian Islam. See especially Chapter 5.

mujahidin Warriors who engage in holy war.

al-Mukmin Pesantren See **Ngruki**.

Muslimat NU The women's branch of the Nahdlatul Ulama. See Chapter 5.

Nahdlatul Ulama, NU Literally "Revival of the Religious Scholars." The Traditionalist umbrella organization. Its Reformist counterpart is Muhammadiyah. The NU was also, in the past but no longer, a political party. See especially Chapter 5.

NASAKOM An acronym for Sukarno's attempt to create a new ideology blending nationalism (*nasionalisme*), religion (*agama*) and Communism (*komunisme*).

Nasyiatul 'Aisyiyah The young women's branch of Muhammadiyah. See also **'Aisyiyah**.

Ngruki Used to designate the *pesantren* al-Mukmin, although Ngruki is actually the neighborhood in Yogyakarta, Central Java, where it is located. This *pesantren* is the best known of the minority of *pesantren* which have encouraged and possibly facilitated violent extremism. See Chapters 5 and 6.

nyai The wife of a *kiai*; also a female Islamic teacher or scholar.

orthodox In scholarly usage sometimes refers to those who accept the authority of the four classical legal schools (*mazhab*) in Sunni Islam. The term is of limited utility in Indonesia because it is not relevant to the most important variations in political opinions and religious practice.

Outer Islands Rebellion (1957–58) A failed regional rebellion, including insurgencies in Sumatra and Sulawesi, which helped to discredit and marginalize political Islam, especially Reformist Islam. See Chapter 3.

Padri War (1821–38) A struggle in the Minangkabau country of West Sumatra between traditional rulers and Islamic reformers newly returned from the holy places armed with fundamentalist Wahabi doctrine. See Chapter 2.

Pancasila The five principles Indonesia's national philosophy, in the preamble of its constitution. beginning with Belief in One Supreme God, and establishing that Indonesia is neither an Islamic nor a secular state, but rather a multi-religious state. See especially Chapters 2 and 4.

perda An acronym for *peraturan daerah*, meaning "regional regulation." Regulations passed by city or district (*kabupaten*) governments empowered by decentralization; some have been based on local interpretation of sharia (Islamic) law while a much smaller number in Christian areas have reflected Christian objectives. See Chapter 7.

PERMESTA, Piagam Perjuangan Semesta Alam (Universal Struggle Charter) The 1957 Sulawesi insurgency which became part of the Outer Islands Rebellion. See Chapter 3.

Persis, Persatuan Islam Founded in 1923, before Muhammadiyah, Persis espoused a fundamentalist doctrine similar to Wahabism but apparently not connected with Saudi Arabia.

pesantren Islamic boarding school. See especially Chapter 5.

PETA, Pembela Tanah Air (Defenders of the Fatherland) A non-sectarian military force established by the Japanese which was an ancestor of the Indonesian Army. See Chapter 2.

preman Thug or hoodlum, sometimes employed by Islamic extremists to intimidate or to make money by illegal means.

priyayi The middle to upper class, nominal Muslim Javanese who dominated the Dutch colonial bureaucracy, one of three terms used by anthropologist Clifford Geertz to describe cultural-religious lifestyles on Java. See also *abangan*, *aliran*, *santri* and Note on Terms.

PRRI, Pemerintah Revolusioner Republik Indonesia (Revolutionary Government of the Republic of Indonesia) The government of the short-lived 1957–58 Outer Islands Rebellion.

ratu adil The "just king" of Javanese mythology.

Reformist A broad, imprecise category of Indonesian Muslims, also referred to as Modernists, represented by the umbrella organization Muhammadiyah, who are less accommodating of local custom than the Traditionalists and, in recent years, more influenced by fundamentalist doctrines from the Middle East. See Chapter 1 and Note on Terms.

RMS, Republik Maluku Selatan (the Republic of South Maluku, or the South Moluccas) A secessionist movement launched by Christian Ambonese in 1950. The movement failed, but helped to create Muslim-Christian tensions which were a factor in the post-Suharto strife in Maluku. See Chapter 6.

Salafi, Salafism An imprecise category meaning those seeking to return to the practices of early Islam. A minority of Salafi known as Salafi Jihadists espouse the use of violence. At the other extreme of the movement are those who eschew politics and favor a strict regime of religious study.

Salafiyyah A confusing term which has been used to mean different things. Literally "as done by the previous generation," it has been used in Indonesia by conservative, apolitical *pesantren* which refused to be integrated into the state educational system, but also by members of the Salafi movement who were in fact invoking a different set of ancestors in support of a radical fundamentalist agenda.

santri Literally a religious scholar, but used by Clifford Geertz in his typology of Javanese socio-religious life styles to designate a class of strictly observant Muslims, including merchants, landowners and clerics, both Traditionalists and Reformists; See also *abangan, aliran, priyayi* and Note on Terms.

Sarekat Islam (SI) Never consistently Islamic, Sarekat Islam was Indonesia's first mass organization, formed by batik merchants in 1909 to protest ethnic Chinese competition. It rapidly became broadly anti-capitalist and anti-colonial.

In 1923 the Muslim political party PSI (Partai Sarekat Islam, later Partai Sarekat Islam Indonesia) was formed from SI elements. See Chapter 2.

sayyid Title used by descendants of the Prophet, including by ambitious Arab immigrants from the Hadramaut.

shahada Literally "witness" or "testimony." The profession of faith, a declaration that there is no God but Allah and that Muhammad is His messenger. It is the first of the Five Pillars of Islam and the critical step in conversion to Islam.

shahbandar A senior port official in pre-colonial Indonesia. Such officials, often foreign Muslims, are thought to have played an important role in Islamization. See Chapter 1.

shaykh See *sheik*.

sharia The entire corpus of Islamic jurisprudence, beginning with the Five Pillars of Islam, hence including by reference Islamic values. Often incorrectly assumed by non-Muslims to refer to a global, agreed-upon Islamic law code. For Indonesians it has often been used to denote certain elements of Islamic law, including those applying to burial, marriage, and inheritance, for which day-to-day Islamic practice differs from that of non-Muslims. See especially Chapter 5.

sheik or *shaykh* Leader, elder or chief; in Indonesia, usually refers to Sufi leaders or masters, those who lead Sufi observances.

Shia, Shiism Some Muslims disputed the succession to the fourth caliph in the mid-seventh century, resulting in an enduring division in the international Muslim community. A scattering of Indonesians converted to Shiism after the Iranian Revolution in 1979; the vast majority are Sunni, as are about 85% of the world's Muslims. The distinction between Sunni and Shia Islam is essentially political, not doctrinal.

silsilah An intellectual genealogy linking a Traditionalist cleric with his teacher and his teacher's teacher and so on, part of what is needed for a *kiai* to establish his legitimacy. See Chapter 5.

Srivijaya A seventh- to thirteenth-century trade-based empire with its capital at Palembang in southern Sumatra. One of a succession of maritime states, including, more recently, Malacca and modern Singapore, located on the Straits of Malacca, the primary India-China sea route.

Sufi, Sufism Islamic mystic, Islamic mysticism. Sufism is strongly linked with Traditionalist Islam in Indonesia. It is about a *methodology* of religion, mysticism, not a doctrine, and is usually but not always politically moderate. See Chapter 5.

Sunni The majority branch of Islam which (in contrast to the Shia) supported the succession of the Prophet's companions. Almost all Indonesians are Sunnis.

Tablighi Jumaat A puritan, fundamentalist group with Sufi roots founded in India in 1927, active recently in Indonesia and in many other Muslim countries.

taqlid Custom or convention; see **ijtihad**.

tarbiyah Education. See also **Gerakan Tarbiyah**.

tarekat A Sufi order or brotherhood. Today not all Sufi practitioners are affiliated with *tarekat*, but those who are not may lack full legitimacy in the eyes of other Muslims.

Tasawuf Sufism; Islamic mysticism.

Traditionalist A broad category of Indonesian Muslims whose style is relatively accepting of customary practices and often associated with Sufi mysticism; represented nationwide, but strongest in East and Central Java. The major Traditionalist organization is the Nahdlatul Ulama, similar in scope and functions to the Reformist organization Muhammadiyah. See especially Chapter 5 and Note on Terms.

TNI, Tentera Nasional Indonesia (Indonesian National Army) The Indonesian armed forces (all branches).

UIN, Universitas Islam Negri (State Islamic University) The UINs are at the top of the state Islamic University system. See Chapters 4 and 5.

ulama Religious scholar, similar in meaning (in Indonesian) to the Javanese term *kiai*.

usroh also **usrah** Cell-type organizational structure used by the Muslim Brotherhood organization in Egypt and later by Reformist activists in Indonesia.

Utan Kayu A Jakarta complex combining features of a *pesantren*, think-tank and media center, established after the 1994 banning of the magazine *Tempo* by its editor, Goenawan Mohamad, and besieged unsuccessfully by Muslim vigilantes in 2006. See Chapter 7.

Wahabi The form of Islam that is the state religion of Saudi Arabia, puritanical and favoring a literal interpretation of scripture and early tradition, similar in style to the broader Salafi movement.

wakaf An Islamic charity.

wali songo Nine quasi-mythological, saint-like figures, teachers and holy men, who established Islam on Java and are still revered today.

wayang Theater performed by people or puppets, most famously shadow puppets whose images are projected on a screen while a puppet master (*dalang*) chants the narrative. Indonesian *wayang* is usually based on one of two Indian epics, the *Ramayana* and the *Mahabharata*, but is sometimes adapted to Islamic themes. *Wayang* is a hallmark of Javanese culture; however, variants are found elsewhere in Indonesia and in other countries as well.

Indonesian Political Parties

This list includes important Islamic political parties as well as a select group of non-Islamic parties. Parties currently in existence are marked by an asterisk (*), followed by the percentages of the national vote that they received in the 2004 and 2009 parliamentary elections. These percentages do not add up to 100 because some of the total vote went to minor parties which are not listed here.[1]

Gerindra* (2004: NA; 2009 4.5%) Partai Gerakan Indonesia Raya, Great Indonesia Movement Party. The recently created party of retired General Prabowo Subianto, most famous for his alleged role in the 1998 Jakarta riots; in 2009 it presumably drew votes primarily from the PDI-P.

Golkar* (2004: 21.6%; 2009: 14.5%) "Golkar" is an acronym for *Golongan Karya*, meaning "functional groups." The army created Golkar in 1964. In 1971 Suharto developed it into one of his trilogy of government-sponsored parties, together with the PPP (for Muslims) and the PDI (for nationalists and Christians). The concept of "functional groups" drew on communist terminology and referred to social and professional categories such as workers, peasants, artists, etc. It might have been assumed that Golkar would fade away after the fall of Suharto. It has, however, remained powerful, partly due to its government-created national organization, but also because many (including many Muslims) are attracted by its quasi-secular image.

Hanura* (2004: NA; 2009, 3.8%) Partai Hati Nurani Rakyat, People's Conscience Party. Like Gerindra this new party is primarily the personal vehicle of a retired general, in this case former army chief General Wiranto, and presumably drew voters primarily from PDI-P.

Masyumi Majelis Syuro Muslimin Indonesia, Indonesian Muslim Consultative Council. An umbrella organization created by the Japanese in 1943, Masyumi initially included the Traditionalist NU. It became a political party after independence. With the withdrawal of the NU in 1952, Masyumi became a predominantly Reformist party. It was banned by Sukarno in 1960 along with the socialist party (PSI), primarily for complicity in the 1958 Outer Islands Rebellion.

NU Nahdlatul Ulama, Revival of the Religious Scholars. The pre-eminent Traditionalist organization, NU participated directly in politics after it split from Masyumi in 1952, until 1984, when it reverted to its role as a social and religious organization, similar in status to its Reformist counterpart, Muhammadiyah (see glossary). The PKB is composed mainly of NU adherents.

PAN* (2004: 6.4%; 2009: 6.0%) Partai Amanat Nasional, National Mandate Party. PAN is a theoretically nationalist party with a mainly Muslim constituency, created by former Muhammadiyah leader Amien Rais in 1998. Its supporters include radical Reformists as well as some religiously conservative Traditionalists.

Parmusi Partai Muslimin Indonesia. Created in 1968, Parmusi was Suharto's first attempt to create a pliable home for Reformist Islam to replace the banned Masyumi. It lasted only until 1973 when it was folded into the PPP.

PBB* (2004: 3%; 2009: 1.8%) Partai Bulan Bintang, Crescent Moon and Star Party. PBB is militantly hard-line, an heir to the brand of Islam encouraged by former Masyumi members after that party's continued exclusion from politics under Suharto.

PBR* (2004: 2%; 2009: 1.2%) Partai Bintang Reformasi, Reform Star Party. A minor Reformist Muslim splinter from the PPP.

---

1   2004 figures are National Election Commission figures from Saiful Mujani and R. William Liddle, "Leadership, Party and Religion: Explaining Voter Behavior in Indonesia," *Comparative Political Studies*, Vol. 40, No. 7, July 2007, p. 832. (Figures for two minor parties. PBB and PBR, are from an earlier draft of this article.) 2009 figures are primarily from Mujani and Liddle, "Muslim Indonesia's Secular Democracy," *Asian Survey*, July–August 2009, esp. pp. 576–82.

PD* (2004: 7.5%; 2009: 21%) Partai Demokrat, Democratic Party. Future President Yudhoyono created the PD in 2001 in order to contest the 2004 parliamentary elections. It is vaguely nationalist and largely urban. It was the biggest vote-gainer in 2009, a direct result of Yudhoyono's personal popularity; it has little organization.

PDI-P* (2004: 18.5%; 2009: 14%) Partai Demokrasi Indonesia, Perjuangan, Indonesian Democratic Struggle Party. Founded by Megawati Sukarnoputri in 1999 as a replacement for the PDI (without the "-P"). Suharto had created the PDI in 1973 by amalgamating the old PNI (Partai Nationalis Indonesia) founded by President Sukarno, with Protestant, Catholic and minor left-wing nationalist parties, in order to achieve his three-party system. Today's PDI-P, like Golkar, attracts many Muslim voters, and, with Golkar, is sometimes seen as constituting a vaguely secular bloc.

Perti Persatuan Tarbiyah Islamiyah, Union for Islamic Education. A minor party founded in West Sumatra in 1930 by ethnic Minangkabau Sufi teachers from a major brotherhood, the Naqshbandi. It is noteworthy primarily because it was an early example of Sufi participation in politics.

PK See **PKS.**

PKB* (2004: 11%; 2009: 5%) Partai Kebangkitan Bangsa, National Awakening Party. Abdurrahman Wahid founded the PKB in 1998. It is officially multi-religious, but most of its support is still from NU adherents.

PKI Partai Komunis Indonesia, Indonesian Communist Party. Once allegedly the world's largest communist party, destroyed by the Indonesian Army in 1965–66, with help from Muslim youth groups in Java.

PKS* (2004: 7.3%; 2009: 8%) Partai Keadilan Sejaterah, Prosperous Justice Party. It was founded as the PK (Justice Party) in 1998, building on networks established by the campus-based *tarbiyah* (Islamic learning) movement; admired by some for its brainy leadership, sophisticated organization and emphasis on clean government; suspected by others of soft-pedaling or concealing Islamic extremist goals. It was the only Muslim party to gain vote share from 2004 to 2009.

PNI Partai Nasionalis Indonesia, Indonesian Nationalist Party. Founded in 1927 by Indonesia's first president, Sukarno, folded into the PDI by Suharto in 1973, renamed the PDI-P by Sukarno's daughter, Megawati Sukarnoputri. The PDI-P remains a major secular/nationalist party.

PPP* (2004: 8.2%; 2009: 5%) Partai Persatuan Pembangunan, Unity and Development Party. It began in 1973 as Suharto's second attempt to keep political Islam under control, this time by putting it all in one party. The PPP absorbed the former PSII, Perti, Parmusi, and, for a time, the NU. Muslims were understandably offended by the absence of any reference to Islam in the PPP's name. However, like the other components of Suharto's trilogy, PDI and Golkar, the PPP has survived the New Order thanks partly to inherited organization. Today the PPP has both Traditionalist and Reformist supporters. It is nominally a pro-Islamic state party, but the depth of its commitment to this goal is questionable.

PPTI Partai Politik Tarekat Islam, Muslim Tarekat Political Party. A breakoff from Perti, and similarly Sufi-dominated, it gained favor under Sukarno and, under Suharto, managed to become part of Golkar.

PSI Partai Sosialis Indonesia, Indonesian Socialist Party. A small but influential party dominated by westernized intellectuals, banned by Sukarno (along with Masyumi) in 1960 for complicity in the Outer Islands Rebellion.

PSII Partai Sarekat Islam Indonesia, Indonesian Islamic Union Party. Elements of *Sarekat Islam*, Indonesia's first mass movement, formed the *Partai Sarekat Islam* in 1923, which became the *Partai Sarekat Islam Indonesia* in 1929. Known as the *enfant terrible* of Indonesian politics for its blend of Islamic fervor and erratic nationalism, the PSII dwindled to minor party status after Indonesian independence and was absorbed in the PPP in 1973.

Index

Indonesian personal names are in most cases listed under the first name (Abu Bakar Ba'asyir, not Ba'asyir, Abu Bakar). In a few cases where a prominent individual is known primarily by his last name, that is the primary listing (Nasution, Abdul Haris, not Abdul Haris Nasution). The index is designed primarily as a guide to important issues and topics. It does not cover the glossary or the guide to further reading.